the
other face
of
LOVE

The Guitar Lesson. Balthus. 1954. Collection
particulière, New York.

Endpapers: *A Man*. Antonio Pollaiuolo. Drawing. Louvre, Paris.

the other face of LOVE

by Raymond de Becker

Translated by
Margaret Crosland & Alan Daventry

GROVE PRESS INC.,
NEW YORK

ACKNOWLEDGMENTS

The Bibliothèque Internationale d'Érotologie and the author would like to acknowledge the valuable and enlightened help they have received from: Dr. F. Albertini, Jacques Baratier, André Baudry, José Benazeraf, Maurice Bessy, Eric Bourgeois, Hervé Bromberger, José-Manuel Capuletti, H-G. Clouzot, Marc Daniel, Alain Daniélou, Gilbert de Goldschmidt, Max Jurth, A. de Mandiargues, Gilbert Mahieu, J.-J. Pauvert, Geza Radvanyi, Nicholas Ray, Angelo Rizzoli, J. Tardieu, Roger Vadim, Gilles Velon, Roland Villeneuve, Patrick Waldberg, Raouf Zarrouk. Also to the following magazines and film producers: *Arcadie*, Athletic Model Guild, C.C.C., *Cinémonde, Crapouillot, Mattachine Society, Gloria, Krau, Madeleine Films; Minotaure, Paris-Théâtre*, Warner Bros.; and the photographers Alinari, Anderson, Boudot-Lamotte, Brogi, R. Droog, Giraudon, A. Grimm, Pierluigi, J. Robuchon, Roger Jean Ségalat, and Pino Zac. Finally, we gratefully acknowledge the aid received from the following institutions, galleries, and museums: Albertina Graphische Samlung (Vienna), Alte Museum (Berlin), Bibliothèque Nationale (Paris), British Museum (London), Cinemathèque Française (Paris), Cook Gallery (Richmond), Galleria Nazionale (Rome), Glyptoteket (Copenhagen), Institute for Sex Research (Bloomington), Museo Nazionale del Bargello (Florence), Musée Condé Chateau de Chantilly (Chantilly), Musée Thomas–Dobrée et Musée Archeologique (Nantes), Musée des Beaux-Arts (Ghent), Musée Guimet (Paris), Museu Nacional de Arte Antiga (Lisbon), Louvre (Paris), Museo Nazionale (Naples), Galleria degli Uffizi (Florence), Museum of Olympia (Greece), Galleria delle Terme (Rome), Musée de Peinture et de Sculpture dit Des Augustins (Toulouse), Nationalmuseet (Copenhagen), Nederlandsfilmmuseum (Amsterdam), and Pinacoteca (Turin).

CONTENTS

Introduction

Part One
The Universality of a Historical Fact

Part Two
Christianity: Exception and
Parenthesis

Part Three
The Contemporary Eruption

The Berdache Dance among North American Indians. After George Cathelin (1796–1872), Club des Librairies de France, Paris.

INTRODUCTION

Deep within every individual and society can be found—as a sign of hope, judgment, or contradiction—eroticism, the crossroads where love and sexuality converge without always meeting. And deep within eroticism, the ultimate sign of scandal or supreme stimulus to thought, lies homosexuality (or, as cautious people describe it, homophilia), the love of boys for boys, of girls for girls.

Censorious critics sometimes complain about the licentiousness of our era. Although their lamentations are hardly new—they reappear with each century—these critics do not seem to see that if a certain licentiousness does exist in moral standards today, it has not given rise to any new ethic, and the majority of philosophers and legislators continue to view the situation with hardly any more discrimination than in the past. Western civilization remains antisexual, or at least asexual, and is still incapable of finding a place for eroticism in the hierarchy of its values. This failure naturally increases licentiousness, since everything that is not connected in some way with the intellect is bound to proliferate in a wild, primitive, if not animal way, and increase the scandal through the very fact of its disassociation. Nothing is more revealing from this point of view than a certain aspect of the French mind, which is content to solve all problems through jokes or songs, and which, like the Renaissance mind (although less profound and less sure of itself), tolerates everything without ever justifying anything.

The reason for such a contradiction is surely the fact that laxity of morals does not succeed in being accepted by an attitude that remains imbued, if not with evangelism, at least with a form of asceticism whose origins are more remote and could date from the Babylonian Captivity. This antisexual tradition, which goes back further than two thousand years, assumed the appearance of a universal tradition as long as Europe could imagine that it represented the world and was not merely a brilliant province in a misunderstood or despised universe. The discovery of this universe necessitates, at the very least, a confrontation, an exchange, and, presumably, a parallel readjustment of values. Considered from this point of view homosexuality attains the dignity of a paradigm, for, in the face of twenty centuries of Christian tradition, it finally appears as the supreme heresy, the absolute sin, the example of what is opposite. It belongs, naturally, to the whole group of criticized sexual values, that is to say all the relationships that do not have procreation as their objective; but the fact remains that premarital or extramarital sex relationships and, even more so, sexual aberrations within marriage, are more easily accepted socially than homosexuality, especially male homosexuality.[1]

Western provincialism has considered this latter in turn a heresy, a crime, or a perversion. Since the beginning of sexology (and psychology),[2] the crime has become an illness, the illness has turned into a deficiency, the deficiency into a type. No conclusions have been reached as to whether this anomaly is innate or acquired, or as to whether it is socially compatible or not. However, the study of primitive peoples as well as that of the great non-Western civilizations reveals an infinitely more modest if not more commonplace attitude toward homosexuality: the one adopted toward a daily phenomenon deserving neither the honor nor the indignity that our moral arbiters attribute to it. We have to discover whether this commonplace character is in keeping with nature or, on the contrary, whether homosexuality leads people to

[1] Dictionnaire de Sexologie (Paris: J.-J. Pauvert, 1962).

[2] J. M. Lo Duca, Histoire de l'Érotisme (Bibliothèque Internationale d'Érotologie, No. 1; Paris: J.-J. Pauvert, 1959).

extremes which, according to the point of view adopted, might be those of vice or genius.

At this juncture it is essential to consider certain historical phenomena: that of Greece and, to a lesser extent, that of Japan. The close link between the civilizations of these countries and homosexuality is striking. To admire Greek civilization and yet condemn the homosexuality that occupies such an important part in it is a sign of bad faith which can no longer be excused either by ignorance or stupidity. The same thing is true of Japan, or at least the Japan of the Samurai and the Bushido. To disapprove of homosexuality is to reject at the same time Plato, Aristotle, Aeschylus, Sophocles, and many others; to cling to the heritage we believe to come from Greece is to admit the sexual reality that conditioned it. Whatever attitude is adopted, the result is a heartbreaking conclusion: hypocrisy or unawareness cannot go on forever.

An examination of primitive, pre-Christian, or para-Christian civilization is, however, only of interest to the extent to which the Christian phenomenon itself is examined in depth and from a realistic angle. Could it have happened, during centuries of Christian faith, that homosexuality completely disappeared or was found only among social outcasts? How can we explain the condemnation of a reality other cultures seemed to consider commonplace or even superior? Must we think, as psychoanalysts often suggest, that homosexuality is linked to the archetypal mother-figure, that is to say an incestuous attachment which could lead the son to reject any liaison likely to detach him from the woman he originally loved? Or could it be that the manifest hostility of the Christian world to this variety of love is part of a latent homosexuality which refused to recognize itself? Have not some commentators seen in the friendship of Christ and St. John—a friendship crowned with the love of Mary—the most classic example of the homosexual triangle described by psychoanalysis? How can we explain the passionate friendships of some of the Desert Fathers, or the Fathers of the Church, whose quarrels and reconciliations are reminiscent of the games played by lovers unaware of their own feelings? How can we believe that the Devil—who all through the Middle Ages continually showed his bare behind—did not express the depths of a reality that could not be consciously realized at this period? How can we imagine that the accusations which for example were leveled at the Knights Templar did not correspond to some truth their contemporaries did not succeed in understanding? In other words, the exception made by the Christian church may have been no more than anxiety caused by a reality which did not dare or could not come into the open, a reality in which the friendships between the Fathers, the relationships in monastic orders, and the celibacy of the priests, just as much as the prosecutions for sodomy, were only divergent and complementary aspects.

The end of the nineteenth century and the start of the twentieth have seen the development of two movements—one philosophical and literary, the other medical and scientific—which have been concerned with homosexuality. From Magnus Hirschfeld to Hans Giese, by way of Freud, Kinsey, and Jung, the same research has shown that the pathological character of this type of love remains a matter for discussion and must be appreciated by reason of its artistic and cultural achievements. In the same way, from André Gide to Jean Genet, from Oscar Wilde to Jean Cocteau, there has been an attempt to achieve awareness—the first time this has happened since the time of Plato.

Sexologists, after having met only homosexuals who wished to be cured and who therefore went to see doctors, made inquiries among those others who believe themselves satisfied with their lot or are, at least, sure enough of themselves to refuse treatment and to demand that society reform itself instead. As a result, the most daring among the sexologists, convinced that any person who takes his destiny in his own hands has no further need for medicine, now invite homosexuals to define themselves and state their function in the world.

Such is the magic circle that everyone hesitates to enter. For such an invitation, contrary to what many homosexuals think, does not signify that contemporary science justifies their particularity in an absolute manner, finding it innate or congenital, and decides that it is superfluous, if not successful, to carry out any treatment that would suggest modifying it.[3] It is unanimously felt in scientific circles that laws which in certain countries still condemn sexual relationships between consenting and responsible adults should be abolished, and tolerant, comprehensive opinions developed in their place; yet opinions differ on the question of the biological, psychological, and social effects of a way of conduct which is accepted and no longer condemned, although its nature is not understood.

It would be a mistake therefore on the part of homosexuals to complain about the tolerance demanded on their behalf by science, without also taking into account the questions raised by science. Is it true that homosexuality, whether tolerated or not,

---

[3] The laboratories of the Faculty of Medicine in Prague (under Dr. Jan Raboch) are said to have perfected a method of rational diagnosis for homosexuality from the time of the subject's childhood (Bibliothèque Internationale d'Érotologie).

could possibly correspond to an infantile stage in evolution? Is it true that anxiety and frustration would be inherent in it, quite apart from the attitude of society? Must it be considered that the maturation of the human species implies the abandonment of the many sexual types which were accepted at early stages of civilization, demanding instead a progressively more exclusive orientation toward monosexual and monogamic structures? Or, on the contrary, must it be considered that a certain androgynous quality, a certain bisexuality, probably makes up a constant element within humanity and could exist equally well at the end of civilizations as at the beginning? Does there exist within homosexual union a social link, an aim which could justify it in the eyes of society just as having children justifies heterosexual union? In the case of two people of the same sex, is there any substitute for children?

These are some of the problems which will be raised in this book and will no doubt make it just as suspect to the enemies of homosexuality as to the apologists. Homosexuality seems to us all the simpler because the attraction which forms its basis is often more spiritual than physical, and because the eroticism that it permits sometimes remains "Platonic" and identifies itself with an eroticizing or a spiritualizing of the flesh, with an overaesthetic attitude that confers upon form an absolute predominance over the totality of reality. As a result we must ask to what extent homoerotic aestheticism—at the same time that it produces works or leads forcibly to raptures of which the average mind has rarely any idea—does not imprison those responsible for it within a vitrified vision of the world, a vision which ends in solitude. Solitude of the being, but perhaps also the exaltation of the image that one has of it, and as a result,

indefinite progress because of the perpetual refusal imposed by the demand for the impossible: these are the contrasts suggested by homosexuality as much to the society which observes it as to those who consent to its mirages. More so than in the case of heterosexuality, which finds its immediate end within itself, we must allude here to the eroticism which surrounds the sexual act, precedes it, accompanies it, or follows it, often without achieving anything, and sometimes even censuring it. Artistic, political, or military exaltation, religious or mystical emulation, a certain kind of fetishism revealed in sports or in clothes, will therefore attract attention as much as techniques which are specifically sexual, and the nature of possible pleasures.

Step by step, we shall try to describe along parallel lines the problems of both male and female homosexuality, although the latter has left fewer traces in history and has hardly formed the object, like the former, of important philosophical thought. In spite of these minor differences, this twofold enquiry will lead toward the myths of bisexuality and the androgyne, myths which can be discovered at the beginning of civilizations. For it is not really impossible to legitimize a form of behavior or place it within the hierarchy of values except by integrating it with its archetypes, if they exist, and by comparing it with these "exemplary attitudes" to which, in periods of crisis, the unconscious does not cease to refer.

Going beyond historical and geographical investigations, and beyond statistical inquiries or psychoanalytical explorations, we shall find ourselves obliged to approach the world of myths and ontology itself, if only on a cautious basis, in order to know whether or not Gilgamesh and Enkidu, Set and Horus, Castor and Pollux, Zeus and

Ganymede, Jesus and St. John reveal archetypal case histories into which ordinary everyday homosexuality can be integrated.

Love is blind, as everyone knows. However, according to legend, the bandage he sometimes wore over his eyes was not too thick for him to see his victims through it and aim at them effectively. We shall try to follow Eros in his wanderings, remaining blind enough to lose ourselves while in search of him, but lucid enough to discover where he is going and to discern the nature of his passion.

Today, more than ever, the love of boy for boy and of girl for girl remains the privileged sign of contradiction which, at the twilight of two thousand years of Judeo-Christian civilization, and deep in the heart of the liberties which rightly or wrongly love demands in our time, is either the symbol of an anguished return to primordial asceticism or of an evolution toward an ethic free from the idea of sin and the complex of the terrible Father bequeathed to us by the Bible.

During the ritual Bison Dance, a character representing the devil has to be "covered" by certain males of the tribe in order to assure the latter of a satisfactory hunting expedition.

Fresco from the House of Vetti, Pompeii. Pentheus, according to one version of the myth, introduced homosexuality into Thebes. The women did not forgive him and the Bacchantes massacred him.

PART ONE
The Universality of a Historical Fact

European values will lose their privileged position of universally accepted norms; they will return once again to the level of local spiritual creations, that is to say deriving from a certain historical trajectory and conditioned by a clearly circumscribed tradition. If Western culture does not wish to become provincial, it will be obliged to enter into contact with other non-European cultures, and to try not to make too many mistakes about the meaning of terms.

Mircea Eliade

Silenus and Young Satyr. Borghese vase.
Louvre, Paris.

I

Natural and Unnatural

or
Concerning Animals and Primitive Peoples

Nothing hurts homosexuals more than hearing their particular characteristic described as "against nature," or "unnatural." This attitude, which is always that of the man in the street, is so firmly entrenched that homosexuals themselves cannot entirely succeed in breaking away from it; either they recognize it by rebelling against it or they deny it by means of endless arguments of a more or less scientific nature. When André Gide published *Corydon*, his first care was to prove that the attraction of one sex for its like was not found only among men but occurs among many different species of animals. Cocteau, in fact, went so far as to see a form of sexual freedom among plants, an advantage which nobody had imagined them as enjoying. It is not difficult for homosexuals to invoke the aid of scientists on these points, although it is, to say the least, questionable for anyone to attempt to justify human behavior by invoking that of the animal or vegetable kingdom, and to ratify the superior through the inferior. But homosexuals are no different in this respect from those of their fellow men who seek spiritual security through the fact that their conduct conforms to what they believe to be the laws of nature. Anyone who looks for some identification with universal structures is much consoled by finding in the animal or vegetable kingdom, even in the construction of the atom, some correlation or analogy with his own inner demands. If André Gide had known anything of atomic science he would not have failed to advance in support of his particular characteristic some argument based on the existence of those corpuscular elements which, unlike positive or negative electrons, are characterized by an absence of complementary qualities which has earned them the delightful name of neutrons. The possibility that homosexuals could be regarded as human neutrons, although it does not alter in any way their problem of existence in the world, is something that could increase the moral comfort of anyone who regards it as essential to act in conformity with nature and not against it.

3

The reason why this kind of argument is ridiculous is because men forget that according to all appearances they are part of nature themselves; therefore if some aberration develops within them it is caused by nature acting within them. I admit that I have never been able to understand why intelligent men fail to see how absurd and pretentious it is to mention something which could exist outside nature or in opposition to it, because we can have no knowledge of anything which is not within nature; we are phenomena of nature and an integral part of it. Therefore when we mention breaking the laws of nature we should not forget that these laws are only projections of our own minds, partial comprehension of the world through an understanding which can never be complete or absolute, an understanding that advances gradually, satisfying its immediate needs. We have never finished discovering nature and we could not do so without identifying ourselves with it or by becoming God. This is why the laws of nature, as we call them, are never any more than a series of approximations whose only meaning is to help us to increase our power over ourselves and our environment.

For centuries the Western Christian world believed that nature's only sexual intention was that of propagating itself. The Catholic Church however, in accepting the rhythm method of the scientists Ogino and Knaus, has had to recognize that mere erotic pleasure can become an end in itself, at least for married couples whose general intention is to help each other and build a family. But people still think that it would be "against nature" to find pleasure with others of the same sex as themselves, even if this pleasure is found in the total love of one person for another and in the general intention of helping him and taking responsibility for him. For a long time, too, it was thought that this condemnation could be justified by the fact that homosexuality was found in a small number of tainted people, whose peculiarity would find no basis in the animal world or among primitive human societies. As an individual crime and perversion it could only be, from the social point of view, an ultimate phenomenon of decadence. But these attitudes are no longer tenable today.

Without taking into consideration the immense variations in the sexual behavior of animals, it has been established by now that homosexuality exists among nearly all species of mammals that have formed the subject of sufficiently detailed research. What is more, it exists just as much between females as between males, although in many species relationships between the former do not end in orgasm, while between the latter they do. I do not know if this offers any great encouragement to homosexuals, but it is a fact that among rats, mice, guinea pigs, rabbits, hedgehogs, martens, bovine species, antelopes, goats, horses, pigs, lions, sheep, apes, even the anthropoids, females cover females and males cover males. Some writers have observed these activities among bats, porpoises, dogs, baboons, hyenas, and elephants, although they have found such practices to be more frequent among males than among females. Neither do these activities occur only from time to time, as one might have believed. It can happen that they occur to the exclusion of others, but exclusively homosexual behavior, which has been observed among monkeys, lions, baboons, porpoises, and hedgehogs, appears to be limited essentially to males. If homosexuality is perverse, then we are forced to find nature itself perverse, and the designs of Providence obscure. In this case the devout must hastily revise their opinions and philosophers must reconsider their conception of nature, if they cling to the notion of universal harmony and the finality of divine intentions; unless, that is, like new incarnations of Prometheus, they believe that man should detach himself from this perverse creation, remodel it according to his own lights, and thus substitute himself for a Creator who is so incompetent that He cannot successfully produce the unerring instinct which leads the bull to the cow, the he-goat to the she-goat, and the pig to the sow. Neither is there any need to mention hermaphroditism, which is even more unnatural, revealing one animal to be both male and female at the same time, or alternately one and then the other, like the annelida or certain mollusks, which can exchange alternately their eggs or their sperm.[1]

Could it be that the noble savage and so-called primitive peoples reveal a surer instinct than these aberrant species of animals, and a respect for natural laws which only decadent societies reject? On this point too, unfortunately, it appears that many accepted opinions should be revised and we must learn that at the very dawn of history the effects of original sin were greater than the upholders of an optimistic philosophy might suspect.

It is not possible today, however, to establish a complete picture of sexual life among primitive man. Ethnology has not yet reached the stage when there is no terra incognita on its maps of the world. This fact is even truer when we consider types of amorous behavior which are regarded by the Judeo-Christian tradition as abnormal. Most observers of so-called primitive societies belong to this tradition; they adhere to its beliefs, are subject to its prejudices, and

share its taboos. Their personal equation leads them to regard with indifference if not repugnance the way of life that their own tradition condemns. This tradition leads them to look in other directions and when reality is such that they cannot escape it, they tend either to underestimate its implications or to interpret it in a way which coincides only with our type of perspective. These difficulties are even greater in the case of male ethnologists when, for example, they have to observe types of erotic behavior between women. These drawbacks have not, however, prevented the establishment of the fact that homosexuality is just as widespread among primitive humanity as among civilized humanity and that it causes within primitive societies an equally wide variety of social attitudes.

We are compelled, in fact, to accept this second point, and nothing would be more absurd than to go from one extreme to the other and imagine that among primitive peoples ignorance of or failure to observe natural laws, such as the Judeo-Christian tradition imagines them to be, could correspond to a paradisiacal kind of freedom. Primitive life, which is freer than ours, is still burdened with taboos of all kinds and sexual life is the first to be affected by them. These taboos, however, which touch on all aspects of sexual life and not only homosexuality or erotic relationships regarded as abnormal by our local tradition, appear to obey criteria different from ours, criteria which are linked to the thought behind the practice of magic or animist beliefs which it would be rash to describe in this context.

Edward Westermarck believes that homosexuality occurs, at least in sporadic fashion, among almost all peoples, and Kinsey has stated that there exist sixty or so primitive societies where there has been evidence of certain homosexual behavior

---

[1] J. P. Scott, "Animal Sexuality," in *Encyclopedia of Sexual Behavior,* Albert Ellis and Albert Abarbanel, eds. (New York: Hawthorn Books, 1961), p. 133.

among the women, although this appears to remain fairly rare. Among the Mohave Indians in the southwest United States, however, cases of exclusively homosexual behavior among women have been observed, in addition to official approval of this behavior by the group. Ford and Beach[2] have observed that out of a sample of seventy-six primitive societies sixty-four per cent admit homosexuality from a moral point of view, at least for certain people.

In Africa, mutual masturbation is generally practiced and admitted between boys, but public opinion appears to condemn it after adolescence. On this topic W. D. Hambly reports the remarks of one of his interpreters in Angola: "There exist here," he apparently said to Hambly, "men who desire men and women who desire women. People find that very bad. . . . There are also men who dress as women. They scent their hair with palm oil and go with the other women to grind the grain on the rocks."[3] One of my explorer friends has told me that among the tribes found near Lake Chad there are groups of homosexual nomads who, in the northern part of the area, go from town to town in order to abandon themselves to prostitution, and who are feted like royalty everywhere. In the Congo, in one of the Ubangi tribes, the men regard women as existing essentially for procreation and boys for pleasure.[4] In Polynesia, although data about homosexuality is rare, it has been established that in the Marquesas Islands, for example, a certain number of men practice homosexuality without incurring the slightest social disapproval. More curious and more difficult to explain is the transvestism practiced by some of these homosexuals who live close to the chiefs and on whom are imposed the same duties and the same taboos as on the wives of the aristocrats.[5] Claude Lévi-Strauss states that in the tropics, among the Nambikwara Indians of Brazil, there exist homosexual relations to which the natives give the charming name of "untruthful love." These relations are authorized among adolescents whose situation vis-à-vis each other is that of "crossed cousins," that is, one of them is destined in the normal way to marry the other's sister. But these "cousins who make love," as the natives describe their frolics, seem to continue their relationships after marriage, with the result that one can frequently see men who are husbands and fathers walking lovingly together in the evening, arm in arm. At first their union gives rise to greater publicity than heterosexual relationships. These lovers do not retire into the bush like couples of opposite sexes but abandon themselves to their pleasure by a campfire beneath the amused gaze of their neighbors.[6]

The "untruthful love" of the Nambikwaras is a kind of official acceptance or socialization of homosexual relationships and presents a true pattern of pederastic marriage. Now this kind of marriage has existed and does exist in many societies, although it usually appears linked to religious attitudes, a fact to which we shall refer later. Among American Indian tribes, men were frequently discovered disguised as women, playing the same part vis-à-vis their warrior husbands as a wife burdened with domestic tasks. Before their conquest by the white man certain native communities

[2] W. D. Hambly, *Source Book for African Anthropology* (New York: Kraus, 1937).

[3] *Ibid.*

[4] Romano, *L'Aventure de l'Or et du Congo Océan.* Edition Toison d'Or.

[5] Bengt Danielsson, *Work and Life on Roraia* (Mystic: Verry, 1964).

[6] Claude Lévi-Strauss, *Tristes Tropiques* (New York: Atheneum, 1964).

in Australia possessed special rites and taboos relating to marriage between a man and a young boy.[7] This practice however seems to have been found most frequently among the shamans or medicine men of Manang Bali and the Chukchi, peoples among whom homosexuality is common. This is why the latter, who live in the extreme northeast of Siberia, choose their shamans, who are priest-magicians, almost exclusively from among homosexuals who dress as women, perform women's work, and marry men.[8] Homosexuality is even obligatory among the shamans of the Manang Bali and the Dayaks of the Borneo seaboard, who also take husbands, while in the island of Rambree, near Burma, the magician marries a colleague, and sometimes takes a wife with whom both men live, together. The identical custom is observed among the Patagonians and the Araucans, where magicians are usually inverts. Mircea Eliade, in quoting most of these cases goes as far as to put forward the hypothesis according to which natural evidence of homosexuality is the factor which among primitive peoples determines the vocation of shaman, and Westermarck used to say that for these peoples effeminate characteristics have always suggested the possession of supernatural powers. Knowledge of magic was considered then as a substitute for the absence of virility, a substitute deserving of honor and respect. George Cathelin, during the nineteenth century, described and illustrated several homosexual scenes among the Prairie Indians.[9] In particular they performed various ritual dances, the most sig-

nificant of them being that of the berdache, I-coo-coo-a. This personage also wore women's clothes all his life and, because he accepted this degradation and performed certain tasks described by others as menial, he enjoyed various advantages and was considered simultaneously as a "medicine man" and a sacred being. During the dance, young men with special tastes or men who had acquired the privilege, committed on the I-coo-coo-a acts which can be imagined, after which they offered him a sumptuous feast. During the so-called Bison's Dance, the aim of which was to prepare the hunt by means of imitative magic, another sacred personage played the role of the Demon who had come to upset the ceremony. He arrived naked in the midst of the crowd and in a state of overexcitement which Cathelin refused to describe. It is amusing to note that this Demon had first to fail in his attacks on the women and it was only when he was overcome by medicine "superior" to his own that he was to attack the male dancers disguised as bison, assume the posture of a bison himself, and allow the others to cover him. Every dancer passed in this way over the Devil, while deafening applause rose from the crowd. These Indians believed that this homosexual rite was necessary before the Great Spirit would send the bison which the tribe needed. There was another and equally interesting detail: When the Demon had been outraged in this way the women seized "magic wands" and broke them into pieces. The Greeks themselves, particularly Herodotus and Strabo, mention a type of hermaphrodite medicine man who is said to have existed among the Scythians. While they feared the "feminine malady" of those whom they called Enarees, the Scythians are said to have honored them, prostrating themselves before them in order to keep their affection. According to Ham-

---

[7] D. W. Cory, *The Lesbian in America* (New York: Macfadden, 1965).

[8] Mircea Eliade, *Myths, Dreams, and Mysteries* (New York: Harper & Row, 1967).

[9] George Cathelin, *Drawings and Notes on the Habits, Customs & Life of the North American Indian.*

mond, every tribe of Pueblo Indians in New Mexico needs an effeminate priest for the celebration of the rite and particularly for the springtime orgies, during which male homosexuality plays a large part. These priests, who are called *mujerados,* are usually chosen from among the strongest men. In order to make them effeminate they are first subject to as much masturbation as possible and made to ride on horseback continuously; the genital organs gradually become feebler and pollution becomes so frequent that the result is impotence, atrophy of the testicles and the penis, the disappearance of hair, and a change in the voice. After being transformed in this way the *mujerado* is no longer a member of men's society, and he identifies himself with the women. However, he is held in great honor by everyone during the religious celebrations and during ordinary times he is used for pederastic purposes by distinguished Pueblos.

Although transvestism and effemination are in themselves distinct phenomena of homosexuality, and while the costumes adopted are by no means always homosexual (many of them being virile by nature or in appearance), it is not without interest to note that from the dawn of civilization this link between homosexuality and religion —which will often be mentioned in this study, although its significance cannot yet be defined—gives rise, apart from the practices mentioned, to myths which seem to have a universal application. One of the most curious is certainly that of the "divine rascal,"[10] the story found by Paul Radin among the Winnebago Indians in Nebraska, and discussed by Jung and Kerenyi. In it a hero, a young tribal chief, is described as making himself a vulva and breasts, putting

on women's clothes, marrying a boy from a neighboring tribe, getting pregnant by him, and giving birth one after the other to three fine children. On the frontiers of myth and reality Don C. Talayessva, a Hopi Indian who belongs to this old corn-growing civilization which, according to Lévi-Strauss flourished three thousand years before our era, has described in an astonishing book the initiation ceremonies in which he took part, notably as "leader of the clowns."[11] He tells how young boys would dress as girls, with belts, moccasins, and ceremonial blankets, adorning themselves with jewels which included suns attached to their foreheads. He tells how he won the "first round" on a "Katcina," a sacred personage disguised as a woman. And to a white man who was indignant at this ceremony, he replied: "White Man, you find this indecent, but for us it has a sacred meaning; the old Katcina represents the Virgin of the Maize, and we must make her fertile so that our maize will grow big and our people will live in plenty." Unfortunately he does not explain why the Virgin of the Maize must be incarnated by a man rather than by a woman. Whatever the reason, myths of this kind (with which there are analogies in Oriental and Roman religions), as well as medicine-man customs, must go back to very ancient beliefs concerning primitive bisexuality, of which the memory and the notion only survived in the Christian West within esoteric movements strongly tainted with heresy, such as Gnosticism, the Cabala, or Alchemy. This is also the explanation as to why, in secret societies, both for men and women, the initiation of boys and girls was often carried out by homosexual priests or Lesbian priestesses, and did not have as its

---

[10] Paul Radin, *Le Fripon Divin: An Indian Myth* (Geneva: 1958).

[11] *Sun Chief: The Autobiography of a Hopi Indian,* ed. Leo W. Summons (New Haven: Yale Institute of Human Relations, 1942).

sole object the achievement of maturity necessary for the state of marriage, but the capacity to assume, as an adult, all sexual forms of life, including the most "libertine," that is to say, in ways allowing a deeper relationship between mankind and what is sacred.

It would be inconceivable otherwise that these secret societies were always founded on the most severe segregation, that they celebrated rites of death and resurrection linked with the sexual nature of their initiates, and often abandoned themselves to warfare of which the struggles between the Greeks and the Amazons were perhaps the final manifestation. During the night, men would attack the houses where young girls lived in secret, and oppose the palming of cards in which the candidates indulged under the supervision of "initiation mothers"; the latter, in a state of intoxication, riding broomsticks and chanting obscene songs, indulged in attacks on men who dared to show themselves on the day of their ritual banquet, undressing them, treating them brutally, and forcing them to pay a fine before they could regain their liberty; all such behavior would be inconceivable if secret societies of both sexes had not pursued, each one for their own purposes, a kind of emancipation, at least of a temporary sort, as regards the other sex. This emancipation was linked to certain ritual circumstances and to periods of seclusion which could suddenly turn into orgies, during which homosexual practices assumed considerable significance.

It is not by any means true, however, that primitive societies reveal only sacred or ritual homosexuality. They also reveal profane homosexuality, if one can use such a term, although we remain ignorant of the type of eroticism it expresses. Cathelin, who has already been quoted, describes among the Prairie Indians a group of boys with no sacred characteristics who stood apart from the chiefs, warriors, and doctors. They were called the "Beaux." They were the dandies who are found in all tribes, who are hardly pressed to take part in fighting or hunting, but show themselves off in the villages, where they display their beauty and elegance. They wear splendid robes, their preference being for swansdown, duck feathers, tresses of scented herbs, and all kinds of ornaments which have no significance beyond personal adornment. These coxcombs are often described by the men of the tribe as "old women" or "faint hearts," although it should be added that there is nothing pejorative about this description. The "Beaux" do not go in for sport any more than fighting but, riding on piebald or dapple-gray ponies, with saddles of white doeskin stuffed with bison hair, they go to watch others playing games and applaud them. Cathelin has described one of these fops who, he said, "wore a robe of wild goatskin so fine and so white that it looked like silk, all embroidered with ermine, and ornamented with quaint dyes in the most delightful colors." He added that the ephebe was tall, well-made, and graceful, holding a wonderful pipe in his left hand, while in his right he held a fan with which he fanned himself. A whip with a horn handle and a fly-swatter hung from his wrist. And he concludes: "There was nothing savage about him, nor anything which could shock the most refined mind."

These displays of primitive frivolity would not be unworthy of our great cities. They are complementary to religious homosexuality, which one might perhaps be tempted to dramatize, although they do not allow us to make premature generalizations. In any case it appears that homosexuality, which was practiced by most primitive peoples, usually tolerated, and sometimes admired, was never attacked or condemned in the same way as it was by Judeo-Christian tradition. From the cultural point of view let us note an early connection between homosexuality, the vocation of the medicine man, tendencies toward magic, and initiation ceremonies for men and women.

Totem. Folk-art. Wooden statue found in the Pyrenees.

II

Mesopotamia, Egypt, and Palestine

The knowledge we possess of homosexuality among animals or primitive peoples gives us no clue concerning the nature of the emotion underlying this type of erotic behavior. However, in one of the oldest existing epics, which goes back to the second millennium before our era, the *Epic of Gilgamesh*—a Babylonian poem of which the most recent texts date from the second period of the Assyrian Empire, during the seventh century before Christ—we can hear for the first time the profound music of homosexuality, a music in which psychoanalysts could find many of their themes, but which also leads us toward some of the most frightening aspects of man's metaphysical destiny.

Gilgamesh was neither a medicine man nor a prostitute, but a king, a powerful and much-feared warrior. Religious prostitution did exist in Babylon and Nineveh, among both men and women, and was practiced in the shadow of the temples. But this is something different, and the archives of Boghazkeui have revealed a document which is at the same time a love story and a quest for immortality and the subterranean world. Gilgamesh is the great Babylonian hero, some of whose gigantic portraits can still be admired in our museums and especially in the Louvre. Neither was there anything effeminate about Gilgamesh. He was a person so important that no one dared to vie with him. However, his dreams revealed to him what reality did not. He dreamed on several occasions that while he was "preening himself before the valiant" someone resembling a champion of divine stature fell on top of him and when he tried to lift the other man he found him too heavy. He tried to free himself from the oppressive weight of this body but did not even succeed in budging it. His comrades—the craftsmen and the people of Erech—then gathered around the champion, paid homage to him, and kissed his feet. And in the end, Gilgamesh himself embraced him "as one embraces a wife" and deposited the champion at his own mother's feet.

The mother of Gilgamesh was very wise. She interpreted the dream and told her son that the champion he found too heavy for his strength was the man she had made into his companion, that this companion would watch over Gilgamesh as over a wife, and would always come to his friend's aid, that his strength would weight the entire country, and that he would never abandon Gilgamesh. And when Gilgamesh dreamed again about a double-bladed ax that fell on him and over which he watched as he would over a wife, his mother told him again that this ax was a man whom she was going to bring into his presence and who would be his companion forever. Psychoanalysts would have difficulty in finding, long before the time of Oedipus, a more admirable confirmation of the link which they are certain exists between a homosexual liaison and men's attachment to their mothers.

However, the real mother disappears from the epic. Gilgamesh meets in reality the companion of whom he had dreamed. He is called Enkidu, and his strength is greater than that of the hero. They fall in love with one another and set out in search of the herb of immortality, facing monsters and obstacles neither would have dared to challenge on his own. Gilgamesh continues to dream, except that it is no longer his mother, but his friend, who interprets his dreams. He wakes in the middle of the night and asks, "My friend, did you not call me? Why did I wake up? Did you not touch me? Why am I anxious? Has a god not passed by? Why is my body without strength? Oh Enkidu, my friend, I have seen in a dream. . . ." And Enkidu again interprets his friend's dream.

The most violent episode in the epic is certainly that in which the two friends confront a woman. The latter has assumed the appearance of Ishtar, who was the Babylo-nian goddess of pleasure. She intends to have her revenge and asks her father to create a celestial bull which could overcome the hero. The celestial bull disperses a hundred men, then three hundred, but the two friends kill it. Ishtar curses Gilgamesh, but Enkidu throws the animal's organs in her face, while the goddess threatens to castrate him in her turn. Then Gilgamesh utters one of the great songs of masculine misogyny:

Thou art no more than a ruin, he said, that gives no shelter to man against bad weather, thou art only a banging door that cannot withstand the storm,
thou art only a trap that conceals acts of treachery,
thou art only blazing pitch that burns the hand of him who touches it,
thou art only a water bottle that drowns him who carries it,
thou art only a scrap of limestone that lets the ramparts fall into ruins, . . .
What lover of yours did you ever love for ever?
What man whom you have possessed ever knew good fortune?
Listen, I will recount the endless list of your lovers.
The good Dumuzi, your lover when you were young.
. . .
And when you have loved me, you will treat me as you treated them!

In Babylonian mythology, the god Dumuzi can be identified with Tammuz or Adonis, that is to say one of the gods who died young because of a woman. Gilgamesh, in fact, refuses to accept such a fate. And, as Enkidu in his turn curses the courtesan, the assembled gods deem that so many crimes should be punished. It is Enkidu in the end who must bear the violence of their wrath and die. This time it is not Gilgamesh who dreams, but his friend. The latter sees his arms covered with feathers like the wings of the birds which in Mesopotamia are the symbol of death. He begs Gilgamesh to follow him "to the house which one enters with no hope of leaving, along the road which leads only toward it and never back...." But he must enter the subterranean world alone while Gilgamesh, in vain, goes on in search of the herb of immortality. And when many years later he returns disappointed to Erech, his royal town, and when, near death, he wants to know the ultimate reality, he asks the gods to allow his friend to come up from the underworld and reveal it to him. After this prayer has been granted, an astonishing dialogue takes place:

Tell me, my friend, implored Gilgamesh, tell me, my friend, tell me the law of the underworld that you know.
No, replied Enkidu, I shall not tell you about it, my friend, I shall not tell you; if I were to tell you the law of the subterranean world that I know, I should see you sit down and weep.
Very well, replied Gilgamesh once more, I am ready to sit down and weep.
That which you cherished, Enkidu then confided, that which you caressed and which brought happiness to your heart, like an old garment is now devoured by the worms.
That which you cherished, that which you caressed and which made your heart glad, is today covered in dust.
It is all plunged into dust, it is all plunged into dust.

We have given substantial extracts from this four-thousand-year-old poem because they give deep insight into the homosexual relationship, whereas animal sexology or mere comparative ethnology allow us to see only external and superficial aspects. In the epic of Gilgamesh, the origins of this relationship are found in the loving recognition of superiority. Gilgamesh, the all-powerful sovereign of his kingdom, finds a savage whose strength is so great that he has to bow before him, but Enkidu, the savage, must also bow down before the social strength of his partner. Curiously enough, it is the hero's mother who presides over this love affair and defines it. However, although the partners are under the maternal wing, at least at the outset, they find in this relationship the strength to oppose Ishtar, the goddess of pleasure, who intended to stop them in their quest for immortality. The fact that Enkidu must die while Gilgamesh can pursue his course, that he is perpetually the shadowy interlocutor to whom the hero speaks (in addition to being the one who descends into the underworld and reveals its nature), also foreshadows the theme of the Ka, the Double, which is found among the Egyptians; that of the Dioscuri among the Greeks; the Dadophores in the cult of Mithras; and that of the Shadow in contemporary depth psychology. Everything takes place as though Gilgamesh were discovering in Enkidu a shadowy dimension of himself, the revelation of his hidden and unconscious depths, from which he must all the same turn away, at least temporarily, in order to accomplish his masculine vocation. He only finds them at the moment of his final isolation and his last demand. The homoerotic relationship appears within this perspective as the discovery of a force superior to that imagined by the conscious ego. This force implicates the final fate of the being, helps to overcome the obstacles or temptations of a life that is too easy, and allows, at the end of existence, the final dialogue with the interior Double who is incarnated by the friend in external life.

There is no homosexual writing written

Pharaoh Senusret I embraces his friend Phtah.
Pillar from the temple of Amon, Karnak. Twelfth Dynasty.

before the time of Plato so explicit and profound as this. Many ecstatic erotic drawings have survived from Egyptian times, showing tender embraces between Pharaohs and young boys, or women in disguise who, like Queen Hatshepsut, are shown as men

and endowed with false beards; these are all documents proving the existence of homosexuality even in the most elevated strata of society by the Nile. There is however no Egyptian literature which, like the *Epic of Gilgamesh*, celebrates homosexual love as the lofty destiny of the soul. There is only one tale from the New Empire—and several inscriptions in the temples reveal its antiquity and authenticity—which describes, in the form of a popular tale, sodomist relations which are supposed to have existed between Set and Horus, according to one version the sons of Osiris and Isis. According to this story Set is supposed to have invited Horus to "spend a happy day in his house" which his brother accepted willingly. In the evening, "a bed was set up for them, and the two friends lay down upon it." Now it happened that during the night Set tried to abuse Horus, but the latter gathered his brother's seed into his hands and went to ask his mother for help. The latter, when she saw Set's sperm, uttered a loud cry, seized hold of a knife, cut off his hands, and threw them into the water. Isis later procured him some more hands, and is said to have collected Horus' sperm, although the story does not explain how. Then, in the morning, she apparently went to Set's garden and after telling the gardener that the two men ate only lettuces together, she apparently spread Horus' sperm over them. The text says that Set, having eaten these lettuces, "conceived from the seed of Horus." However, he did not know what had happened and he wanted to prove his superiority before a court which tried him for the abuse committed on his brother, for this abuse was considered as "an outrage to the vanquished." Since Horus denied the facts, they proceded to evoke the seed of both men. Thoth, "the master of divine words," called first upon the seed of Horus, which replied to him "from the

14

depths of the water, within the marsh." As for that of Set, he caused it to issue from his forehead in the shape of a golden disc, which was seized by Thoth, who placed it on his own head as an ornament, and it became the moon god.

This tale is still very mysterious, although there can hardly be any mistake about some of the observations to be drawn from it. We learn in the first place that in Egypt sodomy was considered, at least for those who were subjected to it, as an outrage reserved for the vanquished. This was the reason why Horus collected Set's sperm in his hands rather than allow it to penetrate him and also the reason why he went to complain to Isis. Psychoanalysts will be very satisfied to again find the presence of the mother in the background of homosexual relationships, a presence which was also restored in striking fashion by the archaic Greek sculptors, whenever they represented Castor and Pollux. The most surprising thing however is probably the fact that the story does not regard the experience as negative for Set, who was the "active" partner in it. He conceives from the sperm of Horus and in the end this sperm emerges from his forehead in the form of a golden disc which is appropriated by a god. It looks therefore as though we should read into this story the idea of sublimation, a transformation of the creative force, and regard the forehead as representing some form of spiritualization. It is true that the fruit of this sublimation escapes the sodomite and becomes divine property, which might suggest the dispossession and depersonalization to which the homosexual and his creation are often submitted. It is highly significant that in this case the creation should be the moon, if we remember that according to ancient belief the moon was "a collection of dead souls, a receptacle," writes C. G. Jung, "where

The Pharaoh makes an offering to the ithyphallic Amon. Pillar in the temple of Luxor. Reprinted from "Annales du Service des Antiquités de l'Egypte," Vol. XXX, Cairo, 1930.

sperm was preserved and which, as such, was also a place where life originated and [a place] of significance to women."[1] From the perspective opened up by Egyptian mythology (which, as has frequently been

[1]C. G. Jung, *Archetypes and the Collective Unconscious*, R. F. C. Hull, trans. (Bollingen Series XX, No. 9; New York: Pantheon Books, 1959).

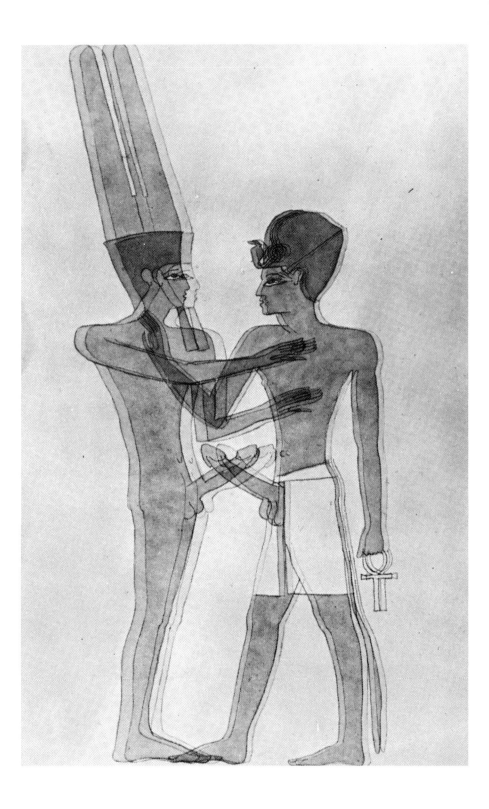

16

pointed out, foreshadows the tendencies to spirituality revealed in Plato and in Christianity), homosexuality in the active partner can be the method chosen by life to preserve and accumulate itself, thanks to a sublimation accomplished independently of the subject's wish and the result of which escapes him by becoming truly collective.[2]

Apart from this mythology it would be unjust not to mention a delicate theme which Egypt was the only nation to popularize, namely that of the Ka or the Double. It would no doubt be ridiculous to interpret it in the exclusive sense of material sexual relationships, for its significance was in the first place religious and metaphysical. The Ka always accompanied the Pharaoh to the life beyond, and all men had to be reconciled with it after death before they could achieve the strength of virility in immortality. The Ka was sometimes shown as a mere black shadow, but the fact that it was more frequently represented by an adolescent proves that in real life the latter must have possessed the power of revelation and fascination which is attributed to the idea of the Double or the Shadow. Egyptian iconography shows us these adolescents bearing oriflammes and following the Pharaoh into the other world, and their conventional attitude in itself has a grace and tenderness which was later rediscovered by the Middle Ages, although in a less profound manner, thanks to the feudal institution of the page boy.

[2] The details of this story are taken from the account of it given by M. Lefebvre, in *Romans et Contes de l'Egypte ancienne*, pp. 195-197, quoted by M. Philippe Derchain in *La Lune, Mythes et Rites*, published in the collection *Les Sources orientales*, ed. du Seuil.

Alexander the Great before the god Nim at Karnak. Oscar Reutersvärd. Watercolor with depth illusion.

Offering to the ithyphallic Amon. Thebes. Seventeenth Dynasty. After Denkma. Bibliothèque Nationale, Réserve, Paris.

The Pharaoh embraces the ithyphallic Amon. Pillar from the temple of Luxor. After David Pattee.

Among the Hittites, who possessed the most ancient civilization of Asia Minor, legal marriage existed between men and boys, except for the fact that the boy apparently did not bring any dowry with him.[3] There is even a Hittite play which seems to deal with pederasty, although the extracts we possess are not adequate to give a real impression of what homosexual feelings might have been in this old civilization. The most interesting problem, however, remains that of the Hebrews, whose antihomosexuality taboo has been inherited by the Christian West.

The situation does not seem to have been particularly clear before the Babylonian captivity, about the seventh century B.C. It is possible that the Hebrews regarded homosexuality as originating from Canaan and that their nationalist feeling, wishing to retain a state of segregation, rejected foreign customs and ways of life at a very early stage. However, neither the Code of Alliance nor the Book of Deuteronomy regarded it as a crime. In the same way, the male prostitutes, who were called Kelebites, or "Dogs," had a house within the walls of the temple of Jerusalem, as well as in other local sanctuaries, until the time of King Josiah; their function was an integral part of the Jewish religion (II Kings 23:7). We have to go back to Leviticus, which comes earlier, to discover an edict that a man should not "lie with mankind, as he lieth with a woman." "Both of them have committed an abomination," says the text; "they shall surely be put to death; their blood shall be upon them." (Lev. 20:13.) One can however only assess the significance of this ban by remembering that it is included

___

[3] Dr. Margarete Reimenschneder, *Die Welt der Hithiter* (Berlin: 1954).

Papyrus No. 10018. British Museum, London. On the pretext of initiation ceremonies, Egypt already shows exhaustive homosexual scenes.

without any particular emphasis, in a long list of other prohibitions. Thus in the same chapter of Leviticus the following are condemned to death: "every one that curseth his father or his mother"; "the man that committeth adultery with another man's wife" (the adulteress herself is also condemned); the man "that lieth with his father's wife," his daughter-in-law, or his mother; or "if a man lie with a beast," etc.

All these sins are regarded on the same footing and from the very severity of the punishments inflicted upon those who committed them, one must infer that such acts occurred frequently among the Hebrews of the period. The most curious fact is that many of these prohibitions are justified by the fact that the guilty party "hath uncovered the nakedness" of his partner. An obsession with nakedness seems to have been fundamental in the development of taboos among the Hebrews. Again in Leviticus (18:6–19), there are no fewer than a dozen prohibitions referring exclusively to nakedness. It is forbidden to uncover the nakedness of one's father and mother, one's aunt, sister, granddaughter, uncle, sister-in-law, brother, and of any woman "having her sickness." Genesis (9:18–25) already has told how Noah, having drunk wine, "uncovered" himself and cursed Canaan because Ham had not covered him and had only told his brothers who, in order to cover up their father with his garment, walked backward and averted their faces so that they would not see him in this state. Such anxiety is rare and no doubt pathological.

It is however impossible to understand the significance of Jewish legislation on sexual matters without taking into consideration this anxiety and obsession which form the background to it. The question is all the more interesting from our angle because it is precisely to the Canaanites that the Jews attribute the introduction of religious sodomy into the temple of Jerusalem, an innovation which dated from the time of the earliest kings and continued until the

The Pharaoh behind his god. Pillar from Karnak.

reform of Josiah (640–609 B.C.). In this instance also the ambiguous nature of legislation at this period is clearly revealed: Sodomy carried out with a boy of less than nine years and one day was no longer considered a sexual crime and, instead of being punished by death, in the same way as sodomy with an adult, it led only to flagellation. In the same way, although the taboo relating to nakedness only applied in the case of boys and not girls, there was no law in existence that condemned female homosexuality. It was a long time before it was considered unsuitable for a Lesbian to marry a priest and a tardy order laid down disciplinary punishments, which were moreover light and rarely applied, for female homoséxuality.[4] These inconsistencies show to what extent Judaic legislation in this matter obeyed criteria unconnected with true sexuality.

[4] R. Wood, "Sex Life in Ancient Civilizations" (pp. 127–128), and Rabbi Samuel Glaser, "Judaism and Sex" (p. 579), in *The Encyclopedia of Sexual Behavior, op. cit.*

Priest of Osiris clad in a phallic panther-skin. Papyrus of Ani. British Museum, London. *This is reminiscent of the greeting between an Indian monk and a lay scholar.* Khajuraho. Tenth century. Temple of Vishvanâtha.

The famous incident of Sodom and Gomorrah also proves that the homosexuality which the Hebrews held in abomination was most of all that exercised in a violent manner by foreigners; the reason seems due, to a great extent, to the Hebrews' desire to protect their nationals from the manners and customs of the neighboring peoples, of whom homosexuality was precisely one of the characteristics. The virtuous Lot did not hesitate, in order to save his guests from the lust of the Sodomites, to offer them his two daughters who were still virgins, and to invite them to do as they wished with them (Genesis 19:8). Women were held in such low esteem at this time that it seemed more proper to sacrifice to frenzied men the virginity of their daughters than that of their male guests. It is true that according to the Bible the latter were nothing less than angels. And with angels we come to an abyss of ambiguity which the Jews were not the only ones to enjoy: Byzantium, the Middle Ages, the Quattrocento, and the Renaissance were to use these enigmatic apparitions, possessing alternately a terrible, flamboyant beauty, an exquisite sweetness, or a nauseating mawkishness as a means for plunging into subtle theories and of celebrating a type of adolescent beauty whose rustle of wings, light, fiery glances, and sumptuous apparel occasionally triumphed over the somewhat frigid perfection of Greek classical nudity. The fact remains, as Kinsey has observed, that oral-genital relationships and homosexual activities remained associated for a long time with Jewish religious rites, while their general condemnation of all such sexual relation-

ships occurred only after the return from captivity in Babylon, when a terrifying wave of nationalism led the Jews to abolish customs which might have assimilated them to foreign peoples.

The retention, until a late stage, of sacred prostitution, the severity of the laws, the already-mentioned obsession concerning nudity, as well as the nationalist fear of

Amenhotep IV, the Reformer. Sculpture. Karnak. Reprinted from Henri Chevrier's *Travaux de Karnak* (1929–1930). Cairo, 1930.

22

resembling foreigners, show to what extent the possibility of homosexual love must have caused a strong and anguished disturbance in the Jews. The Bible itself describes this emotion in the narrative of the love of David and Jonathan, and leaves no doubt as to the real nature of that love, although it may have remained chaste. It is true that the love relationship between David and Jonathan possessed neither the depth nor the durability of that between Gilgamesh and Enkidu, but in its archaic simplicity it reveals a freshness and purity which also makes it into one of the great love stories of humanity.

It was immediately after his victory over Goliath that Jonathan fell in love with the young hero who, in the First Book of Samuel (16:12—17:42) is described as "ruddy, and of a fair countenance" and as "withal of a beautiful countenance, and goodly to look to." David takes the head of the giant he has slain to King Saul and Jonathan, the heir to the throne, is seated at his father's right hand. From that moment, says the Bible, "the soul of Jonathan was knit with the soul of David, and Jonathan loved him as his own soul." From that moment also Jonathan took sides against his father, whose jealousy was awakened over the young man. It was Jonathan who allowed David to escape from the King's enmity, in the name of the naïve oath which bound them together: "And as touching the matter which thou and I have spoken of, behold, the Lord be between thee and me for ever" (I Sam. 20:23). Things went so far that Jonathan, who was destined to reign,

David and the head of Goliath. Guido Reni. 1607.

"stripped himself of the robe that was upon him, and gave it to David, and his garments" which, according to the ancient oriental conception, symbolized the gift of his personality. He gave him "even to his sword, and to his bow, and to his girdle" (I Sam. 18:4) and, although he did not yet know that the prophet Samuel had decided to remove Saul from the throne and put David in his place, Jonathan begged him at the moment when he was leaving for the combat:

And thou shalt not only while yet I live shew me the kindness of the Lord, that I die not: But also thou shalt not cut off thy kindness from my house for ever: no, not when the Lord hath cut off the enemies of David every one from the face of the earth. So Jonathan made a covenant with the house of David, saying, Let the Lord even require it at the hand of David's enemies. (I Sam. 20:14–16.)

He accepted the idea that David might replace him on the throne, which, from the psychoanalysts' point of view, corresponds to a complex for self-effacement, which is an indication of homosexuality. Jonathan continues in humble fashion to make the gift of his person to the one who is the chosen of his soul, and to save David from the attempts on his life prepared by his own father. And when, on Mount Gilboa, he perishes at the hand of the Philistines together with his brother and Saul, David mourns his death in a funeral lament whose quivering emotion can still move us today:

How are the mighty fallen in the midst of the battle! O Jonathan, thou wast slain in thine high places. I am distressed for thee, my brother Jonathan: very pleasant hast thou been unto me: thy love to me was wonderful, passing the love of women. (II Sam. 1:25–26.)

This friendship presumably did not go as far as sexual relationships, although the

23

Dancing Maenade. School of Brygos. Wine-cup. Approximately 540 B.C.

Bible speaks of kisses, embraces, and secret encounters, but the episode cannot however be regarded as a mere piece of adolescent infatuation, for at the period of their friendship David and Jonathan knew the love of women and were able to compare it to the feelings they were experiencing. David had married successively Michal (Saul's daughter, who loved David and had saved his life), Abigail, and Ahinoam the Jezreelitess, while he was leader of a band of men. Similarly, when he died, Jonathan already had a son. Their feeling assumes, therefore, a real significance, especially since, in a society where the father-complex was particularly strong, Jonathan's revolt against Saul confers on his love for David a truly liberating value. Perhaps in the first glance that they exchanged on the day of their meeting, and in the love that overwhelmed them, the two friends had an intuition of that subterranean part of the being which, as we have seen, revealed itself to be the true meaning of the relationship between Gilgamesh and Enkidu. After his victory over Goliath, David no doubt saw unconsciously in the young prince the confused and scintillating image of his own royal destiny; while Jonathan also sensed in the docile hero who uttered divine commands, the proximity of his own encounter with renunciation and death. For it is a curious fact that, just as in the epic of Gilgamesh, Enkidu dies in order to allow his friend to accomplish his earthly destiny, Jonathan has to die so that David can acquire royal status. Enkidu however, after becoming an inhabitant of the underworld, can still reveal the secret of Hell to his friend, but Jonathan's memory will be perpetuated in the house of David only through the daily presence at the King's table of a little cripple by the name of Mephibosheth, who was none other than the son of his dead friend.

Hebrew legislation was brutal and frenzied; the story of David and Jonathan gives it a reality that is more human, more affectionate and subtle, proving that the Jews were as sensitive as other peoples to the fascinating power of love between people of the same sex.

Amazon. Detail from *Magnosia ad Maeandrum*
(V, pp. 40-41). Louvre, Paris. The Amazon
theme is universal and belongs, no doubt, to the
fantasy of sex-warfare and its extreme manifestations, male and female homosexuality.

Harmodius and Aristogiton. Attributed to Kritios and Nesiotes. Museo Nazionale, Naples. Athens and Greece placed their liberties under the protective patronage of the couple Harmodius and Aristogiton, who were famous for their assassination of a tyrant.

III
Greece and Rome

Greece is particularly interesting from our point of view, not only because pederasty was raised to the status of an institution leading to philosophical reflection of an outstanding kind, but also because it was the location for a type of female homosexuality which was less talked about but was no doubt complementary to pederasty. It seems interesting to evaluate this complementary quality because it can throw light on certain backgrounds common to both male and female homosexuality.

Long before Sappho, the woman poet of Lesbos, gave her name or that of her native island to the taste that women develop for each other, the minds of the Greeks were preoccupied with the curious phenomenon of the Amazons. Whether this phenomenon belonged to history or legend is less interesting than the importance it acquired in Greek mythology or art, in which it reflected the mental fantasies or certain psychological aspects of ancient man.

According to legend the Amazons, who were masculine and warlike women, are supposed to have inhabited the banks of the Thermodon, a river in Asia Minor, living in three separate tribes based on the capital cities of Themiscyra, Lycastia, and Chadesia. Before this, if we believe Sallust, they apparently inhabited the banks of the Don in Thrace. The ancient writers maintained that these women burned away their right breasts so that they could shoot more easily with a bow and arrow. They only consented to sexual relationships with men once a year, in order to perpetuate their race. They established these relationships every spring with a neighboring mountain tribe, the Gargarensians. From the children born of this intercourse they kept only the girls, massacring the boys or sending them to their fathers. Between times they had homosexual relationships among themselves.

Although certain writers have contested the truth of the Amazon legend, it cannot easily be refuted because it has appeared on other occa-

Fresco. House No. 2, Pompeii, Reg. IX, Is. V. Effeminacy and transvestism were never well received. Achilles learned something about them from the court of Licomedes where he lived disguised as a woman.

sions, at different periods, although it must be admitted that the historical observations behind it are as vague and uncertain as those of the ancients. This is why when the first Europeans penetrated into Brazil they described the Marañón River as the "River of the Amazons" because they apparently encountered female warriors along its banks. Gaspar de Carjaval, a Spanish priest, asserts that he saw them, describing them as "very muscular" and going about "quite naked, covering only the private parts," with bows and arrows in their hands and fighting like ten Indians. They also offered themselves to men only once a year, on the day of their annual feast. They then bathed in the waters of a lake called Yaci onaroua, or Moonbeam, and, if they had a daughter after this brief union, they sent the father a lucky stone which they found on the bed of the lake and which was supposed to be only mud hardened by the light of the moon. According to legend, the Brazilian Amazons experienced a period of supremacy over men, and this supremacy could only be abolished by the action of a hero. The latter, named Yurupari, is said to have called the men of the tribe together and initiated them into the Rite of the Sun. It is a significant fact that Yurupari, whom the Indians regarded as a god, was said never to have touched a woman. This legend shows how the homosexuality of the Amazons appears to find its opposite pole in the homosexuality of men, both types of behavior revealing themselves as the most sensitive extremes in the general struggle for hegemony between the sexes.

The fact that certain authors, such as Weigall, have denied the existence of the ancient Amazons as a historic fact and made them into mere priestesses of Cybele, does not affect the psychological hypothesis that

we have just put forward and, if anything, confirms it. The primitive drawings at Lydia show these priestesses dancing, armed with battle-axes, and with their bows and buckles hanging from their waists. Athenaeus asserts moreover that the inhabitants of Lydia were the first people to practice the operation that renders women sterile, which is supposed to have allowed them later to employ female eunuchs instead of male ones. In the same way that emasculation caused secondary female characteristics to appear in the shamans or the priests of Attis, the above-mentioned operation, when carried out on the priestesses of the ancient Goddess-Mother, induced masculine characteristics which led later to the legends about Amazons with mustaches. If this version is accurate, it tends to show that the homosexuality of the Amazons probably had a religious origin, and that as with the shamans, in whom its purpose was to bring out intuitive feminine qualities, its purpose was to bring out in women warlike qualities of a masculine nature.

It looks as though the Greeks were particularly fascinated by this appearance of masculine qualities in women, and that they were even terrified by them. The Greeks

Amazon fighting. Detail from Herculanaeum. Museo Nazionale, Naples.

Treasury at Delphi. The Amazon queens proclaimed themselves daughters of the god Mars and the stories about them are all accounts of warfare. In the stories dealing with Antiope (who attacked Theseus and was conquered by him on the bridge of Thermodon), or with Penthesilea (who was killed by Achilles in the Trojan War), or with Thomyris (who is said to have caused the death of Cyrus), violence remains their destiny and accompanies them everywhere. However, throughout this merciless struggle which ancient man seemed to be waging in order to gain his supremacy, it is possible to sense not only the fear of being vanquished, but the base and pleasurable desire to be conquered. This desire, which corresponds to the masochistic tendency of certain feminine men to be overcome and destroyed by masculine women, appears later in Rome, in the *Aeneid*. Before the Amazon Camilla dies, Virgil describes, in fact, with obvious enjoyment and anguish, the humiliations she inflicts on many warriors and the massacre which this brings about. He even describes Arruns, her conqueror, as horrified by his victory and fleeing in a state of joy mingled with fear:

> Thus, before enemy arrows can pursue him, the wolf who has slain a shepherd or a young powerful bull, rushes away at once to hide, taking lonely paths on the high mountains: aware of the boldness of his exploit and keeping his quivering tail between his legs he reaches the woods. In the same way the desperate Arruns hid from the gaze of others, and content that he had fled, he mingled with the crowd of warriors.[1]

This pleasure in emphasizing a certain boastfulness or a certain cowardice among men is all the more significant in Virgil because the poet never succeeds in throwing

---

[1] Virgil, *The Aeneid*, XI, 806–815.

must have understood, either in a real, historical sense or a psychologically subconscious sense, that the triumph of the Amazons could only be achieved at the cost of suppressing their own masculinity. This is why much of Greek art shows scenes of extreme violence between men and women, as can be seen on the friezes of the mausoleum of Halicarnassus, on the temple of Phigalia, or on the metopes of the Athenian off his own homosexuality. Consequently, we can see behind it the anxious fear of woman, along with the secret desire to be vanquished by her and the refusal and revolt inspired by this feeling. During the eighteenth century, Heinrich von Kleist did not hesitate to go to the end of this fantasy, to reverse the story as told in the legend, and to remove one of the disguises from it, by making Achilles die at the hand of Penthesilea.

The sadistic aggression of the Amazons foreshadows that of the warlike heroines of later ages who, wearing man's dress like Joan of Arc, Mathilda of Tuscany, Jeanne de Montfort, and many others, show a violent revulsion against heterosexual relationships and display a super-virility calculated to humiliate their indolent contemporaries, but who also reveal Lesbian tendencies which were, at least, latent. It foreshadows the kind of liaison or marriage in which the man, dominated by the woman,

Wounded Amazon. Antique cameo. Bibliothèque Nationale, Paris.

prefers practices such as *fellatio, cunnilingus,* or *coitus per anum* to the usual sexual relationships. Lastly, it explains to some extent the criminality which certain psychiatrists[2] believe they have noted as a frequent factor in female homosexuality.

[2] Frank Caprio, M.D., *Female Homosexuality* (New York: Grove Press, 1962).

Harornobor. Print. Musée Guimet, Paris. We find the Amazon theme in Japanese art, as well.

31

Sappho. Antique cameo.

The tendencies of Sappho appear less aggressive and come closer to a certain bisexual quality. Sappho was born at Mytilene on the isle of Lesbos during the sixth century B.C., living from approximately 612 until about 558; it is known that she gave rise to the terms "Sapphism" and "Lesbianism" which are the usual names for female homosexuality. Unfortunately we know little about this poet whom Plato regarded as "the tenth Muse," whom Socrates reportedly delighted in calling "Sappho the Beautiful," and whom Strabo described as "miraculous." Thanks to the Christians, who decided that her work would have a dangerous influence on the morality of which they had set themselves up as guardians, we possess only six hundred out of the twelve thousand verses she composed. The first destruction to which they were subject took place during the period of Gregory of Nazianzus, and another large quantity of her books were burned in 1073, on the orders of Pope Gregory VII, with the result that at the end of the nineteenth century all that

was known of her work was two Odes: one dedicated to Aphrodite, found among the work of Dionysius of Halicarnassus, and the other, "To a Beloved One," which had been preserved by Longinus. Since that time, important excavations carried out in Egypt in the tombs of Oxyrhyncus led to the discovery—in the packing surrounding contemporary sarcophagi—of several other fragments of her work.

It is true that the violence of the attacks by the Christians has led us to imagine two Sapphos, one who might have been a courtesan and likely to behave in a disorderly fashion, and the other who was a genius. Since, however, there can be no doubt about the meaning of most of the "Sapphic" poems, those who supported this theory were forced to make the courtesan and the poetess into one and the same person. It has been proved today that there is no historical foundation for these pious falsehoods and that the loves of Sappho cannot be disassociated from the special nature of her genius.

According to tradition she was ugly. Her eyes and hair are said to have been darker than fashion required, and she is supposed to have been so small in build that she was forbidden to have children. Ovid attributes to her the words, "If nature has unkindly refused me beauty, my genius makes up for this lack. . . . I am small in stature but my name can fill the whole world." Horace speaks of the masculine Sappho, although Athenaeus asserts that she was "a most womanly woman." Her ugliness was no doubt of that attractive kind in which the charm is due to delicacy, refinement, and the expression of the eyes. Plutarch celebrated her "expression mingled with ardor" and Swinburne "her Lesbian beauty in the small brown body possessed of eternal fire."

Sappho belonged to the aristocracy of Lesbos, and it appears that her father died very young, during the war which his country fought against Athens. It was during this war that her mother, Cleis, retired to Mytilene with the child and her three brothers. The little girl is said to have been jealous of them and tried to dominate them. During this early part of her life, which coincided with a period of war during which women enjoyed an exceptional degree of liberty, Sappho probably found the young soldiers she met somewhat unattractive, for nothing is known of any attachment she felt for a man. She was, however, loved by Alcaeus, a poet like herself, all of whose advances she repulsed, and whose homosexual liaisons were notorious. It looks as though a certain degree of rivalry separated the two artists who, after having been attracted to each other at first, tried to assert themselves by each taking refuge in homosexuality. Sappho was involved in the plot by the aristocracy against the tyrant Pittacus and was exiled to Pyrrha, then to Sicily, where she seems to have lived in Syracusa. There she married a rich merchant by the name of Cercolas, with whom she is said to have experienced some happiness. However, the poems she wrote at this period prove that the marriage must have remained unconsummated, for she cries "I shall remain a virgin (*aiparthenos*) for ever." However, we know today how much truth there was in these protestations of virginity.

When she was able to return to Mytilene she gathered round her young girls to whom she taught versification, singing, and dancing. It looks as if her house, which was placed under the protection of Aphrodite and the other goddesses of love, may have had a certain religious character which justified it in the eyes of contemporary society. She is said to have invented while there a new poetic meter and the so-called "Sapphic" line. Her poems were accompanied by music which she composed herself and played on her lute. The young girls with whom she surrounded herself were *hetairae*, a term which later signified courtesans, though its precise meaning is "intimate companion," "close friend." The names of several of her *hetairae* are known to us. The liaisons that she had with some of them were often tragic. For Atthis, who had fallen in love with a boy, she wrote:

He seems to me to rank with the gods, this man who sits opposite you and hears at close quarters your sweet voice and your adorable laughter. Ah, my heart within my breast is completely carried away at the thought. For as soon as I look at you, my voice at once fails

Achilles and Penthesilea. Cameo. Bibliothèque Nationale, Cabinet des Médailles, Paris. The legendary story ended with the victory of the male over the female, but certain authors, such as von Kleist, expressed latent masculine masochism and reversed the conclusion by making Penthesilea massacre Achilles.

me, my tongue is silent, and an intangible fire circulates beneath my skin. My eyes can no longer see. My ears buzz. I am bathed in sweat. A quivering overwhelms me. I am greener than grass. I am motionless, I seem to be well nigh dead. But one must resign oneself to everything. . . .

When jealous of a girl whom her loved one prefers: "Who is this peasant who has bewitched your heart? She does not even know how to lift her skirt above her ankles." And of another girl she writes: "I am utterly weary of Gorgo."

Her compatriots, flattered by her genius, offered her a house and a vast area of land. She said moreover: "I myself love a life of elegance, and for me riches and beauty are part of the desire to see the light and the sunshine."

As the years passed she appears to have grown somewhat tired of her *hetairae*. She felt the need to justify herself. "My feelings toward you, my beauties, do not change," she wrote, and "Today I want to sing for my *hetairae* the songs that please them." But in the end, legend has it that she fell in love with a young sailor named Phaon whose beauty was apparently wonderful. He despised her and fled from Lesbos. She wanted to pursue him to Sicily. Ovid then described the young man as saying:

Neither the girls of Pyrrha nor those of Mytilene nor the host of other women in Lesbos delight me any longer. Anactoria and the white-skinned Cynda are hideous to me; Atthis has no charm for me. Traitress! He who was the object of many women's longing, you alone possess him.

When she arrived on the island of Leucadia, Sappho must have understood how vain it was for a woman of fifty-five to pursue, against his wish, a youth of twenty. She climbed up the white stone cliff where a

Apollo. Piombino. Bronze. Louvre, Paris.

temple of Apollo stood, and threw herself into the sea.[3]

Although the information we possess about Sappho is sufficiently explicit concerning the orientation of her feelings, it is no more than allusive as far as the nature of Lesbian practices are concerned. Lucian of Samosata was more explicit in his *Dialogues of the Courtesans*. While describing Megilla, who was also born on Lesbos, he causes a young woman by the name of Leaina to tell how she came to spend the night with the rich Lesbian friend who shared her house. Lucian shows the two women covering their guest with kisses, embracing her as a man embraces a woman, biting her tenderly, and introducing their tongues into her mouth. Leaina asserts that she had the impression of having intercourse with an athlete. Megilla uses the masculine form of her name and says, "I am called Megillo and I have married Demonossa who has become my wife. Have you ever seen a man more handsome than I am?"

In addition to this evidence from literature, Greek painting and many vases from the fifth century B.C. bear witness to the frequency of Lesbian love in the Hellenic peninsula, but this information is, however, out of proportion when compared to that which has been transmitted to us concerning male homosexuality, about which we possess many legislative texts, a quantity of erotic and amatory literature, philosophic thought of principal importance, and evidence of the most solid kind concerning the significance

[3] Arthur Weigall, *Sappho of Lesbos* (London: 1952).

34

that it possessed in political or military spheres.[4]

Some authors have wondered whether pederasty was a phenomenon which developed late in Greece or whether it dated from remotest antiquity. Lucian, for instance, believed that there was no pederastic love in earliest times, and he wrote in his *Amores*:

> It was essential at that time for men to be united with women, so that the human race would not die out for lack of reproducing itself. But the variety of knowledge and the desire for virtue generated within us through the love of beauty was only to blossom in the fullness of time, in a century which carried out investigations on all points, and pederasty flourished along with divine philosophy.[5]

This point of view, which can perhaps be justified as far as the moral and institutional aspects acquired by pederasty in Greece are concerned, can no longer be held today, when the comparative study of civilization shows that homosexual practices exist among all peoples as a spontaneous phenomenon. This study does not show that these customs appeared at a particular stage of historical evolution, but it does show that they were recognized more or less officially by moral and social laws. As a result it seems futile to discuss where such practices originated, which race transmitted them, and at what point they were first observed. Since they are inherent in human nature it should be said rather that they exist every-

[5] Lucian, *Amores*, xxxv.

[4] The most complete study on this question is *L'Histoire de l'Amour Grec dans l'Antiquité* by M. H. E. Meier, the French edition of which has been augmented to a valuable extent by a selection of original documents and several complementary essays by L. R. de Pagey-Castries (Paris, 1952). A large number of facts included in this chapter have been taken from this work.

Apollo. Glyptoteket, Copenhagen. During the Hellenistic period there were many works of art making use of the hermaphrodite theme.

Apollo. Glyptoteket, Copenhagen. During the Hellenistic period there were many works of art making use of the hermaphrodite theme.

where, at all periods, and among all peoples—who sometimes condemn them, sometimes tolerate them, sometimes even encourage them, according to their degree of moral evolution and their particular demographic or social necessities.

In the case of Greece, the homosexual character of a great number of religious myths, as well as the passionate friendships described in the Homeric epics, and even more so the existence of homosexual customs among peoples of very different cultural levels, show to what extent the moral and institutional pederasty of the classical period was rooted in customs dating from immemorial times. Greek mythology did not limit itself, in fact, to offering veneration to Hellenic divinities of an androgynous nature and of a vague bisexuality; it applied itself to describing in a precise and explicit manner the homosexual relations of the greatest of the gods. Zeus himself, the father of Olympus, showed the example with Ganymede, thus presenting the archetypal example of the amorous liaison between the older and younger man, the great and the small, the immortal and the mortal, an archetype which gave such powerful inspiration to the pedagogic Eros of Socrates and Plato. According to Plutarch, Herakles had so many lovers that it would be impossible to enumerate them all, the most famous having been Hylas and Iolaos, to whose tomb boys in love would go, even in Aristotle's time, to swear solemn fidelity to each other. Apollo, Hermes, Bacchus, and Orpheus (whom women are said to have

Bacchus and Ampedo. Museo Nazionale, Naples.

36

assassinated because he taught pederasty to the Thracians), as well as Pan himself reveal how all the gods of Olympus fell in love with boys and disputed with mortals over the most handsome of them.

It is true that the epics of Homer supply fewer details about the friendships of Achilles and Patroclus, Orestes and Pylades, or Theseus and Pirithous than the epic of Gilgamesh gives us on the loves of the Babylonian hero and his friend Enkidu. Nevertheless, Lucian was no doubt right when he asserted in his *Amores* "that they did not love each other for the mere pleasure of looking at each other and listening to each other sing." Furthermore, these great examples of brotherhood in arms gave rise later to relationships of a sufficiently explicit nature to prevent us from spending any time on conjecture about practices in Homeric times. For the history of Greece is full of these military couples whose love led them to heroic exploits, and one should not forget the famous Theban Guard instituted by Epaminondas; the three hundred companions who made up this body of elite were all lovers or loved ones who remained invincible until the battle of Chaeronea, when they were wiped out by Philip of Macedon. It was also *de rigueur* among the Thebans that the lover should offer his loved one a complete set of military equipment, and in Elis they were placed next to each other on the battlefield, so that this proximity should inspire them to behave in a heroic manner. In Chalcis it was customary to point out the tomb of Cleomachus of Pharsala, who in the seventh century B.C. succeeded in destroying the Eretrian cavalry thanks to the inspiration he gained from the sight of his lover during the battle. This was the reason why the Chalcidians used to sing this song, which is quoted by Plutarch in his *Erotica* (Chapter xvii):

O young men to whom fate has granted
    beauteous grace and valiant fathers,
Do not forbid courageous men to enjoy your
    youth,
For the benevolent Eros flourishes along
    with beauty
In the cities of the Chalicidians.

There is no doubt therefore that a kind of military pederasty existed in Greece from the most ancient times, but we should not conclude as a result that homosexuality in this country always possessed this heroic quality or that at a later period it became exclusively bound up with philosophy. The different Greek city-states possessed degrees of civilization and types of morality so diverse that the most varied types of homosexuality also flourished. The Boeotians for example, whom the ancients regarded as the coarsest of the Greeks—although it was they who devised the graceful fables telling of Narcissus and of the love of Herakles for Iolaos, and it was they who produced both Plutarch and Pindar—tolerated the corruption of boys which, in theory at least, was condemned in the other cities. Xenophon says that among them, as among the Aeolians, men and young boys had "relationships similar to those of husband and wife," but Pindar asserts that this type of relationship was encouraged in order to modify a way of life that was too brutal. In Sparta, pederasty was part of the educational system, as Xenophon says, and the government prescribed this kind of love to the extent that boys of aristocratic origin who had no lovers were punished, and handsome youths who preferred a rich lover to a poor and honest man were fined. However, if all show of affection and even the most intimate relationships were authorized by law, those who were responsible for corruption and those who submitted to it were punished by exile and sometimes by death. The lover had to defend his loved one in public assemblies, in the same way as the latter had assisted the former on the battlefields. The reserve inherent in homosexuality as practiced in Sparta, however, seems to have been the exception, for in the other Dorian states, where it did not always have the political importance that it acquired in Sparta, it invariably revealed itself as more lascivious and coarse.

In Crete, for example, it was usual for relationships between boys to begin with abduction. Three days beforehand, the lover advised the parents and friends of the loved one of his intentions. When the day arrived the parents and friends gathered together, and if the lover appeared to them unworthy, they tried to prevent the abduction; if the contrary was the case they resisted only for the sake of form, and pursued the ravisher as far as his own house. The lover was made to give a present to his beloved. Then he had to take him away to the country and for sixty days he had to house and maintain all those who had been present at the abduction and offer them the pleasures of the hunt. The law did not allow the lover to keep the boy longer than two months; once this

Dionysus. Symbolic discovery of our time. During excavations carried out by order of the Pope in the Basilica of St. Peter, with the intention of opening up the Apostle's Tomb, this gigantic Dionysus was discovered—it has the air of an actor in a Fellini film.

Graffiti by homosexuals at Thera (names of various couples on the Rock of Friendship). After Dr. Magnus Hirschfeld, *Die Homosexualität im Altertum* (Albertina Graphische Samlung, Vienna, 1927).

Violent games. Fifth century. Paris.

Youths dancing. Fourth century. Paris.

period was over he had to take him back to his parents, give him a military outfit, a bull, and a drinking vessel, and finally take his leave. The boy then had to sacrifice the bull to Zeus, and afterward it was his turn to invite all those who had followed him to the country to a great feast. He had to say if he had been well treated by his lover, in which case their relationship could continue. On the other hand, if he had received violent treatment, he had the right to dismiss the brutal man and demand reparations. Abduction also existed in Chalcidia, which is moreover the source of the legend describing the abduction of Ganymede by the father of the gods.

In Athens pederasty existed before the time when it was the subject of meditation on the part of the philosophers or when it was celebrated by writers and poets. From the time of Solon there were regulations about it, and it is an interesting fact that it was forbidden to slaves. Solon himself, one of the seven Sages of Greece, had been the

lover of Pisistratus, and both Plutarch and Athenaeus have quoted one of his poems, which leaves no doubt concerning his tastes:

You will know love for boys in their
    delightful youth,
Desiring their thighs and their tender
    mouths
You will know love for boys until
    a stray hair grows like down on their
    faces,
Cherishing their sweet breath and their
    thighs.

Although homosexuality in Athens was reserved essentially for free men, it would be naïve to imagine that it was merely Platonic or simply in accordance with the ideal set out by the philosophers. Male prostitution was widespread, and it was also something of a profession, forming the object of a particular tax which was ratified every year by the Senate of the Five Hundred. Aristophanes refers to the Athenian magistrates who had the special duty of supervising the young under the amusing name of "arse inspectors." There were many young men who sold their bodies, either for money or for a horse or a hunting dog or some exotic bird. The names they were given varied from "little prostitutes," to "tarts" or "old rags," "skins," "leather bags," or "arses." There were in existence contracts which were signed by witnesses and deposited with third parties, contracts in which the boy set out his conditions and the favors he would bestow. In addition to this free-enterprise prostitution, if it can be described as such, young and handsome slaves worked in brothels on behalf of their masters. In the same way there was no lack of well-born young men ready to be kept by rich protectors and live as concubines with their "husbands." This type of elegant semiprostitution was regarded almost as severely as the other, but the line of demarcation between

Skyphos. Circa fifth century. London.

what was called by agreement "pure love" and "impure love" was often vague and difficult to define. The fact remains that the prostitutes and the kept youths were generally despised, whatever the degree of tolerance they finally achieved in social life. A free Athenian who had come of age could not prostitute himself without being punished by death, and if he abandoned himself to this fashionable semiprostitution consisting of kept youths, he found himself always at the mercy, not only of public disapproval,

Alcibiades mutilating a Hermes from a crossroads, during a night of orgy. Copenhagen.

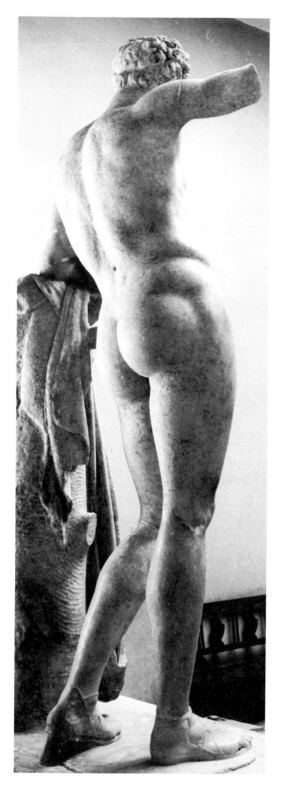

but of the denunciations which everyone had the right to make. Anyone who was found guilty could be condemned for infamous conduct for life and deprived of his civil and political rights. Slaves were forbidden to be prostitutes. By the same virtue, although procuring was forbidden to freeborn youths, the law did permit the sale of young slaves for the purpose of debauchery, and even allowed them to be castrated. On the other hand, anyone who corrupted a minor without the consent of his father or his tutor, or outraged a freeborn youth even if he were of age, could be condemned to death and executed on the same day that he was sentenced. It is true however that social life developed in such a way that, according to Aeschines, it became necessary for the law to make it clear that politicians who had prostituted themselves publicly or had led a life of debauchery could no longer make speeches in the people's Assembly.

This development, as well as the legislative system to which reference has just been made, show to what extent homosexuality had penetrated throughout the whole of Greek life and how far it had spread into the most widely differentiated strata of society. And in fact it is difficult to mention the name of any famous Greek without adding the names of his lovers. In this sphere politicians compete with philosophers, and poets with soldiers. We have already mentioned Solon. Themistocles and Aristides were rivals also over a handsome boy by the name of Stesilaos. The adventures and disappointments of Alcibiades are well known, as well as the insult to which Socrates submitted him. Demosthenes had the reputation of spending just as much on

Hermes. Praxiteles. Museum of Olympia, Greece.

courtesans as on boys; when he was married he fell in love with the handsome Knossian whom he established, without scruples, in the conjugal home; he dressed with care, wore short mantles that were overelegant, and flowing tunics which some people regarded as more suitable for a woman than for a man. The greatest tragic poets were not immune to the craze. In *The Myrmidons* Aeschylus celebrated the loves of Achilles and Patroclus, while he also composed a *Laius* which depicted the liaison between the father of Oedipus and Chrysippus, the son of Pelops. Sophocles described in *The Women of Colchis,* the love of Zeus for Ganymede and wrote about pederasty both in his tragedy *Niobe* and his satirical drama *The Lovers of Achilles.* He himself was inclined toward love affairs with men until he reached old age, and Athenaeus recounts the homosexual adventures he still had when he was sixty-five; he only gave them up when he was very old and had become impotent, which caused him to say, "I have

The Embrace of Eros. Antiquarium, Berlin.

escaped from the pleasures of love like a slave from his master." Euripides was the lover of the poet Agathon (whom Aristophanes reproached for being a foppish, effeminate creature) and he wrote, no doubt in order to please Agathon, the tragedy of *Chrysippus,* in which he described how Laius abducted this son of Pelops and the link which united them beyond death. The most famous of the Greek sculptors, Phidias, loved his pupils Agoracritos of Paros and Pantarces of Airgos. Among the poets, Alcaeus, whom we have already mentioned in connection with Sappho, celebrated and practiced pederasty, like Anacreon, Ibycos, Pindar, and many others. All the poems of Anacreon are erotic in character, although they are full of a delicate reserve: "Boy with the virginal gaze," he cried, "I am mad with love for you, but you never listen to me. You do not know that in your hand you hold the reins of my soul...." And in the *Anacreontia* we can read this portrait of the old man in love:

Diskobolos. Myron. Fifth century. Louvre, Paris.

Another hermaphroditic *Apollo*. Glyptoteket, Copenhagen.

When I see a group of young men, I grow young again and, old though I am, I join in the dance.

Cybele, I beg you, give me flowers: I want to make a garland for myself. Away with hoary old age! I shall be young and dance with the young.

Bring me the juice of the grape, and everyone will see a vigorous old man who can talk, drink and commit delightful follies.

Pindar, whom contemporaries described as possessing "an excessively amourous temperament," is known to have loved Agathon in his youth, to have fallen in love while middle-aged with a flute player by the name of Diodorus and, when he was eighty, with a certain Boulagoras of Phanagoreion. He died in the arms of Theoxenes of Tenedos for whom he had written this song:

O my soul, it was in his time, when I was young, that I should have gathered the flowers of love. But who would not have burned with desire when he saw the face of Theoxenes with its marble-like glow? Otherwise a man would be black at heart forged in iron or steel in a fire of ice, or be despised by Aphrodite of the provocative eyes, or be a prey to the exhausting thirst for riches, or be the blind slave of imprudent women. As for me, passion devours me utterly and I melt like beeswax whenever I see an adolescent boy in the springtime of puberty. Yes, Persuasion and Grace dwell in Tenedos with the son of Agesilas.

It would be impossible to mention all the Greek poets who celebrated the love of boys, leaving behind them work that varied from the slight and licentious to the serious and melancholy, including epigrams and amatory letters. Theocritus of Syracuse, Addeus of Macedon, Asclepius of Samos, Callimachus of Cyrene, and Philostrates are some of those whose names and fragments of work have come down to us. This poetry lasted from the seventh century B.C. to the third century A.D. Sometimes it was coarse, as in the case of Addeus of Macedon, who was not afraid of writing:

When you meet a boy who pleases you, you must take action at once. Instead of concealing your intentions, take hold of his balls. Being polite, saying "I respect you, I want to be a brother to you," is a form of prudishness which can only prevent you from reaching your goal.

44

This kind of poetry becomes roguish with Strato of Sardis who found that in bed "a sad and shameful attitude" is only suitable in the case of common boys and recommends "preliminary kisses, play before getting down to serious love making, lascivious desires, tickling and embracing." Sometimes the poems were melancholy and delicate, such as that written by Meleager of Gadara:

O sacred night, O lamp, sole witnesses of the vows that we exchanged! He swore he would love me forever; I swore I would never leave him. You can bear witness to this mutual promise. But now he says these words were writ on water, and you see him, O lamp, in other arms than mine.

As for the philosophers, most of them practiced pederasty and celebrated it in their work. It was not only Socrates, Plato, and Aristotle whose thought was of capital importance in the understanding of this type of love; the Cyrenaics, the Cynics, the Stoics, and the Epicureans concerned themselves with it in order to justify it, condemn it, or try to ennoble it. Among the great men of Greece, however, Pericles alone definitely loved only women. Contrarily, Aristophanes—whom Plato made responsible, in the *Apologia* and the *Phaedo*, for the condemnation of Socrates — was alone among the poets in detesting pederasty and turning it to ridicule, at least in its impure and effeminate forms: there is no work of his in which he fails to satirize it and *The Guests, The Knights, The Clouds, The Frogs, The Wasps,* and *The Thesmophoriazusae* are all plays which supply valuable information about Athenian society at the period when sophists, libertines, and gossips were triumphant there. It is all the more entertaining, as a result, to find Aristophanes himself in *The Symposium* partaking in a dialogue with Socrates and justifying

Narcissus by the Fountain. Fresco. Museo Nazionale, Naples.

pederasty through the famous myth according to which early man was by nature a hermaphrodite.

It would be a mistake however to think that there was some connection between moral freedom during the time of Aristophanes and the failure of the Greek cities to unite against the Macedonians and resist them. For the same practices existed among

45

Faun pursuing a boy. Museo Nazionale del Bargello, Florence.

victors and vanquished; Philip and Alexander were homosexuals just like Demosthenes and no doubt to a greater extent. The homosexuality of the Macedonian princes was well known and was apparently of a brutal and violent nature. Several of them were assassinated by their male favorites. Archelaos, King of Macedonia, was slain by two men whom he loved, Cratias and Hallanocrates of Larissa, because he had offended them deeply. Philip himself was killed in 336 A.D. by one of his bodyguards named Pausanias. The latter reproached him for not having avenged him for the insult caused by one of the King's other lovers who, out of jealousy, had handed him over to his grooms; the latter had taken advantage both of Pausanias and of a female prostitute.

Alexander the Great was inclined to love affairs with men from his earliest youth and Athenaeus, Plutarch, and Epictetus assert that after wishing to be loved for himself alone he was not above buying handsome slaves for his pleasure. He loved passionately the eunuch Bagoas, as well as Hephestion. Athenaeus tells how at the theater he happened to kiss Bagoas in front of the spectators, a gesture which gave rise to

applause and cries of "Encore!" whereupon the King obeyed the crowd and kissed his beloved a second time. On various occasions he was seen to dance with him. But when his deeply beloved Hephestion died at Ecbatana his grief was so frenzied that it brought him near to madness. For three days Alexander remained in the room where his friend had died, without eating, without sleeping, and without ceasing his lamentations, until the corpse, in a state of decomposition, had to be torn away from him.[6] According to Plutarch, he ordered that as a sign of mourning the manes of horses and mules should be cut off immediately, that the crenelations on the walls around the city should be knocked down, and that the doctor who had failed to save his friend should be hanged. Epictetus adds that he caused the temples of Aesculapius to be burned down so that the god of medicine should be punished for his incompetence. His frenzy only subsided on the day when Jupiter Ammon ordered that Hephestion should be revered and that sacrifices should be made to him as to a god.

Although homosexual freedom could be associated with the decline of Greece, the Athenians had never failed to regard pederastic love as the origin of their liberty. In *The Symposium* Plato causes Pausanias to say that if the barbarians condemned love for boys, it was because tyrannical power tends to forbid it, in the same way as it forbids the love of knowledge or physical exercise. For in fact "it is not to the advantage of those in power to allow the development, in those who submit to this power, of lofty thoughts or of close friendships or attachments, which are the usual outcome of love." Two facts deserve to be remembered in this connection. The first occurred during

[6] See Maurice Druon, *Alexandre le Grand ou le roman d'un Dieu* (Paris: 1959).

the forty-sixth celebration of the Olympic Games, that is to say at the end of the sixth century B.C., and conjures up memories of the great ritual murders of the most archaic periods. While an epidemic was raging, Epimenides is said to have ordered the Athenians to make a human sacrifice in order to purify the city of an ancient blemish. A handsome adolescent boy named Cratinos is said to have offered of his own free will to die for his country, and his lover, Aristodemos, is said to have followed his example. The sacrifice of this homosexual couple was regarded as having saved the city, which in later centuries devoted a fervent cult to them. In the same way the murder of the tyrant Hippias in A.D. 514 was attributed to two lovers, Harmodius and Aristogiton. In actual fact the young men, who died in the plot that they had contrived, only killed the brother of Hippias, who was himself driven out of Athens four years later. The incident had, however, made such an impression that the tyrannicidal lovers were the first to have their statues in the Agora, and a tomb on the road to the Academy; to become the objects of a cult and of commemorative feasts. There was even a law which obliged every citizen to take the following oath against anyone who might attempt to overthrow the democratic government:

I shall kill with my own hand, if I can, any man who overthrows the Athenian democracy. . . . And if anyone other than myself carries out this murder I shall regard him as dutiful toward the gods and the spirits. If on the contrary any man, either in carrying out the murder or in attempting to carry it out, happens to die, I shall do good toward him and I shall honor both him and his children, like Harmodius, Aristogiton, and their descendants.

And shortly after the Persian War, Callistra-tus composed in their honor a song which could be heard, apparently, at even the least important banquets, and became the theme song of Greek love:

I shall carry the sword in a branch of
    myrtle
like Harmodius and Aristogiton
when they killed the tyrant
and set Athens free.

Dear Harmodius, no, you are not dead;
you live in the Blessed Isles
with the swift Achilles,
with Diomedes, son of Tydeus.

I shall carry the sword in a branch of
    myrtle
like Harmodius and Aristogiton,
when at the feast of the Panathenians,
they slew the tyrant Hipparchus.

Your fame shall be eternal,
dear Harmodius and dear Aristogiton,
for you have slain the tyrant,
for you have set Athens free.

Hermaphrodite. Fresco. Pompeii.

It is therefore against this background of reality and the diversity of pederastic customs in Greece that we should understand and assess the philosophical meditation on the subject of homosexuality, principally in the work of Plato. It is not this thought which allows us to grasp the reality of Greek love, for the philosophy was only the reflection of it and not the cause, and its merit and significance lie in the fact that it brought into the light of consciousness a phenomenon experienced by everyone; that it attempted to integrate that consciousness into the hierarchy of social and moral values admitted at that time; and to transform it into a way of accomplishing destiny, and into a stage in absolute knowledge. But this speculation can only be appreciated inasmuch as we do not lose sight of the whole background of material facts to which we have referred—and which supply material for it—and if we do not omit to mention the homosexuality of Socrates and Plato themselves.

It is true that there has been discussion on this question, at least so far as Socrates is concerned, and if one can admit that Plato's description of the night which Alcibiades and the philosopher passed together was to a large extent an attempt to prove something. Socrates had been condemned, as everyone knows, following the accusation that he had corrupted young men—a crime for which, as we have seen, a man could be denounced. Moreover, at the period when Plato was writing, further posthumous accusations had been made against the master. Some people said that Socrates was responsible for the misdeeds of Alcibiades and in particular for the mutilation of the statues of Hermes (which the handsome dandy had carried out), the divulging of the Mysteries (of which he had been guilty), the disastrous Sicilian expedition (which had been his

Antinous. Delphi. Antinous was Emperor Hadrian's lover. He was deified, and a town was founded in his honor and named after him. In the temples priests performed cures in his name by making him appear to patients in dreams.

decision), and lastly for his recent acts of treason. By showing Socrates as resisting the advances of Alcibiades and indoctrinating him, Plato was suggesting that if the young man had gone wrong, it was rather because he had not followed the example of his master. By an irony of fate, the denunciation of which Socrates was the victim had been made by Anytus, the philosopher's unlucky rival with the same Alcibiades. It was a matter of jealousy disguised as the defense of virtue. However, some people have thought that the philosopher—whose ugliness was proverbial, with his protruding eyes and snub nose, his whole appearance resembling that of a satyr—had only used the passion of his age for the love of boys as

48

a pretext to find the most favorable background for his teaching. However, it is known for certain that when he was young, Socrates was loved by his master Archelaos and that during his maturity and until his old age, he pursued many handsome youths in assiduous fashion. In particular he was in love with Charmides, the son of Glaucon, with Euthydemus, the son of Diocles, with Phaedrus, Agathon, and above all, Alcibiades. It is obviously difficult to know to what stage he took his love, since Plato in fact tried to exonerate him from the accusation of homosexuality of a corrupting nature. But he left no doubt that Socrates experienced carnal desire for the boys with whom he was in love and that his affection was far from being purely spiritual. The details surrounding the dissertations attributed to him by Plato, details which reflect the daily life and habits of everyone, are much more revealing than the dissertations themselves. When Socrates admits that contact with Aristobulos' naked shoulder gave him a visceral shock, or when, after Charmides had looked at him with an expression he could not describe, a glance beneath his clothes showed him that he was on fire and no longer master of himself, we do not need any drawings to help us grasp the situation and we understand better how, in *The Symposium,* Socrates was able to state that he understood love and that the gods had given him the gift of discerning at first glance who was in love with whom.

There is no doubt that Socrates tried to introduce a spiritual quality into homosexuality, to disassociate it from sensuality and use it as a springboard for the universal contemplation of the Beautiful. It is impossible to set out in detail here the viewpoints of Plato and, through Plato, of Socrates, and even more so to discuss them. Let us recall only that these viewpoints can be found in

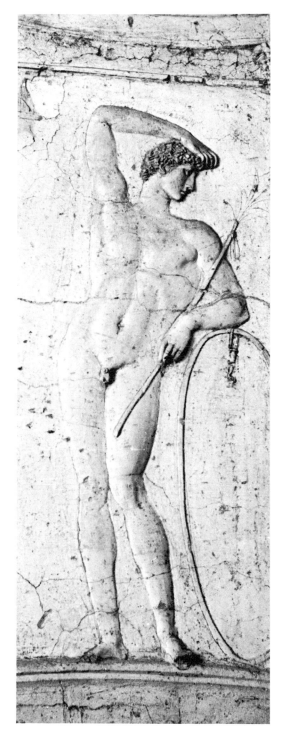

An ephebus. Stucco. Pompeii. The youth depicted as a god.

49

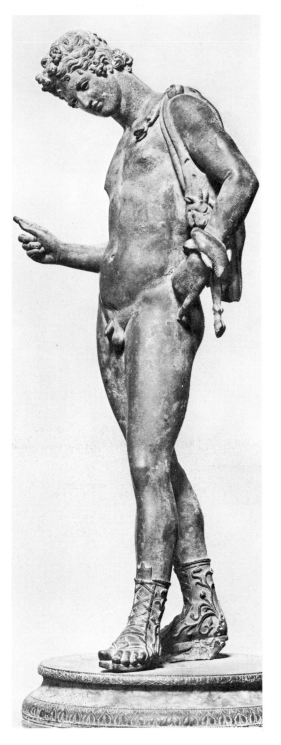

The Narcissus of Pompeii. Museo Nazionale, Naples.

The Symposium, Phaedrus, and Lysis and that it is already remarkable that love between man and woman is hardly mentioned, for the dialogues deal almost exclusively with the love for boys. It is not less surprising that it should be a woman, Diotima of Mantineia, who confirms the superiority of this love over that between opposing sexes. For it should be noted that *The Symposium* deals in principle with all forms of love and that homosexuality is considered precisely in connection with so-called normal love. Neither is "normal" love in any way despised. "The union of man and woman," says Diotima, "is a divine thing. It is the presence of immortality within mortal life: fecundity and procreation."

Plato, we know, causes every guest at *The Symposim* to make a speech about love, but he clearly lends his support to the description given by Socrates of the opinions of Diotima. However, the opinions of Phaedrus, Pausanias, Eryximachus, Aristophanes, or Agathon do not contradict in any way the teachings of the extraneous woman from Mantineia. They should be described rather as complementary or as situated at those inferior degrees of initiation which she herself regards as the indispensable point of departure for any later ascent. Phaedrus praises homosexuality for the courage it incites in battle and states that the lover is more divine than his favorite, for he alone is possessed of the god. Pausanias distinguishes between the celestial Aphrodite and the popular Aphrodite and asserts that the followers of the latter love women as much as boys, and love body more than soul; he finds that the perverse man is he who, deprived of constancy, allows himself to be won over by money or power of a political kind. In all these attitudes both men are merely talking around this revelation by Diotima, for whom the first degree of initiation consists of progressing from the physical beauty of one boy to that of several, and from there to larger objects of love. In the same way the myth evoked by Aristophanes is integrated in the whole ensemble of the Platonic conceptions and cannot be disassociated from them. This myth presents primitive humanity as having been composed of three kinds: the males, the females, and the hermaphrodites. All of them are said to have been round and double in shape, and they were so daring that the gods decided to crush them. Zeus was therefore said to have cut them in two, which gave rise to the need for each being to find his other half and his original unity

Augustus and Caesar. After a cameo published by Hancarville. After Lo Duca, *Histoire de l'Érotisme, (De Erotica I)* J.-J. Pauvert, 1959.

again. It is a curious fact that the sexual organs of these first representatives of humanity are supposed to have been located not at the front of their bodies but outside, with the result that they would have no progeny and would reproduce themselves by penetrating not into each other but, like grasshoppers, into the ground. It was only later that the father of the gods apparently moved their genitals to the place where they are situated today. Whatever the reason, men who were halves of those combined beings called hermaphrodites are said to have become lovers of women; women who were halves of primitive women are said to have been inclined toward women by becoming tribades; and the halves of the original males are supposed to have gone out in search of their other male halves. "As long as there are young **boys**," says Aristophanes, "they will love grown men, will take their pleasure in sharing their beds and embracing them . . . once they have grown up they will reveal themselves to be men by engaging in affairs of State. Once they have become men they will love boys and will be satisfied to spend their lives together in a state of celibacy." He makes it clear that their ideal is never to leave each other, night or day, and to become such a close partnership that they can lead a common existence together as though they were one being only, and after dying together, still be one, in Hades. Copulation, if it took place between the opposite sexes, should allow reproduction and the increase of the species, and if between males, should allow "a satisfaction that leads to action."

This idea was later taken up again and explored more thoroughly by Socrates who, distinguishing between the celestial and the vulgar Eros, stated that a twofold desire for procreation did exist. One of these, which was concerned with the body, would turn for preference toward women and would ensure immortality through the procreation of children. For, as Diotima said, "the aim of Love is not the Beautiful, it is procreation and the giving of birth within Beauty." Poets, artists, inventors, and statesmen should then seek out beautiful bodies through contact with which they will be able to procreate works of art, for "they will never procreate in ugliness." Now they undertake to become educators. So that after having loved only one beautiful body they become transformed into "lovers of all beautiful bodies, thus calming the impetuousness of their love in respect of one individual." "The straightforward practice of love for young men" makes them ascend as though by stages: from fine bodies to fine occupations, from fine occupations to fine knowledge, and from fine knowledge to the essence of Beauty, simple and eternal, without shape and without face, present in all things and estranged from them, dominating life and death and identifying itself with the Divine. To those who allege that love for boys is a frenzy, Plato replies that the frenzy is the effect of a divine favor and the source of the greatest good. Only this frenzy is capable of making us see, through terrestrial beauty, the beauty that is eternal.

It is certain that Plato, although he does not condemn sexual intercourse between the lover and the loved one, acknowledges sexual relations only as a stage in this ascent of the soul which he sets out in detail. Some authors, such as Léon Robin, have believed that through the spirituality of love Plato sought only the end of sensuality. It is no doubt more accurate to think that the Platonic tendency, while accepting the initial reality of carnal love, proposed to remove the carnal element and to sublimate it. Plato, and to a greater extent, Plotinus, prepare the way for Christianity and a disassociation between soul and body which finally assumed the aspects of the tragic neurosis of the western Middle Ages. In *The Republic* Plato again offers as a reward to warriors the right of embracing and of being embraced by the handsomest boys. But in *The Laws,* his last work, he finds sensual love abominable and admits only spiritual love. Much could be said about this development, which takes place, in fact, in the philosopher's most Utopian works (works which also include suggestions of the most disorderly communism and racism). Few commentators have pointed out to what extent this social Utopianism is certainly linked to the erotic Utopianism which aims at detaching the mind from the body. Nietzsche deserves to be heard when he accuses Socrates of being one of the aspects of Greek decadence. For Socrates, who was an incorrigible chatterbox, finally suggested that love could be reduced to talk and that talk could be identified with creative work. These great philosophers were beginning to realize the difficulty of maintaining the unity between body and soul: they found themselves at the beginning of a cycle of which we are at the end. The fact remains that Socrates and Plato had the immense merit of attempting to devise a form of eroticism, of "thinking out" a phenomenon which until then had been lived out in unconscious fashion, of trying to work out the responsibilities of the partners, and of integrating them in a hierarchy of values acceptable to all.

It is more important to remember this attempt, the first ever made, than the conclusions it reached. The *Eros Socraticus,* which finally identified itself with a pedagogic type of love, with the love of the older man for a younger one, is far from helping to solve the problems caused by homosexuality today. It did not even succeed in solving the

Bronze. Châlon-sur-Saone. Bibliothèque Nationale, Paris. Young Ethiopian slaves were appreciated by the Romans for their chatter as well as their beauty.

range of problems caused by homosexuality in Greece, of which we have seen the extremely wide variety. This was because it restricted itself to defining the duties of the adolescent and the mature man while there existed in Greece liaisons between adults which could not fit into the Platonic setup. Socrates himself supplied the example of this by pursuing Alcibiades with his attentions. Similarly, Euripides, who at the age of seventy-two loved the poet Agathon, who was then forty; or Permenides who, having passed the age of sixty, fell in love with the philosopher Zeno, who was also in his forties. What can we make of Pindar's love for Diodorus when he was twenty-four? These unknown quantities, which are quite natural, still leave us with the problem of creating an erotic system and finding a place for homosexuality in a hierarchy of values. Socrates and Plato made it clear that it was dishonorable to be won over quickly or to allow oneself to be seduced by the attraction of money or political power, and added that the only honorable way of yielding to one's lover was to do so out of esteem for him and in the hope of self-improvement; at the same time they said that "the thing" was neither beautiful nor ugly in itself, but became beautiful if it was carried out in a beautiful way. Thus Socrates and Plato established moral rules which were more important than their metaphysics and which can still be put forward today to all those who seek to find themselves through love.

In view of these attempts to integrate erotic love within general ethical systems, it is not particularly interesting to consider what the situation of women could have been at this period. For although they were usually confined to the house and excluded from everything concerning culture and the interests of the country, one cannot regard this situation as a cause of homosexuality

54

but rather as a consequence of the homosexual tendencies of most Greeks. Furthermore, it is incorrect to imagine, as some people did in the past, that Greek homosexuality wanted women to remain uncultured and could not tolerate the idea of a cultivated woman. Very much to the contrary, it was in regions like Ionia (and even in Athens) where this segregation of women was practiced, that homosexuality never acquired the dignity of an institution. In the Dorian states, on the other hand, where women were honored and took an active part in social life as well as in the upbringing and education of men, homosexuality did acquire this characteristic to an advanced extent. The result is that pederasty appears it be a phenomenon independent of the cultural or social position of women, and resembles a spontaneous emotional tendency which can be seen through the most widely different political and moral structures.

In Greece, as we have mentioned, the philosophers attempted the sublimation of homosexuality; the inhabitants of Megara, when they wished to commemorate a lover, organized a contest around his tomb every spring to see which boy could give the sweetest kisses, and the winner went home to his mother wreathed in garlands. The Romans, on the other hand, practiced homosexuality with the heavy and brutal sensuality that was characteristic of them.

From the sixth century onward, homosexual orgies had become usual in Rome, although the law punished by death every act of violence in this sphere. Although we possess only isolated pieces of information relating to the Roman Republic, we can see from the time of the Empire the importance which had been acquired by this aspect of love. Caesar—the dandy, the writer, the strategist and politician of genius—was the lover of Nicomedes, the King of Bithynia, a fact so well known that his soldiers used to sing as they accompanied him:

Caesar conquered the Gauls, Nicomedes had
  conquered Caesar.
Today you can see the triumph of Caesar,
He who has conquered the Gauls,
But you can't see Nicomedes, who has con-
  quered Caesar.

Curio called Caesar "a husband to all wives and a wife to all husbands," but he liked to announce that his soldiers, even if drenched in perfumes, were the best of all. Sulla had already warned Caesar against this "young man with the inadequate girdle," a fashion which in Rome was regarded as characteristic of effeminate men; and when a senator treated him as a woman, the conqueror of Gaul had replied that Semiramis had reigned over Syria and the Amazons over part of Asia.

Even Augustus, who otherwise conducted himself so well, was accused of having prostituted himself for three hundred thousand sesterces to Aulus Hirtius; during the public games the crowd had brought the house down applauding an actor who, pointing out a priest of Cybele who was playing the timbrel, had recited this line which they believed contained an allusion to the Emperor's way of life: "Can you see how that eunuch controls his drum with his finger?"

According to Suetonius, Tiberius had trained very young children, his "minnows," to stay between his legs while he was swimming, so that they could lick and nibble him until he gradually became

Pan and his Pupil. Variant. Galleria delle Terme, Rome.

excited. He was said to have offered his genitals to lively babies who were not yet weaned, so that they could suck those organs instead of the breast. One day, seduced by the beauty of the acolyte who was assisting him during a religious ceremony, he could not wait for the end of the service, took the boy aside, and enjoyed both him and his brother, who was a flute player.

Caligula took advantage of young men who were sent to him as hostages. He was alternately the lover and the loved one of Lepidus and was intensely attached to Mnester, the actor. He kissed Mnester during the show and if anyone made the slightest sound while the artist was dancing, he had the offender dragged out of his seat and beat him with his own hand. It was a significant fact that Caligula identified himself with Jupiter, and on nights when the moon was full begged the god to come and embrace him and share his couch. He conversed with the master of the gods, threatened him, and one day was heard to call out: "Take me, or I shall take you."

Nero solemnly married Pythagoras and later Sporus, a young freedman whom he had previously had castrated. During the feasts given for their betrothal the Romans paid the handsome *castrato* the honors reserved for an emperor. Sporus conducted himself very well: he assisted the Emperor until the time of his final setbacks, he was one of the four people who remained faithful to him when he fell from power, and he encouraged Nero to commit suicide.

Galba, who overthrew Nero, preferred strong, mature men. When one of his favorites announced to him in Spain that his rival was dead, Galba did not restrict himself to embracing the man warmly in front of his soldiers, but also begged him to have his pubic hair removed at once, and then led him away. Otho, who was called Pathicus,

prostituted himself with his friends. Titus, whose good conduct was renowned, maintained hosts of favorites and eunuchs. But the scandalous behavior of the emperors did not stop at homosexuality, as is well known. The degradation of this form of love was only one aspect of a more general degradation, the prime cause of which was absolute power and the intoxication to which it led.

Heliogabalus seems to have been the only emperor who was exclusively homosexual, and in a passive way. This great priest of the sun, who had been put on the throne at the age of fourteen through his mother's ambition and the sensual admiration of the Legions, never succeeded in having sexual relations with a woman. His two marriages were both failures. He had been initiated into homosexuality by a masseur who remained faithful to him until he died, and he began by falling desperately in love with a wagoner. Afterward he would fall for favorites who were always of a lower class. After the charioteers he came to actors, cooks, locksmiths, and finally a latrine-cleaner. He gave them all state posts and they seem to have carried out their duties no worse than those who regarded themselves as brought up for this purpose. At Rome in the year 973, Heliogabalus thought out an incredible scene: He summoned the prostitutes of Suburra to his palace, gave the young ones to his guards, and then forced the old ones to undress in front of his most handsome favorites so that the splendid nudity of the latter put the misery and deformities of the former to shame.

However, the dignity of pederastic love, even in the imperial palaces, was saved by the liaison which united Hadrian, the greatest of the Caesars, to Antinous. In her fictional *Memoirs of Hadrian* Marguerite Yourcenar has described the handsome, young Bithynian as he appeared one evening

Hippolytus. Fragment of a sarcophagus. Louvre, Paris.

in Nicomedia, during a recital of poetry in the gardens of a Roman noble:[7]

A little apart from the others a young boy was listening to those difficult strophes, half-attentive, half in dream; I thought at once of some shepherd, deep in the woods, vaguely aware of a strange bird's cry. . . . I kept him on after the others had gone.

Hadrian then lived "a few fabulous years" in the company of this passionate young savage who, like a living image of beauty, had attached himself to the Emperor "like some animal or a familiar spirit." But as time passed Antinous imagined that he was obstructing the career of his friend the Emperor. He decided, as a final proof of love, to sacrifice his life to him. He went out silently one day in Hadrian's boat and drowned himself in the Nile. Marguerite Yourcenar's Hadrian says:

I descended the slippery steps; he was lying at the bottom, already sunk in the river's mud. . . . Everything gave way; everything seemed extinguished. The Olympian Zeus, Master of All, Savior of the World—all toppled together, and there was only a man with graying hair sobbing on the deck of a boat.

The depth and dignity of this love somewhat rescue the homosexual practices of the Romans from the depravities that covered them with shame. With the exception of Virgil, whose tendencies are known to us (although the incidents of his life are not), one cannot maintain that Horace, Catullus, Tibullus, or Martial raised its reputation. They preferred women to boys

[7]Marguerite Yourcenar, *Memoirs of Hadrian*, tr. Grace Frick (New York: Farrar, Strauss, 1963).

57

and their homosexual relationships seem to have occurred only infrequently or during orgies. Much will be forgiven Catullus, however, for the touching accents inspired by "'Juventius all made of honey" who despised him and who, in order to punish Catullus for having snatched "a little kiss sweeter than ambrosia," wiped off his fingers "the drops with which his lips were covered" as though the trace of the poet had been no more than "the loathsome saliva of a shameless female wolf."

No doubt Petronius, in his *Satyricon*, gives a fairly accurate description of Roman manners in the early years of the Christian era and of the "serene immodesty" which characterized them. His hero, Gito, the narrator's lover—whose name came to mean catamite, a boy who accepted the role of favorite—goes from one love to another with such ease that his friend no longer knows whether he should be angry with him for circumventing his girlfriend or angry with her for corrupting his favorite. Succulent flesh, exquisite flagellations, leather phalli introduced into the softest depths complete the warm voluptuousness procured by Gito:

What a night that was, O gods! O goddesses!
How soft that bed! a fiery embrace!
And through our burning lips our vagrant
Souls passed one to the other. Flee, mortal
Cares! For I shall die of pleasure.

It is true that the outlook of the period was different from ours. Nothing proves it more clearly than the erotic *graffiti* found by Roger Peyrefitte at Pompeii. They were the work of "young men of the Venus of Pompeii," who proclaimed themselves "happy young men" (*juvenes sumus felices*) in no way ashamed of the homosexuals among them whose principal preoccupation was "the enjoyable thing"; proud of saying if they had done it five or six times, whether a certain man "makes love to the boys splendidly or not"; and, after so much proof of lasciviousness, leaving these splendid statements: "Perish the man who does not know how to make love!" And "May he who forbids love-making perish twice over!"

In addition to the abovementioned, however, male prostitution had developed to such an extent in Rome that it overwhelmed everything else. Apart from the open prostitution which was practiced, especially along the Via Suburrana, the Mons Esquilinus, the Vicus Patricius, the Porta Trigemina, etc., homosexual brothels, which were often situated beneath theaters and circuses or in certain taverns, offered their clients effeminate young boys, called *pueri,* who played the passive role, and hairy, muscular adults named *dranci* or *agentes in paedicatione,* who played the active role. Among the aristocracy the richest men kept harems of boys, and in an amusingly paradoxical way it was fashionable to call them *paedagogia.* The favorites who officiated in them were usually recruited in Africa, and the Alexandrines seem to have been the most sought after, the most admired, and the most expensive; the Syrians and the Moors were also appreciated for their chatter and their roguish beauty. But these *pueri,* who were often insolent and bold, introduced an obscene and coarse atmosphere into Roman homosexuality that was partly responsible for the general moral degradation of which Christianity took advantage. For homosexuality in the Roman world had moved continually further away from Greece. There had been no effort to introduce any nobility into it, to think about it and raise it above the coarsest and most material sensuality. It is understandable therefore, that spirituality had been

58

neglected to such an extent that some compensation was sought in the mystical asceticism of the new religion. Since there was no longer any attempt to conceal these excesses or to form any links with the highest aspirations of the soul, they can only have led to boredom.

From the fourth century onward, the Christian emperors, Constantine, Valentinian the Younger, and Theodosius proclaimed edicts making homosexuality a crime punishable by death. In 536 and 544, Justinian published in Byzantium two new laws threatening to inflict torture on all those who would not repent of this "illicit" luxuriousness, "impious behavior, which is abominable and hated by God." The ancient world was dead. The Middle Ages were born.

Hermaphrodite or Sphis Contemplating his Metamorphosis. Cameo. Bibliothèque Nationale, Paris.

59

Incision of the scrotum, after *Traité de Chirurgie.* Cherefettin Saboundjouoglou. 1465. Bibliothèque Nationale (Ms.), Paris.

IV
In the Moslem East

The fact that Islam has adopted an attitude toward homosexuality different from that of Christianity is all the more interesting because these two societies, at least as far as the characteristics of their religions are concerned, emerge from the same root of Judaism. Among the Jews nationalist motives led, as time went on, toward moral severity and the strengthening of sexual taboos, but among the Arabs the tendency was toward a greater indulgence and adaptation to the life actually led by peoples who had been converted to the Moslem faith. Islam very soon became a great universalist religion, not only as far as its aspirations or its aims were concerned, but in relation to historical reality. Judaism on the other hand always remained, from a material if not from a doctrinal angle, a national religion in which tendencies toward segregation and spiritual hegemony predominated.

As far as homosexuality is concerned, the presence of Jewish taboos in Islam is revealed by the fact that in the Bible and the Koran the destruction of Sodom and Gomorrah is described in identical terms. The Suras which refer to the event record without any comment the legend of Abraham and the moral judgment which is implicit in it. As far as the Lot of the Koran is concerned, the Sodomites are guilty of baseness which nobody in the world had committed before them. "Will you have carnal relations with men? Will you practice brigandage? Will you commit the blameable act in your gathering?" (XXIX: 27-29). And elsewhere it repeats: "Through covetousness you will commit the fleshly act with men and not with women. Truly, you are a people without faith" (VII: 79-81). In another Sura the Sodomites are treated as "a race of transgressors" (XXVI: 165-66) and, in yet another one, as "a bad and perverse race" (XXI: 74). However, we do not find in the Koran, any more than in the Bible, any direct link between the homosexual ways of the Sodomites and the decision taken by God to destroy their city; in fact the link is less direct. The decision is motivated by the Sodomites' general lack of piety, the outrage that they have committed on the Lord's messengers and, most of all, by their lack of faith. In the Suras this last assumes a concrete aspect; the Sodomites have sacrificed a camel which Allah had sent them as a sign, so that they should do it no harm and save themselves by saving it. It is their pride, rather than their baseness, which becomes the cause of their downfall (VII, 71–73 to 76–78).

The fact remains that apart from this story of Biblical origin, there is no explicit condemnation of homosexuality anywhere in the Koran. The thing that is forbidden outright is "baseness," understood expressly as referring to adultery. Obviously "he who fornicates is committing a sin" (XXV: 68); "Allah has no love for scandal" (II: 201–205); and all believers are invited to behave with decorum and chastity, in return for which they are promised "a vast reward" (XXIV: 38). But apart from adultery, fornication is only related to luxuriousness in the most general way. Certain commentators on the Koran have tried to include homosexuality, but these interpretations cannot be based on any precise text. Furthermore, if a Sura forbids believers to force their female slaves into prostitution (XXIV: 33), there is no corresponding directive concerning male slaves.

Whatever the situation, if "baseness" and fornication are sins and if the Moslem is invited to keep "a pure heart" in everything, the Koran is careful not to inflict punishments as cruel as those in the Bible. The pain of death is nowhere ordered for any carnal sin and the particularly barbarous form of stoning, which the Jews had used, even less so. The man or woman fornicator is only subjected to a hundred strokes of the whip (XXIV: 2), which must have been a considerable relaxation of punishment as compared to the Hebrew code. As far as homosexuality itself was concerned, the Prophet's indulgent and no doubt accommodating attitude toward it is reflected in the Suras describing the delights of paradise. For in the Mohammedan Heaven, the Fortunate Ones, clad in silk, brocade, and bracelets, can enjoy not only "houris with large eyes" (LII: 20–24), but "immortal ephebes, whom you might take for separate pearls" (LXXVI: 19).

There can be no doubt that this Moslem Paradise reflects the desires and tastes of the world of Islam, which was never obsessed with the sins of the flesh and was always sensitive to the most varied forms of love and beauty. This ambivalent attitude of Islam in erotic matters appears in literature just as it does in daily life. The reason why we possess hardly any visual proof comparable to the legacy of Greece is because Mohammed forbade any representation of the human face. In places where this prohibition was not observed, as in Persia or the Moslem parts of India, delicate miniatures give evidence of feelings which the poets did not fail to celebrate. It is possible that homosexual poetry may have reflected only the emotions of a refined milieu, but nothing can tell us more about the way in which homosexuality penetrated daily life during the great Moslem period than the tales of *The Thousand and One Nights*.[1] This masterpiece—a true collective opus by anonymous storytellers—provides us with not only frenzied or fantastic writing, preoccupied with the imaginative and the marvelous, but also with a detailed, harsh, and highly colored picture of the most varied

[1] Enver E. Dehoi, *Érotisme des "Mille et Une Nuits"* (Bibliothèque Internationale D'Érotologie, No. 4; Paris: J.-J. Pauvert, 1959). See also *Dictionnaire de Sexologie* (*op. cit.*), pp. 113–220.

Persian miniature. 1629.

references to young slaves whose beauty is "as bright as the sun," adolescents and young men whose delectable good looks are celebrated by everyone. The enchantment of these meetings does not assume a libertine character on every occasion, and is included in a most natural way in a religious context: "Heaven be praised for uniting two handsome beings," we can read in *The Splendid History of Prince Diamond*, "smoothing away difficulties from their path and solving complications." Friendship of an inspired nature often goes hand in hand with the love of a woman, but this is in order that the woman can be sacrificed to the man in a more subtle manner. Thus, in the affection of Giafar the Vizir and Attaf the Generous, which is described in *The Story of the Magic Book*, both friends sacrifice the woman they love in order to please their male partners. At the start of their liaison they can be seen sleeping next to each other, and Attaf gives up the women in his harem, over a period of four months, so that he will not be inelegant, ungracious, or impolite toward the guest with whom he has fallen in love. When, after many years and endless vicissitudes, the two young men meet again, Giafar, on hearing that Attaf is present in his town, appears "so upset that he looked like a man who has drunk poison. And he no longer knew what he was doing or saying. And he fell flat on his face, still holding in his hand the crystal goblet and the letter from his friend."

The violent feelings which express themselves in this way sometimes go to the lengths of crime. In the same story a sheikh comes to make his excuses for having killed a young man whose body had been found by the police. He justified his action through jealousy. His friend did not stop at taking his money, he said, but he was also unfaithful to him. "He would go and amuse him-

social milieux in the great cities of the Near East in the time of Haroun Al-Raschid. This picture shows that homosexuality was a frequent if not everyday occurrence, which was accepted from the moral standpoint.

In the same way as in Greece, homoerotic emotions revealed themselves through feelings ranging from the most pure to the most licentious. But behind every liaison resulting from natural choice we can sense a background formed by a general responsiveness of which the cause is the beauty of the ephebe, and not only that of the ephebe, a kind of perpetual thrill and wonder concerning masculine beauty as a whole. *The Thousand and One Nights* contains endless self sometimes with Schumuschag, sometimes with Nagish, and with Ghasis and with Ghubar and Ghushi and with many other scoundrels." The poor sheikh is outraged, for everyone boasts openly of having possessed his friend, even the street cleaner and the cobbler. Therefore, when the faithless man descended to the tripe dealer, the sheikh could no longer contain his jealousy. "The world went black" before his eyes, and he killed the ungrateful man, thus freeing himself from his torments. Did the hand of justice fall on the perpetrator of this murder, who in the West would have been regarded as a wretch? Not at all. The Caliph Haroun Al-Raschid was moved by so much misfortune in love and pardoned the fanatic.

These details throw light on the complex aspects of homosexuality in Moslem nations; it is far from being a diversion for men of refinement, or just a pure and highly charged friendship. It spreads to street cleaners, tripe dealers, and cobblers. The fact is that in Damascus men run after men just as often as those in the West run after women. In *The Story of Princess Zuleika*, a vizir of Schiraz, who admits that he is descended from the race of Lot's companions, makes advances in the middle of the street to a student from Damascus. Having learned from the boy that he was over sixteen years of age, he rejoiced and cried: "This is the good age, my child! It's the good age!" He then said to him: "If you have nothing else to do, come with me to the palace and I will introduce you to our king who likes handsome faces; he will appoint you as one of his chamberlains...." To which the bold young man replied with scarcely any hesitation: "By my head and by my eye, I hear you and I obey you." They then held hands, the vizir wondered at the good looks and elegance of his companion

and said in conclusion: "By Allah! If all the young men of Damascus are like you, that city is a region of Paradise and the sky over Damascus is Paradise itself."

Sometimes these fantastic stories, full of miraculous events, contain details likely to interest psychoanalysts. In *The Delightful Sessions of Casual Adolescence* a hardheaded boy crouches on the branch of a tree, makes water, and lets his excrement fall on the head and face of a "great man," who is covered with it. The boy is then carried away, along with his sister, by a giant bird and cries out, "My sister, I am going to tickle this bird's rump." The young girl, trembling with fright, tries to dissuade him. But the boy is obstinate. "I really want to tickle this bird's rump," he insists. And as he does so the bird behaves as the sister had feared: it lets them fall into the sea, from which they can only reach the shore through "the blackness of night" and finally come to "the country of darkness."

Let us leave aside this nocturnal symbolism, in which depth psychology will recognize some of its favorite themes. The poetry of Moslem countries is often allusive and delicate, and is not afraid of the most evocative images:

My lord is the king of beauty and there is not a single corner of his body, the work of the Creator, to be neglected, for everything is equally perfect.

His figure is as delicate as his heart is hard, his long eyes declare war on those who remain indifferent, and kindle flames in the coldest hearts.

His hair is black and curly like so many scorpions, his waist, which is as supple as the ban tree, is as slender as a bamboo shoot.

But when he walks, swaying, his remarkable buttocks tremble like curdled milk in the Bedouins' dish.

The tales of *The Thousand and One Nights* do not omit to mention female ho-

The Two Princely Friends. Sixteenth century. Louvre, Paris.

mosexuality. In *The Story of the Baibars and the Captains of Police,* for example, a woman tells one of the captains, without any concealment, of the love she feels for a young girl and asks him to help her get rid of her friend's father. "Between her and me," she explains, "what happens has happened. And that is a mystery of love. And between her and me a passionate pact has been concluded by treaty, promise, and oath. For she burns for me with equal ardour. Never will she marry and never will a man touch her." The captain of police is somewhat amazed at being chosen as the procurer of one woman for another. He wonders what the love of one young girl for another can consist of, and "how the cucumber can grow overnight on ground which is not suited to it." But the commission does not set him any moral problem, and he is not shocked by it. He is astonished rather at the thought of what "these two gazelles with no penis" can do together.

It is possible to say that practically all Moslem, Arab, or Persian poetry is tinged with homosexuality. Some of the greatest Arab poets, such as Abu Nuwas and El-Mutanabi, have sung the praises of virile beauty and the love of boys. Almost all of them have been aware of it and have celebrated young men as much as women and wine. In many cases (and this is particularly true of the Persians), their inspiration, like that of the Greeks, definitely finds its source in the beauty of faces and bodies and in this external radiance which always seems to fascinate the lovers of the boys. But at the same time there is a deeper pleasure of the soul which was definitely there in Plato but now seems more closely linked to certain aspects of Christian sensibility. A mystical, or at least a metaphysical dimension can be found at the heart of their amorous inspiration, and the beloved whom they celebrate is often simultaneously the being of flesh and blood whose favors they desire and the divine lover whom he incarnates. In certain religious sects, like the Dervishes, spiritual "illumination," which was obtained partly through music and dancing, was also based on love. It is true that the Dervishes, who slept in their cells by couple, were often criticized by orthodox Moslems for the doubtful nature of their relationships, but the fact remains that Djelaleddin Roumi,[2] in showing spiritual illumination by means of loving friendship, expressed a profound tendency of the Near East during the Moslem period and something which is no doubt an essential component of the human soul at all times. But although chastity was, officially at least, recommended to the Dervishes, other esoteric poets, such as the great Háfiz (1320–1389) went as far as to overthrow the values of official morality and to maintain, as he did in his "Divan" that sin is the very expression of life and that nothing else has any value. He was a Sufi and a profound theologian, and compared virtue to a horrible skeleton, stating that if it was sublime to attain perfect purity, it was preferable to commit sins and, by drinking, to destroy this purity. "I have no more money to buy wine," he sang, "but I can sell you, O beloved inn-keeper, my virtue and even the blue gown of the ascetics." And he added, "I want to free the world from the slavery of the chaplet and the stole, and from the rods of the jailer of the spirit." To a young magus, a cup-bearer who reproached him for "staining the essence of the soul through his passion for the lips of boys," he merely replied, "Would we say it was bad if the rose, in spring, was tinted with ruby wine?" And elsewhere he celebrates the lover who comes at midnight,

The Lovers. Persian miniature. Seventeenth century.

"his hair tousled, his forehead damp, smiling and intoxicated, with a poem on his lips and a glass in his hand," bending over him and asking in a sorrowful voice, "Art thou sleeping, O thou who hast loved me for so long?"[3]

In his immortal *Rubáiyat,* Omar Khayyam, as far back as the eleventh century, went further than Háfiz. After having been the most famous learned man of his period as an astronomer and mathematician, this friend of Hassan Sabbah, founder of the Haschichin sect, denounced, late in life, the vanity of asceticism and dogmatism of all kinds. There is no other theme in his hundred and seventy quatrains apart from

[2] Djelaleddin Roumi, Mystic poet and dancer.

[3] Vincent Monteil, "Neuf Qazal de Háfiz," *Revue des Études Islamiques* (Paris: 1954).

this kind of wondering despair provoked by the insoluble enigma of the universe, the impossibility of explaining its mystery, and the unique approach through love—all forms of love. Omar Khayyam, who was a passionate lover of women but retained his lucidity even during his wildest passions, remained appreciative, during his advanced old age, of the charm of young men, whom he seems to have associated especially with a heartrending vision of the precariousness of things. At one point he shows the violet "springing from the beauty-spot which shone like a star on a boy's face"; elsewhere he invites people to tread the ground with care "for this little heap which you are about to crush was perhaps the languid eye of a young boy." And in another place, he describes in mysterious and delicate fashion the happiness of a piece of wood which, after undergoing the torture of being cut up in order to be made into a comb, suddenly plunges "into the perfumed hair of a young boy."

In *The Treasure Without End,* one of the tales in *The Thousand and One Nights,*

Persian miniature. Sixteenth century. Roger Peyrefitte Collection, Paris.

this pre-eminence of love as a way of recognition, if not of illumination, occurs again in the story of a young slave whose beauty was as brilliant as the sunshine and who, clad in a robe of gold brocade covered with pearls and diamonds, presents to the Caliph Haroun Al-Raschid a cup made of a single ruby and filled with crimson wine. The Caliph, after putting it to his lips and drinking the contents, noticed, just as he handed it back to the handsome slave, that it was still full to the brim. He took it from the boy's hands once more and drank it down again to the last drop. The moment he gave it back to the boy, however, it filled itself up again, and this went on indefinitely although nobody poured anything into it. This image of the "treasure without end," of love and its perpetual intoxication, is without any doubt one of the most exquisite fruits of the imaginative treatment of homosexuality by the Arabs.

The great Saladin, the illustrious adversary of Richard Coeur de Lion, was a homosexual by nature. Merchants traveling as far as Afghanistan have stated that the caravans were accompanied by boys dressed as girls, their eyes darkened with kohl, their cheeks rouged, their fingernails and toenails painted with henna; they were transported by camels, in luxurious baskets.

In Turkestan and the Punjab, homosexuality is also a frequent occurrence and in his *Journal de Voyage,* Victor Jacquemont describes the pederastic behavior of Rankit Singh, the "Lion of the Punjab" and his favorite Gulab Singh whom the British set up as sovereign of Kashmir. In Algeria, Morocco, and Tunisia homosexuality has always been practiced, and certain spas, such as Hamammet, are international meeting places. In Egypt homosexuality has been widespread since the Alexandrine period, and the ancient Copts made it an element in

67

Watercolor. Raouf Zarrouk. 1962. Tunis.

their ritual, representing it by two male partridges which fertilized each other alternately. At the period of the Napoleonic conquest, General Bruix could write: "The Arabs and the Mameluks have treated some of our prisoners in the way that Socrates, it used to be said, treated Alcibiades. They had to submit or die." The same experience is related by T. E. Lawrence in *The Seven Pillars of Wisdom*; during the reign of Sahid Pasha, the Dutch consul, Mynheer Van Ruyssenaer, had had to submit to it, both as an active and a passive partner.

All those who during our own times have traveled in Moslem countries know that homosexual practices are as widespread as they were during the time of the Caliph Haroun Al-Raschid. It is hard to find anyone who has not had experiences of this type, even if it is sometimes polite to appear unaware of these tendencies or to make jokes about them. To be honest, the only

persons who show any reserve about them are those members of the middle class who are anxious to imitate the West. Some intellectuals, motivated in this way by a somewhat sordid need to justify themselves, have tried to exonerate Islam from what the West described as a vice or a form of backwardness. Thus, in the review *Planète*, a Persian writer tried to make his readers believe that in spite of internal evidence *The Thousand and One Nights* upheld, in opposition to homosexuality, an idea that men and women were equal, whereas there is no theory in the book about this, apart from an apologia concerning the freedom of love and all varieties of love. In reality, and if not among those who imitate Europe, homosexuality seems to exist in the Moslem East without any concern for morality or any feeling of guilt. No doubt it sometimes appears to be more a question of necessity than of taste, or the result of specific social or family structures. Where harems still exist women naturally have relationships with each other which are largely explained by necessity. E. H. Campbell quotes the case of an Arab chief who had no fewer than three thousand concubines. They were shut up in his vast harem and often had to wait a very long time before it was their turn to be led to the nuptial couch, and it can be understood that in the meantime they tried to console each other as much as they could. In Kuwait, where it is the custom for widows never to remarry, they often employ Negro women who take the masculine role and act in a tyrannical way toward their protégées. But these examples of unusual behavior, however representative they may be of certain social structures, are in no way typical of the moral liberty which reigns in Moslem countries concerning homosexuality, a liberty which offers a contrast to the intolerant attitude of Judeo-Christianity.

68

Women Embracing. Indian. Demotte Collection,
Musée Guimet, Paris.

The Women Friends of Begram. Ivory and bone.   Musée Guimet, Paris.

V
India, the Far East, and Pre-Colombian America

The civilizations of India, China, and Japan are doubly interesting as far as our subject is concerned, because they have, for the most part, remained outside the influence of Judeo-Christianity, and also because they offer observers a field of investigation which is not only of a historical nature but remains an integral part of contemporary reality. There is no doubt also that, due to racial differences, India and the Far East reveal strong contrasts that form the basic material for this investigation, as well as differences in attitude concerning the metaphysical approach to the universe. It is possible that Aryan India cannot be explained without invoking certain ideas of transcendence, but the Far East is closer to a kind of religious paganism and concreteness of thought—which explains reasonably well why China was open to the theories of Marxism. However, problems concerning sexual matters are not regarded there in the same way as they were in the Bible or in the Christian West.

Jean Herbert has mentioned in his books that the civilization of India, at least in those aspects of it which have not been influenced by Islam, possesses no morality in the Western sense of the term. This implies that the notion of sin is practically foreign to it, and morality is reduced more to a question of hygiene, that is to say, to a knowledge of the consequences of the act without any idea of guilt being attached to an imperfect or dangerous act. However, in this civilization which is first and foremost religious, every manifestation of life has acquired a sacred character, and eroticism has not escaped this rule: It has become a vision of the world and a means of accomplishment.

In Hindu polytheism[1] there exists a god of eroticism, Kama, who is considered traditionally to be one of the universal principles and the prime mover, and who is represented as a proud adolescent riding on a parrot. People venerate him in order to be free of desire, for this libera-

---

[1] See Alain Daniélou, *Le Polythéisme Hindou* (Paris: Buchet-Chastel, 1960), pp. 311, 334–350, 452–453, 473–475, 560, 570.

tion can only result from satisfying Eros. "The wise man accepts sensual pleasures when they come, but with a detached heart," says one of the Upanishads. "He is not the victim of desire." True eroticism even finds its archetype in the wonder that the divinity feels at the sight of his own beauty. When Kama looks at the toenails, which are as beautiful as jewels, possessed by Krishna, the divine hero of the *Bhagavad-Gita* and the Hindu epics, he feels truly excited. Abandoning all idea of sexual differentiation he proposes practicing the most severe acts of asceticism in order to be born again as a herdman's daughter and thus be able to caress Krishna's toenails with enjoyment. But the latter, who is in love with himself, had already decided to experience love with his own person, with the result that he causes his own nature to appear in the form of herdsmen's daughters and enjoys himself through them.

The theme of the hermaphrodite is moreover explicit in Hinduism, and Shiva,

The Women Friends of Ajanta. Musée Guimet, Paris.

the great god, is both male and female simultaneously, constantly amazed at his own beauty and capable of union only with himself. The cults of the *lingam* and the *yoni*, that is to say of the male and female organs, are only derivations of this primordial hermaphroditism. Although Hindu mythology celebrates in this way the act of cosmic love in the image of human love, it is the marriage of man and woman which is regarded above everything else as the symbolic support of the universal marriage. This last, however, has already been included in the world of duality, while hermaphroditism is the symbol within it of beginning and end belonging to the One. This is no doubt the reason why the phallus is not considered only as the complementary organ of the vagina, but as the original organ, the father of the world, from whom all beings came, and to whom the seed may return during an act of sacrifice. Agni, the lord of fire, is thus represented as drinking the sperm which spurts from Shiva's phallus.

Hindu mythology also included a god who never married, who was conceived without the participation of any female, and who remains perpetually young. This is Kumara, the Chaste Adolescent, the Leaping One, the Fountain of Sperm (Skanda). His strength is immense and it is stated that his only wife is the army of the gods. Clad in red, armed with a bow and arrows, a sword, a thunderbolt, and an ax, he bestrides a peacock and carries a lance as red as the fire that will destroy the world, a lance that blazes high above his chariot. Women may not be present while he is being worshiped nor take any part in the rites, and it is significant, although this has now been accepted as inaccurate, that some people have thought of identifying him with Alexander the Great and Dionysus of

72

Megasthena. Equally significant is the fact that his worship has incorporated into itself an earlier Dravidian cult, that of the Boy, which was celebrated by means of orgiastic dancing. The worship of Kumara, or of Skanda, the Eternal Adolescent, belongs to various disciplines imposed by the Tantra, so-called of "the left hand" in which as we know use is made of sexual techniques, drugs, and sometimes even urine and excrement. Although in Yoga, Skanda is the name given to the power of sexual abstinence, it is impossible for a psychologist not to recognize in this figure the archetype of the *Puer Eternus* in whom homosexual tendencies supply the fundamental characteristic.

Chhapri, Central India. Twelfth century. *Auparishtaka* practiced by a monk on a princely visitor.

Although certain authors, such as Robert Wood[2] assert that Indians usually have a horror of homosexuality, it can be seen that the problem in India is not so simple. According to information that we have obtained from people who have participated for many years in the life of traditional and orthodox Indian society this revulsion exists only among the separate stratum of Indians who have been westernized and brought up on Victorian puritanism. In milieux which have remained faithful to tradition there are no moral, social, or family problems caused by homosexuality; it is integrated in a religious conception of life that regards all forms of eroticism as divine. For, according to this conception, each desire possesses a god who can simultaneously both satisfy and liberate it. Thus, according to the *Bhagavata Purana*, he who seeks the pleasures of the senses should worship Indra, the King of Heaven; he who desires beauty should worship the celestial Musicians; he who desires luxuriousness should worship the Oblation; and he who wishes to free himself from

desire should worship the cosmic Person. Homosexuals, like everyone else, must seek among the labyrinth of divinities those who can help them and liberate them. These divinities are Skana and Ganapati, the sons of Shiva, whose faithful followers are organized in secret societies. Homosexual acts have their place in the initiation rites of these sects where the members, restricted to men, are sometimes joined together by links which recall certain forms of institutionalization of the religious homosexuality among shamans. Although sexual relations between persons of the same sex have always been tolerated and regarded as sacred in traditional Indian society, sodomy itself seems to have been introduced through Islam, or at least this was the cause which brought it into the open. However, the most ancient texts show oral homosexual practices, quite apart from any Arabic or Moslem influence. In the same way religious sculptures illustrate nonsodomist homosexual practices which are usually executed by monks or hermits: at Khajuraho, in the temple of

[2] "Sex Life in Ancient Civilizations," in *Encyclopedia of Sexual Behavior, op. cit.*

Vishvanâtha, which dates from the tenth century, one can admire for example the approaches made by a monk to a layman who greets him respectfully while allowing his penis to be felt; at Chhapri, in central India, a twelfth-century bas-relief also shows a hermit practicing the *auparishtaka* on a princely visitor. This frequent representation of monks or hermits involved in such acts should not cause surprise: Their tendencies have given rise to jokes in India for centuries, and homosexual practices are called "the ways of Sadhu," that is to say, pertaining to men of religion.

In the *Shushuta*, a medical work which is more than two thousand years old, there are already references to wounds caused to the penis by teeth, wounds which are shown in certain eighth-century temple carvings at Chuvaneshwara near Kattak, in Orissa. The famous *Kama Sutra* of Vatsayana also describes what it calls "oral congress" or *auparishtaka*, which as we have just mentioned is represented in certain religious carvings. This "oral congress" was practiced particularly by hairdressers and masseurs, although the references to the latter in translations of the *Kama Sutra* as "eunuchs" are inaccurate. In traditional India the gender and term "neuter" (*napunsaka*), translated as "eunuch" under the influence of Victorian puritanism, referred definitely to homosexuals. True eunuchs must have been very rare in India before the Moslem period, and in order to keep their harems, the former Hindu princes seem to have used women as soldiers.

The masseurs referred to in the *Kama Sutra* embraced their clients' thighs and drew them closer to them, then touched the joints of the thighs and the central parts of the body. If they then found the penis in a state of erection they pressed it between their hands in order to maintain it in this state. If the client found pleasure in these manipulations the two men proceeded to carry out eight successive operations: *nominal congress*, which consisted of taking the client's penis in the hand, placing it between the lips and touching it lightly with the mouth; *nibbling of the sides*, which meant that the masseur covered the tip of the penis with his fingers, bunched together in the shape of a flower-bud, and pressed the sides with his lips and teeth; *exterior pressure* through which he pressed the tip of the penis with his closed lips and kissed it as though he wanted to pull it; *interior pressure*, in which, by introducing the penis further into his mouth, he pressed it with his lips and then pushed it out again; the *kiss* which he carried out while holding the penis in his hand; *polishing,* by which he first kissed it and then caressed it with his tongue, particularly at the tip; the *sucking of the mango*, when, introducing half the penis into his mouth he kissed it and sucked on it firmly; and lastly the *absorption*, when, with the consent of the client, he introduced the penis fully into his mouth and pressed it down to the root, as though he was going to swallow it.

We should not forget that the *Kama Sutra* is a religious book and only describes erotic practices because of the moral benefit which can be derived from them. It adds that the oral congress which has just been described was also practiced by male servants with their masters, and by citizens of equal rank who knew each other particularly well. The book observes nevertheless that *auparishtaka* should not be practiced by a well-read Brahman or by a statesman. Although the book states that its practice is authorized by the *shastras*, that is to say by religious law, this is only in a way comparable to that in which a medical book can praise the digestive qualities of dogs' meat—the wise man is not forced to eat it as a result. If one is prudent, the book concludes, concerning the adoption of such practices, each man must take his own nature into consideration, and if things are done discreetly, there is no cause to be upset over them.

It is true that if Brahmans are not authorized to practice *auparishtaka* this is not because the act might be considered immoral but only because their mouths are sacred and reserved for celebrating sacred rites; it is for the same reason that Brahmans cannot kiss their own wives. However, although a Brahman is forbidden to practice *auparishtaka* as the active partner, he is quite free to do so as the passive one.

The *Kama Sutra* also describes certain women living in harems who, when they are in love, use their mouths on each other's *yonis*; dress their nurses' daughters, their friends, or their servants in boy's clothes, and satisfy their desires by means of bulbs, roots, or fruit with the same shape as the phallus, or else lie on top of a statue which appears to possess a phallus in a state of erection. Von Mascka, on his side, describes an olisbos[3] made of rubber possessing the size and shape of a swollen penis, often perforated along its length and filled with warm water or milk so that when pressed the effect was similar to ejaculation. Dr. Rustam Mehta, in his *Scientific Curiosities of Sexual Life*, indicates that young girls would sacrifice their virginity to Shiva by deflowering themselves with an iron *lingam* which was kept in the temple. There is no shortage of carvings and ancient vases, some of which are in the Berlin Alte Museum, which show women carrying out various sexual practices between themselves. According to Robert Wood, who has

The Women Friends of Ceylon. Circa 1760. Roland Villeneuve Collection.

already been quoted, there are apparently no fewer than five words in Hindustani for describing a Lesbian. At the same time Havelock Ellis has pointed out that the Hindu poets have described Sapphism with complete freedom and in the crudest manner. In one of their poems a woman even celebrates the superiority of the artificial penis over the pleasures of love-making with a man.

The Buddhists, as we shall see in China, Tibet, and Japan, seem to be even less preoccupied than the Hindus in condemning homosexuality. Claude Lévi-Strauss has described the "childlike religiosity" which is found in their temples on the Burmese frontier: "The priests," he says, "live and sleep in the room used for the celebration of the rites, placing their pots of pomade and their personal pharmaceutical supplies at the foot of the altar, and are not above caressing their pupils between two lessons of the alphabet." Otherwise, male prostitution is no less frequent in India than elsewhere. In the literature there are descriptions of male prostitutes with slim figures, wearing cosmetics, and with dyed fingernails. Travelers have brought back photo-

[3] Cf. *Dictionnaire de Sexologie, op. cit.*

graphs of boys dressed as girls, attached to homosexual brothels in Karachi. In Bombay there is a whole street of these houses where apparently hardly a single Indian village has failed to find representation. This male prostitution is always linked to the art of the theater and to displays of sacred dancing, so much so that in the traditionalist provinces of India it is precisely the young men of the male prostitutes' colony who have the privilege of representing, by wearing women's clothes, the famous shepherdesses in love with Krishna during the spectacles which for one month each year relate the god's ambiguous life.[4] Furthermore, it often occurs in orthodox families that the husband introduces an intimate friend of his into his own home and sometimes lives with him and with his own wife, without these parallel love affairs appearing to create any problem.

One should not be surprised therefore that in India as everywhere else homosexual love has left a legacy of poems, even if this love is sometimes lost in the ambiguity of the two-sided love for the divine lover and the earthly lover. In Rabindranath Tagore's *Cycle of Spring* (a poem which he dedicated to the boys of his ashram in Santiniketan) can be heard accents which do not deceive us:

Gently, my friend, walk gently toward your tranquil dwelling place.
I do not know the way, I have no light.
Dark is my life and dark is the world for me.
I have only the sound of your footsteps to guide me in my solitude.
Gently, my friend, walk gently along the darkened shore
Through the night, carried by the April breeze.

Let the call of the road come with the sound of murmuring,
I have only the scent from your garland of flowers to guide me in my solitude.

In the Far East it is impossible to find any condemnation of homosexuality by the religions which have taken root there. We mentioned earlier the tolerant attitude of Buddhism and the homosexual practices which take place in many Buddhist monasteries and even among the lamas of Tibet. Confucianism, Taoism, or, in Japan, Shinto, have not shown more severity toward homosexuality. It has been pointed out with good reason that Confucius attached extreme importance to friendship in the upbringing of young men, and to a large extent he always placed the love he had for his disciples before conjugal love. In a related way, through the social morality which he defined and which has molded the existence of China, he continued to emphasize the value for the adult of friendships in addition to family relationships. When asked what his ambition was, he replied kindly, "I would like old people to live in peace, all friends to be faithful to each other, and all young people to love those who are oldest." Since a certain Tseng Tien had just played the *seb* to him, and had admitted that his greatest pleasure was to bathe in late spring in the Yi River along with six or seven boys, and afterward enjoy the murmur of the wind in the mountains, Confucius cried, "You are a man after my own heart." When he praised the delights of the family circle this was more for social reasons than for the love of women, of whom he said they were "like people who have been badly brought up: as soon as you are kind to them they become bold; and if you take no notice of them they are hurt."

This feeling for friendship seems to have been, within the structure of Confu-

---

[4] Many of these facts have been taken from the *L'Érotisme divinisé*, Alain Daniélou, (Paris: Buchet-Chastel, 1962).

76

cianism, a compensation for the severe demands made by families. In ancient China this, feeling gave rise to a curious custom, which was related both to homosexual marriage and adoption contracts—that of "dry relationships." Two friends who wanted to seal their friendship and ensure for it some kind of social recognition could declare themselves "dry brothers." The elder, who wished to link himself in the eyes of everyone to his young beloved, declared him to be his "dry" son, *Kann erl-dze*. These "dry relationships" had the privilege of taking the rights of real parents into the family of those whom they united. They were solemnized before witnesses and had the same validity as the most formal deed in writing.

In a little book which is of great value to the understanding of homosexuality in Imperial China, and one which has been authenticated by Claude Farrère, Georges Soulié de Morant has described a "dry" adoption ceremony which he was able to attend and which made a young Peking actor the "dry son" of a minister who was then in office. In this book, entitled *Bijou de Ceinture*,[5] he shows how the actor, whose popularity in the Middle Empire was at one moment fantastic, became the hero of surprising homosexual adventures. Like many country children his good looks had been noticed by the director of one of those theatrical touring companies which travel all over China, and he engaged the boy as a *siang kong*. In the end, the actor finally experienced a most subtle love affair with a boy of his own age, after having repulsed the brutal advances of Prince Li, a member of the imperial family, whose murder he instigated during the Boxer Rebellion.

The *siang kong* or "lords who help"

were in China adolescents destined in principle for the theater, but who were also invited to formal luncheons or dinners in order to provide some gaiety. They were supposed to sing, recite poems, keep the conversation going with witty remarks, and finally to show to anyone who wanted it, the most affectionate or the most sensual provocation. They acted as cupbearers and leaders of games and possessed the right to impose fines on all those who showed that they were not fit for the pleasures to which they were invited. It was asserted in China that the three most highly polished objects in the world were priests' heads polished by the razor, women's thighs polished by rubbing together, and the mouths of the *siang kong* which were polished by kisses. Soulié de Morant describes them as looking like ephebes clad in robes of brightly colored silk, with their hair neatly dressed in long gleaming pigtails and elegant fringes surrounded freshly shaven heads, but with make-up on their faces, and eyes shining with lascivious understanding.

There were schools for *siang kong*, consisting of classes in singing, diction, and bearing. The boys were made to sit on benches made of boxwood sprigs in graduated sizes, in order to prepare them to welcome the pleasures expected of them. And since there were some among them who did not possess enough talent to become artists, the less gifted ones earned their living in cheap restaurants, where they gave the impression of being *siang kong* for the impecunious. In Peking before the Revolution there was a whole street of *siang kong* restaurants where one could see adolescent boys wearing highly colored make-up, who were caressed by the drinkers as they passed by, embraced by admirers who pulled them on to their knees, and then taken later into one of the bedrooms which were always

---

[5] Paris: Flammarion, 1925.

kept for this purpose in the house adjacent to the restaurant.

The great actors were subject to more elegant forms of seduction. Until 1911 feminine roles in the theater were taken by men, since women were no more allowed in the audience than on the stage. No woman—including courtesans, matrons, and virgins —could appear at feasts or gatherings, religious celebrations or in general social life. Women of quality did not even venture out into the street. However, although actors adopted the robes and attitudes of the ladies whose parts they played on the stage, they abandoned them in civil life. Their success was never due to costumes. During the celebrations or the amorous promenades which they adorned with their presence as a matter of obligation, it was their virile qualities that provoked the loving attentions with which the most famous men assailed them.

The love affairs that began in this way were sordid or sublime, according to the nature of those taking part in them. We have mentioned the brutality of Prince Li, who did not hesitate to carry off, imprison, threaten, or bully young men in order to obtain their favors. Others restricted themselves to corrupting boys through the attractions of fame or fortune. An actor by the name of Tsinn-Linn was famous in Peking early this century for having ruined all his lovers, driving one to suicide and another to such poverty that he had to sell his wife and children. In the history of China there is no shortage of emperors, who, until they came to the throne, paid homage to the love of boys. There was also the case of the famous *siang kong* who behaved like Antinous vis-à-vis Hadrian and committed suicide rather than compromise the careers of .friends. On the whole, ancient China, as Etiemble observed in his *Nouveau Singe Pèlerin*, treated "Lesbianism and homosexu-ality with wise indulgence"[6] and there is no shortage of stories describing both kinds of feeling.[7] What has become of these customs in Communist China, which has been suffocated by a Western type of puritanism carried to its furthest extremes? They have gone underground, no doubt, and for the time being it is impossible to say what will happen to them. Moreover, Communist China rejects all forms of eroticism, not only homosexual eroticism, for the country is absorbed by the demands of production which will no doubt remain in force until the nation has achieved economic adaptation to the mechanized universe of today. It could happen, however, that the incredible increase in the population, which has now reached a total of about 710 million, might favor one day for reasons other than mere pleasure, "something like a religion which," as Etiemble wrote, "would rehabilitate homosexual relationships," in order to assist the achievement of birth control.

As far as Japan is concerned, we are fortunate enough to possess literary documents (of which very few have been translated), sufficient to supply us with an idea of what homosexuality was like during the great centuries of Japanese history and especially the Bushido period—that is to say the great feudal age.

A work of inestimable value dating from the seventeenth century has been handed down to us in this connection under the title of *Splendid Stories of Homosexuality*. It came from the pen of one of the greatest writers of Japan, Saikakou Ebara (1641–1693). He wrote many erotic works

---

[6] Paris: Gallimard, 1958, p. 32.

[7] Dr. Wou-Chan Cheng, *Érotologie de la Chine* (Bibliothèque Internationale d'Érotologie, No. 11; Paris: J.-J. Pauvert, 1963).

very late in life, among which are *The Amorous Life of Yonosuke* which first brought him fame, *The Amorous Life of a Woman*, and *The Five Women in Love*. These homosexual stories reflect the customs of the Samurai, as they were, particularly during the twelfth century. But they still existed in Saikakou Ebara's time, and they still exert their influence on contemporary Japan.

The interesting aspect of the *Splendid Stories of Homosexuality* is that they revive the feelings of a period not through the discoveries of ethnologists, which are often superficial, but through the atmosphere of daily life, as the tales of *The Thousand and One Nights* did for the Arab world. These stories reveal not only the feelings of exceptional individuals, but the way in which these feelings were received in the society of the period, and the way in which they passed into everyday life. And what strikes the reader is the natural way in which these feelings were displayed in life; the degree of naturalness is greater, if possible, than that achieved by the Greeks or the Arabs, and was accompanied by refinement, modesty, a sense of ritual, and the profound violence which characterizes the Japanese mind.

In order to place these stories within their context, we should make it clear that homosexuality was encouraged among the young Samurai as much as it was in Greece, and that they regarded love for a woman as something which made a man cowardly, weak, and effeminate. In his humorous preface to the *Splendid Stories of Homosexuality* Saikakou Ebara describes the mythological origin of this type of love:

When this world first began, according to the Nihongue (the mythological history of Japan), there existed something which was shaped like a reed. This thing later became a god. The name of this god was Kounitekotatjino-Michoto (the August Lord of the Eternal Country). After this god, throughout three generations, there were only male gods. And I am sure that this is the origin of homosexuality in Japan. After the fourth generation, the male and female gods began to unite together in a completely unreasonable manner. Then two gods and two goddesses were born. . . . Nowadays, our eyes are dishonored by these women wearing their hair long in the old way, or by these ultra-modern nageshi-mado [this was the seventeenth-century hairstyle], oiled with the oil of plumtree flowers, by their supple hips and their scarlet petticoats. These feminine beauties can only be used for the pleasure of old men in districts where there is not a single handsome youth. A young, healthy, hot-blooded man has no thought for these despicable feminine beauties. If a man is interested in women, he cannot know the blessed joys of homosexuality.

As in Greece, it was honorable at the time of the Samurai to have a young boy as one's lover, and despicable never to have had one. Lords and princes surrounded themselves with pages who were often selected from among the sons of their courtesans. According to an unwritten law, these pages never had the right to love other men except their masters, if they were loved by them. As a general rule sexual relationships were authorized between lovers up to the moment when the young boy became a man. He then cut off the curl which he had worn on his forehead, adopted clothes with short sleeves, and often even changed his name. During the period of the knights the process of becoming a man was described as *genbuku,* but lovers did not separate for such a trifle. They became intimate friends, sacrificing their interests in a mutual fashion and helping each other all their lives. The custom of hara-kiri was frequent, taking place each time any misconduct tarnished these relationships or in cases when death alone could ensure the permanence of love. Relationships which lasted longer than adolescence were however not exceptional, and Saikakou Ebara devotes one of his stories to two old men of seventy:

Hayemon continued to regard Mondo as his young lover. He dressed Mondo's sparse hair with his own hands in the style worn by pages, with much perfumed oil. Mondo's forehead was like a woman's. He took great care of his person. He polished his nails with scented wood and shaved with care. But nobody would have suspected that these two old men had continued their amorous relationship until such an advanced age.

And Ebara commented: "Homosexual love should be quite different from ordinary love between man and woman; this is why a prince, even when he has married a beautiful princess, cannot forget his pages. A woman is a creature without any importance whatsoever, while sincere homosexual love is true love."

In Japan homosexual relationships were not only the privilege of the lords of the Bushido, however. They occurred frequently between priests and, as in China, among actors. The Buddhist dignitaries had attractive pages as lovers and directed them toward the priesthood. Ebara describes the correspondence of a priest which from time to time recalls that of the so-called "Por-

Two Women. Suzuki Moronobu. Early Ukiyo-e school (early seventeenth century).

From a Japanese erotic album. Such pictures were often presented to brides at their weddings.

Two women using a double olisbos. Painting on silk. China. Seventeenth century. R. H. Van Gulik Collection. From *Erotic Colour Prints of the Ming Period,* (Tokyo, 1951).

tugese nun." "I am ready to sacrifice my life for one evening of love with you," he writes to a young man. "One evening of love with you is more precious than a life lasting a thousand years. I would do with pleasure anything that you asked of me. Better to live for half an hour rather than drag out a wretched life." As for the actors, especially those who acted the Noh plays, their life was very similar to that of the Chinese actors. Great freedom of behavior was to be found in theatrical circles and was often not far removed from elegant prostitution. The young actors sold their bodies equally to men and women, and frequented tea houses assiduously. However, true homosexual love affairs were not rare even in such circles.

The image of a dandy of the period is described for us as follows:

He was wearing a big hat decorated with silk and held in place by a pale blue ribbon. His robe, with two wide sleeves, was as crimson as the glorious flowers of the morning. He wore two swords in his belt, their scabbards set with precious stones. He walked casually and carried in his hand a branch of golden flowers. His beauty was such that Guzaeyemon wondered whether the god Roya had assumed human shape or if a peony had come to life and was walking along in the spring sunshine.

The characteristics of this literature consist of a great delicacy and extreme elevation of feeling. Sexual problems are handled without any complications, but in a way that is more allusive than direct. They are always subordinate to love for the person. And if any problems of conscience appear, they do not arise over homosexuality but within the homosexual love relationships themselves. We have already mentioned that certain pages could only love their masters; it can be imagined that sometimes they did fall in love with other men, which led to conflict between desire and duty, fidelity and love, which is precisely the theme of several stories. Or else there is conflict between homosexual love and filial love, as it is described in *The Love of the Two Enemies*.

This story is typical of Japan. It tells of two tragic lovers who one day find themselves separated by the past; the mother of the younger man discovers that the older one was her husband's murderer. She demands that her son should avenge his father, in accordance with the contemporary code of honor. And the young man, although he is torn in two, does not question his mother's demand. He restricts himself to complaining about the wretchedness of life. "You know yourself what you did to my father," he says to his lover. "I know that you could not act in any other way and that you did so on the orders of your master. But as the son of a Samurai, I cannot overlook it. Truly, I am infinitely sorry to kill you and my distress is overwhelming." The friend does not object. He also limits himself to mentioning the strangeness of the world. He has been unaware that he became the lover of the man whose father he killed. "Yes, I am your father's murderer," he admits. "But it will be pleasant for me to die at your hand." He throws away his swords and offers his neck to his friend. The latter, however, insists that he should fight with the same weapons. Now the mother, who has been listening in another room, intervenes. "I admire both of you," she cries. "You are truly men of honor. Make love to each other once more this evening. Celebrate your separation and may tomorrow be the day of vengeance." The young men drink their last cups of wine, rejoice in their last evening, and lie down together on the same bed. When the mother comes to wake them in the morning she finds them lying there in silence. She calls them. They do not reply. She lifts the blanket which covers them: the younger one has pierced his friend through the heart with his sword, running it through his own breast. The tip of the sword can still be seen where it emerges from his back. At the sight of these bleeding corpses the mother remains in meditation. Then, so that she will not find herself unworthy of such love, she kills herself over the bodies of these who have loved each other so nobly.

This story might seem very romantic if we did not know to what extent hara-kiri formed part of daily life in feudal Japan and how often honor demanded it of the Samurai. The story also shows at what level homosexuality was practiced during this period and what formed the moral background for it. The result of this situation was that gallantry and even coquetry were not excluded. "Last spring," a poet relates, "I wrote these verses on the back of a fan where flowers had been painted by the famous painter Unémé Kano: 'My sleeves are continually wet with tears, for my love is without hope.' The compliment that you address me gave me the greatest pleasure: 'The lover who suffers will pass the summer easily with this fan.' You also wrote beneath the poem: 'He who has written it is awaiting his lover.' But, cruel man, you gave the fan to your servant."

Homosexual stories from Japan are almost always imbued with dream and surrounded with this poetic halo, in keeping with Japanese life as it used to be. In this manner, one of them recounts the story of a young boy who was expected to die, to the extent that his parents had already prepared a fine shroud and a beautiful coffin for him. Nobody suspected the cause of his illness when one day he said to his parents, "The man whom I love will pass through this street tomorrow. Stop him and bring him to me." They believed he had become delirious but in order not to thwart a dying man they sent a servant to wait at the entrance to the town and bring back any stranger who might appear. Oddly enough, a stranger did arrive and when he was brought to the house, the father described his son's strange illness. "If your son dies," the stranger asserted, "I shall become a priest so that all my life I can pray for the salvation of his soul. But let me see him before he dies. I want to bid him farewell before he leaves this world." The father took the stranger to the invalid's bedside and the latter, who until then had been utterly exhausted, sat up in his bed, recovered, and became as he had been before. "My body was here," he said to the stranger, "but my soul has always been with you." And he admitted that one night, while he was visiting the city of Takadatji, he had followed the stranger into an inn. "My soul slept with you in the same bed and loved you without uttering a word. Then I put a little of my incense in your sleeve. Is it still there?" The stranger, who was surprised, took out of his sleeve some incense which he found exquisite, but he had not been able to explain where it came from. "I did not know," he said, "that we had exchanged an oath of love." But in order to show him the proof of it, the boy in his turn took out of his pocket another piece of crushed incense. When the two pieces were placed end to end they fitted together perfectly, and their perfume was identical. The stranger was then convinced. The young men then swore that they would love each other forever and even in the afterlife. They both went to settle in the older man's city, the parents of the younger having agreed with pleasure to give him to his lover.

Such stories show how naturally homosexuals lived in Japan, both parents and society admitting the existence of this love just as they did that of other feelings. Japanese homosexual literature was not limited, presumably, to the work of Saikakou Ebara. This writer has, however, the merit of being accessible to us in the translation presented

Women in Moonlight. Huang I-chieh. 1610.   Illustration for a novel of the Ming period.

84

by Ken Sato.[8] He alludes to other works including an intimate journal entitled *My Experiences with Many Men,* and a work in four volumes, *Collections of Stories as Pure as Crystal.*

We possess little information about the sexual customs of pre-Colombian America, although we are certain of a small number of facts. They come from three sources: the Spanish chronicles of the time of the Conquest, whose value is uneven and which are influenced by the circumstances of the war, the prejudices of the authors, and the failure of one civilization to understand another; the pre-Colombian documents which have come to light during the most recent archaeological excavations; and the surviving customs from the past which have been maintained in a more-or-less pure state among the Indians of today.

The difficulty is increased by the fact that several civilizations have been superimposed during the course of time, in Mexico and Peru. It appears in any case that there must have existed a sacred, ritualistic, and institutionalized form of homosexuality and that the prohibitions which attacked it in certain social milieux had no connection with moral preoccupations, in the sense that we understand them.

The Spanish chroniclers, such as Bernal Diaz del Castillo[9] describe this sacred homosexuality which, according to them, was associated with bloody sacrifices that held a place of honor among the Aztecs. They describe "popes," sons of notables who, being deprived of women, practiced sodomy.

From a Japanese erotic album.

[These popes] wore black garments like shrouds over cassocks which came down to their feet, hoods fairly similar to those worn by canons and other smaller cowls comparable to those of the Dominicans. Their hair came down to their waists and with some of them, right down to their feet, full of blood and so matted that it would have been impossible to comb it out. Their ears had been slashed as a sign of sacrifice and they smelt of sulphur and spread an odor of dead flesh that was even worse.[10]

The same author speaks of a temple in Mexico where there was an idol who favored marriages between men and asserts that especially in hot districts and on the

[8] *Contes d'Amour des Samourais* (Paris: Stendhal et Cie, 1927).

[9] See Bernal Diaz del Castillo, *L'histoire véridique de la Nouvelle Espagne,* trans. Dominique Aubier (Paris: Club des Libraires de France, 1961).

[10] *Ibid,* p. 51.

coasts most men practiced sodomy and young boys went about dressed as women, "earning their living by this diabolical and abominable trade."

Max Jurth believes however that homosexuality was first and foremost a privilege of the theocratic emperors and that it was forbidden to their subjects on pain of death, the purpose of this prohibition being to procure victims for the ritual sacrifices. Whatever the situation may have been, the Aztecs made statuettes in gold representing the most varied forms of copulation, including male sodomy. Their supreme god, Ometecutli, and also the Mother Goddess of the Quetchuas were both bisexual.

Pottery with representations of licentious subjects can be found in the reserve stock of the archaeological museum of Lima and in certain private collections, such as those of Kinsey and Larco Herrera. Sodomy is depicted, alongside sexual perversions of the most astonishing types. However, here too it looks as though sexual freedom was more the privilege of the Incas and the ruling classes than of the ordinary people whom the former tried to maintain in a state of obedience, thanks to severe taboos and extremely strict rules pertaining to work and property. If the sovereign was incestuous and polygamous by statute, limitations to sexual life in the lower classes seem to have been merely of an empirical nature. The documents dealing with moral subjects which have come down to us make hardly any allusions to sexual problems, apart from the fact that they regard adultery on the same level as theft. They come down to three precepts: do not steal, do not lie, and do not be lazy. There is no sign that homosexuality could have been the subject of any prohibition.

In the *Crónica del Perú*, Cieza de Léon reports cases of ritualistic homosexuality—young priests who were brought up from childhood as though they were girls and destined to share within the temples the beds of the great dignitaries. Max Jurth notes that in this connection the role reserved for the "chosen ones" was passive, unlike homosexual love in Greece, which exalted the virile virtues of boys who were loved. However this priestly homosexuality did not provoke disdain: we have also seen the same thing occur among the Pueblo Indians of today. On the other hand, it looks as though eroticism has never been very strong among mountain people such as the Quetchuas or the Aymaras. It developed in the coastal regions of Peru and on the Equator and in these areas male homosexuality grew to be part of the ceremonial and became connected, as we have also seen among the Hopi Indians, with a fertility complex. It was no doubt for similar reasons that part of the burial equipment which was placed in the tombs consisted of baked clay pottery where the phallus was the organ most frequently represented and where scenes of homosexual love can be seen.

According to Fred W. Voget,[11] the majority of male Indians must have had homosexual experiences during childhood and adolescence. Techniques used were mutual masturbation or anal penetration in the case of relationships between older and younger men. The use of children by adults was forbidden, although among the prehistoric Mohicans, races living on the Equator, and the peoples of the Caribbean, homosexuality had become institutionalized as a stage in the sexual development of the individual. Houses where unmarried men lived existed for this purpose. Children who had shown a marked preference for the work, games, and

---

[11] "Sex Life of the American Indian," in Albert Ellis and Albert Abarbanel, *Encyclopedia of Sexual Behavior* (New York: Hawthorn Books, 1960), pp. 100–105.

clothes of the opposite sex were closely watched, but no effort was made to bring them back by force to heterosexual behavior. Usually the deviation was regarded as a response to interior nature or as a deeper "call." Homosexual couples formed wherever the custom of transvestism was accepted. Although it was often considered a pleasant luxury it was regarded by certain peoples, such as the Navaho Indians, as a symbol of riches and abundant fertility. Carleton Beals[12] relates that among the Laches and the Caquiteros homosexual unions lead to formal marriages. And he adds that a woman who has more than five male children and no daughters is authorized to bring up one of her sons as a girl. It is the usual practice for homosexual marriages to be based on contracts of common law, although it does happen that some of them are established in accordance with the traditional rules of heterosexual marriage. These ménages are often considered financially advantageous, although in certain circumstances they are exposed to ridicule and obscene remarks.

Homosexual relationships of an occa-sional nature did obviously take place and references have been made to Araucaño hunters and fishermen who would take young boys with them, for sexual purposes, on their expeditions. When they came back they would throw the boys into the sea or the river so that they could greet their wives as bachelors, with the result that their temporary lovers had to swim back to dry land. In the same way homosexuality or transvestism were more acceptable socially among men than among women. In any case, homosexuality and Lesbianism seem to have been more frequent among the coastal races of South America, and even the vocabularies of their languages show evidence of this. The number of terms relating to sodomy and homosexuality is particularly high, and psychoanalysts will no doubt find every consolation in being able to link such a situation with a former matriarchy which, during the time of the Incas, had still left traces. For if the Inca *ayllus* who, as it is known, constituted the social unity in the Empire of the Sun, were directed by male relatives, certain names always referred to maternal rights. And marriage meant that the wife's *ayllu* passed to the husband. Let us mention the fact without attempting to draw exaggerated conclusions from it.

---

[12] "Sex Life in Latin America," *in Encyclopedia of Sexual Behavior, op. cit.,* p. 605.

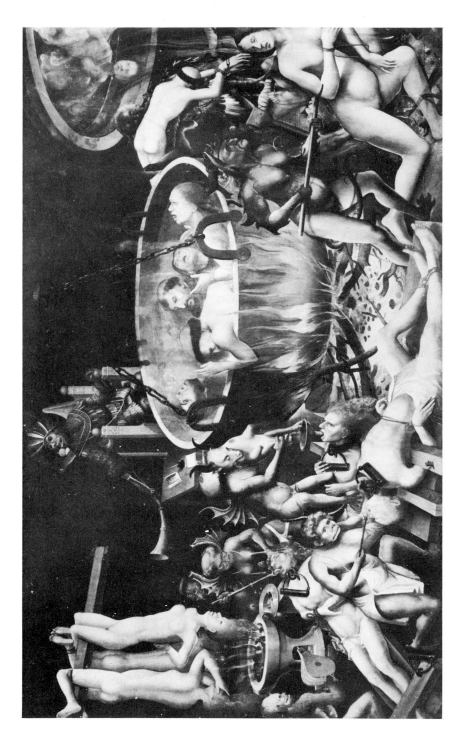

The Inferno. Artist unknown. Portuguese painting. Sixteenth century. Museu Nacional de Arte Antiga, Lisbon.

PART TWO

Christianity: Exception and Parenthesis

As for Christianity, you must believe me on this point: never in my heart have I behaved basely toward it, and since my childhood I have tried very hard, deep within myself, to share its ideal—but always with the final result that it was a sheer impossibility.

Nietzsche

St. John the Baptist. Leonardo da Vinci. Detail.
Louvre, Paris.

VI

The Latent Homosexual
Structure of Christianity

Christianity emerged from Judaism and it would be surprising, in spite of the mutation which it constitutes, to find within it attitudes which are essentially different from those of the Old Testament. The severity of Jewish legislation concerning homosexuality was part of a more general severity toward ways of life of which homosexuality was in one way the symbol and which could have allowed foreigners to assimilate "the chosen people" and to undermine their nationalism. The struggle against homosexuality came late and did not reach its full development until after the captivity in Babylon. It was a nationalist reaction and was only possible because of certain characteristics of the Jews, among which a surprising revulsion against nakedness and an overestimation of the father-figure and his collective image, the Law, seem to have been among the most decisive.

Jesus and the early Christians were Jewish and one can hardly imagine that they were able to free themselves completely from a tradition whose narrowness and inadequacy they certainly resented but which weighed down upon them, nevertheless, with the weight of many centuries. But the Gospels contain no explicit condemnation of homosexuality, and not even any mention of the phenomenon. The tendency in the Gospels was indeed to substitute the demands of love for the severities of the Law, but this tendency was also that of sublimation and spiritualization. Jesus forgives Mary Magdalene all her sins because she loved much and he remarks that "to whom little is forgiven, the same loveth little" (Luke 7: 47–48). But he continues to think that "salvation is of the Jews" (John 4: 22), and it is inconceivable that he would have been able to attack the Jewish law concerning homosexuality other than by silence. For there is no relationship with a woman in his life and the only relationship made by choice mentioned in the Gospels is that which linked him to "the beloved disciple," to the tenderhearted John who, during the Last

Supper, laid his head on his Master's bosom. And when the latter died it was not into the hands of Mary Magdalene nor of any of the holy women who had followed him that he committed his mother, but to John, the disciple whom he loved: "Woman, here is thy son." And to the disciple he said, "Here is thy mother." The son, the mother, and the friend, is this not the triangle in which psychoanalysts believe they can find the classic case of homosexuality?

There has been no lack of writers who have described Jesus as a passive homosexual, but it is not necessary to admit some carnal reality in this sphere in order to discover a structure that excludes women, and a form of eroticism orientated toward one's own sex. In the writings of John this eroticism is more than latent; it is diffuse and on the surface. "For he that loveth not his brother whom he hath seen, how can he love God whom he hath not seen?" (I John 4:20), and "We know that we have passed from death unto life, because we love the brethren. He that loveth not his brother abideth in death" (I John 3:14). One of the gospels of the Apocrypha goes so far as to say: "If you meet your brother, prostrate thyself and worship, for thou hast seen thy god." This wonderment at the divine face of man is a kind of sublimation of the Greek wonderment, but is addressed all the same to men more than to women, who do not ever seem to be mentioned explicitly. "He that hath not loved has not known God, for God is Love," and it is only with difficulty that in this Christianity of John the love of man for man could be condemned.

It was never in fact condemned as such in the whole of Christianity, which could not have done so without denying its essence, but which attempted to maintain it on heights foreign to the realization of its

Detail from Monreale Cathedral. The history of homosexuality in Judeo-Christian times began with the destruction of Sodom.

desire. This is what appeared in the case of Paul, in whom the Jewish tradition became obsessional once more by the very extent to which he tried to free himself from it. For this apostle of the Gentiles continued to believe in the superiority of the Jew: "Because that unto them were committed the oracles of God" (Rom. 3:1–2). And "Glory, honor and peace to every man that worketh good, to the Jew first, and also to the Gentile" (Rom. 2:10). The result was that he continued to echo in spite of himself the old nationalistic discriminations and said, for example of the Romans:

God gave them up unto vile affections: for even their women did change the natural use into that which is against nature: And likewise also the men, leaving the natural use of the woman, burned in their lust one toward another; men with men working that which is unseemly, and receiving in themselves that recompence of their error which was meet. (Rom. 1:26–27).

The fact that, according to him, it is God

himself who leads men to such passions, is likely to raise the problem of responsibility in a strange manner; a certain type of Pauline and Calvinist theology has not failed to do this through the elaboration, not without contradictions, of the theory of predestination. The most interesting thing, however, is to see Paul refer to homosexuality in the same epistle as a consequence of idolatry and at the same time place it on the same footing as "all unrighteousness . . . murder, debate, deceit, malignity; whisperers . . . proud boasters, inventors of evil things, disobedient to parents" (Rom. 1: 29–30). Once again the condemnation of homosexuality forms part of a general attack on sexuality or at least all sexuality which does not have procreation as its object or is only a makeshift. For Paul has no more taste for women. Abstention is good for men, he says, and marriage is only to be recommended to prevent the danger of unchastity (I Cor. 7:1–2). He would have liked everyone to be as continent as he was (I Cor. 7: 7), for "the woman is the glory of the man" (I Cor. 11: 7), and "Neither was the man created for the woman; but the woman for the man" (I Cor. 11:9). On this basis of misogyny, and, to put it plainly, this latent homosexual structure, he establishes, through unconscious anxiety, this general condemnation: "no whoremonger, nor unclean person, nor covetous man, who is an idolater, hath any inheritance in the kingdom of Christ and of God" (Eph. 5: 5).

Let us leave on one side the question of knowing to what extent this general condemnation of the flesh corresponds to an authentic elevation of mankind or to a secret impotence in search of transcendent alibis. "For there are some eunuchs, which were so born from their mother's womb: and there are some eunuchs, which were made eunuchs of men: and there be eunuchs, which have made themselves eunuchs for the kingdom of heaven's sake" (Matt. 19:12). In fact the material eunuch condition to which Jesus seems to prefer a moral eunuch condition was almost always linked just as closely to religious aspirations as to a more or less latent homosexuality, for it was believed to resolve the anxiety caused by the latter state. We have already seen how in ancient times the various cults of the Great Mother were carried out by men who had been castrated. Christianity is in its own way a mother cult also, and the Cross, a symbol of motherhood and devotion to Mary, is necessarily accompanied within it by the Passion of the Son. This domination by the maternal woman, the price paid for the refusal of the woman as lover, is very characteristic of the eunuch state and of homosexuality. Herodotus asserts that castration was invented by Semiramis, the Queen of Babylon, after the death of Ninus and in order to consolidate the power that she had usurped. Pope Leo XIII

Detail. Cathedral of St. Peter. Poitiers. Thirteenth century. During the Middle Ages, homosexuality, which was punishable by burning at the stake, took refuge in the most unexpected places, such as in these stalls in the Cathedral of St. Peter.

93

S · ROCHE · ORA PRO · NOBIS
M · LONS LE SAULNIER

Eighteenth-century print. An angel of the Lord
lifts the robe worn by St. Roch (on the exquisite
pretext of a boil infected with the plague).

94

admitted that the last protectors of eunuchs were the two Sovereign Pontiffs of Islam and Christianity: the Pope and the Caliph. And in fact from Origen to Abelard the history of Christianity is strewn with examples of the frenzy experienced by eunuchs which the Church, it is true, finally condemned. This condemnation came, however, late in the day. In Egypt, the Coptic convents of Gisgeh, Assiut, and Deir el Abiar included castrated Negro boys for centuries. Under the Sultan Abdul-Hamid it was the Christian monks who, in Constantinople, castrated thousands of boys who were destined for the career of eunuch. In Byzantium eunuchs occupied the pontifical throne, and palaces and chapels were full of them. In Russia the members of the Christian Skopzi sect, known as *raskolnikis*, castrated themselves for religious reasons. In the twelfth century in England the priests who supported the faction of Thomas à Becket inflicted the same infirmity on themselves. Eunuchs were not excluded from the priesthood until later. The fear of seeing a eunuch ascend the throne of Peter was for a moment so acute that Benedict III ordered the examination on the *chaise-percée* in St. John's Lateran church: The man elected by the Conclave sat on the chair while his genital organs were examined, after which the examiner made the statement: "Papam virum habemus, testiculos habet." This test was not abrogated until 1513 when Leo X abolished it, because of the stench which permeated the ceremony due to an inguinal bubo that a surgeon had just opened for him.

Nevertheless, the Vatican still continued to use *castrati* in the Sistine Chapel until the eighteenth century. In a treatise which he devoted to them in 1524, a Theatine monk of Verona, Zaccharia Pescaligues, wrote that their voices "imitated that of cherubim in heaven." During the seventeenth century, Orlandus Lassus conducted a group of *castrati* in the chapel of the Elector of Bavaria. Even at the beginning of the last century Napoleon was capable of being moved to tears on hearing the *castrato* Crescenti in *Roméo et Juliette* while in 1829 Rossini wrote an opera for the castrato Velluti. Clement XIV did not forbid them to take part in divine services until 1774, but before his time the Papal States used to castrate no fewer than two thousand boys every year. In Naples the custom was so ancient that barbers used to put up a sign: *Qui si castrano ragazzi a buon mercato* (Boys castrated here cheaply). To what extent were *castrati* used for pleasure? It is difficult to say, although it is certain that they often were. But the essential thing is to see that castration, in connection with art and religion, was also linked with homosexuality and with the anxiety that the latter could produce.

Very fortunately the spiritual aspiration of the early Christians and their reaction against the excesses of the ancient world were rarely expressed through this frenzy. The latter was usually limited to a kind of psychological castration of which the celibacy of the priests and even more so the chastity of the monks were one of the most notable aspects. For it should not be forgotten that this celibacy and chastity are, at least insofar as their regulation is concerned, a phenomenon that is principally Christian. In Buddhist or Tibetan monasteries, for example, celibacy is also demanded of the monks, but homosexuality is nonetheless often tolerated there and sometimes encouraged, to the extent that it helps the monks detach themselves from women and from the world, without leading to an absence of affection which is more natural at the end of the initiation than at the beginning. The psychological castration of priests and monks did not destroy as a result a kind of homophilic eroticism; on the contrary it revealed it and raised it to a degree of exaltation and refinement which until that time had been unequaled. For it is possible to say that Christian anguish, when confronted by homosexuality, led to the introduction into friendship between men of a kind of exasperated tenderness of which Aristotle and the other ancient theoreticians had hardly any idea. This was truly a kind of eroticism, a sublimation of love which (taking a direction that had been pointed out by Plato, it is true), flowered in the writings of St. John, St. Augustine, the Desert Fathers, and the Fathers of the Church, and flourished all through the Middle Ages until the Renaissance.

Christian friendship, of the type found in the Bishop of Hippo, or in Paulinus of Nola, in Gregory of Nazianzus, Basil the Great, Gregory of Nyssa, or John Chrysostom, later in St. Bernard or St. Anselm, is much more than Aristotelian friendship, a feeling of reason, or the expression of a serene heart. It is a loving friendship, a passion which one feels is fed by the flesh and one struggles against it while remaining dependent on it. These warm and eminently human relationships are full of exhortations, declarations, quarrels, formal orders, reconciliations, and disappointments. And Christian friendship does not stop at singing as the Psalmist does: "Ah, how good it is, how sweet for brothers to dwell together!" (Psalm 132, 1). It seeks, as Jean Cassien says, a principle which can render it "indissoluble," a pleasure which grows "with the perfection and virtue of the two friends and of which the knot, when it is once formed, is untied neither by the diversity of desires nor by the struggle between opposing wills." And St. Augustine sees in the *caritas*

Christi and in the love of God a very guarantee of its insolubility: "Happy is he that loves Thee," he says in *Confessions*, "and who loves his friend in Thee and his enemy because of Thee. He is the only man in fact who loses none of the beings who are dear to him, he to whom these beings are dear in him that one cannot lose." In these friendly relationships a true verbal eroticism seeks, even in the caress of words, a joy that the body denies itself. As for example in this poem by St. Paulinus of Nola for his friend Nicetas:

Praise be to God for that great love,
He binds us by its hidden chains,
So strong that nothing shall ever break
The final link!

A firm knot keeps us close
To your loving heart which we embrace;
Wherever thou shalt go, my faithful soul
Shall go with you.

And the love of Christ, who comes down
   from heaven,
Both link our hearts so close
That they are neighbors, even if we are
At opposite ends of the world.

Age, separation, catastrophe, or death,
Shall never take me away from you,
And when our bodies die,
Our love shall live on.[1]

The beauty of these accents, which lasted until the nineteenth century among the German romantics or in Lacordaire, arises no doubt from the challenge that they offer to time and to the enduring quality that they claim, feelings which were somewhat rare among the Ancients who were conscious on the contrary of the extreme impermanence of things. But nature was not always deceived by this verbal eroticism and sometimes admitted the frustration of which

---

[1] *Saint Paulin de Nole et l'Amitié chrétienne* (Paris: Pierre Fabre, 1949).

Herakles and Diomedes. Palazzo Vecchio, Florence.

me in suspense and tortured me by letting me await thee every day." And in the evening of life, when verbal exaltations no longer suffice to conceal the long privations of the heart and the flesh, he says that he has found beneath the ground that has been laid bare and beneath revolting plaster rubbish, "knotty tree-stumps, all kinds of harmful creatures, nests of vipers, his true interior dwelling." "It is now," he says finally, "that I see to what extent I am far from God and to what extent I am dead, if I compare myself with the living."

Christian friendship, such as developed from the Ancient Fathers to the monks of the Middle Ages, varied continually between these two opposite poles. On one side, friendship, homosexual in essence, tended to identify itself with the catholicity of the church, to found a theology in which, as Augustine suggested, the City of God would be nothing more than a universal friendship, a friendship which, as in Ennodes, was even to serve as an example for relationships between the dead and the living. On the other side, behind this immense effort of projection and sublimation, nature, which, especially as age came, discovered its frustrations and dared not admit its failure, except in intermittent cries. Thus Francis of Assisi at the end of his life suspected the fleeting nature of a mystic eroticism which left the flesh unsatisfied. It is not surprising therefore that in spite of the sincerity and the grandiose nature of this effort to attain sublimation, and in spite of the terrible punishments the Middle Ages inflicted on homosexuals, the practice continued to manifest itself, and even on the papal throne.

she was the victim. In vain did Paulinus of Nola write to a friend from whom he was separated: "I dwell in thee and thee in me, unto death and unto life"; this did not prevent him from later expressing his impatience, rancor, and bitterness: "I am weary of inviting thee and awaiting thee.... For nearly two years thou hast kept

The Four Witches. Albrecht Dürer. 1497.

The gallery in the Farnese Palace, Rome. Caracci and Scolari. The caryatids of Renaissance architecture supply pretexts for embraces at all ages.

Satan and his Followers. Henry de Malrost. Illustration for *Le Satanism et la Magie,* by Jules Bois. Paris, 1895.

VII
Was the Devil a Homosexual?

Laws punishing homosexuality did not linger on in Byzantium but they were applied in the West with extreme severity until the end of the Middle Ages and sometimes even as late as the mid-eighteenth century. In the capital of the eastern Roman Empire the fate of homosexuals depended less on the laws than on the whims of the basileus. In the heart of the sacred palace a doubleside was reserved for eunuchs and the use made of them varied according to the tendencies of their imperial master. After Constantine's thunder his son, Constantius, had undertaken to rehabilitate the way of life he practiced himself. And if Justinian returned to the charge as far as severity was concerned, this seems to have been due much more to financial reasons than to moral scruples; since homosexuality was extremely widespread in aristocratic and moneyed circles, it could justify a confiscation of property that was extremely welcome to the treasury. Philip the Fair reasoned in the same way when the Knights Templar became the bankers of Europe. At a certain stage of development antihomosexual laws constitute a choice weapon in the hands of skillful arbiters of power who intend, on moral pretexts, to dispose of burdensome adversaries or seize on coveted riches.

Originally the laws of the Empire seem to have stipulated that persons recognized as guilty of sodomy should be punished by the sword, that is to say, decapitated. But it became customary to hang them, and this tendency was increased by certain municipal arrangements. Later it became usual to strangle them, and after that to burn them. During the Middle Ages sodomy was considered a crime punishable by more than one branch of the law; it was dealt with both by lay and ecclesiastical courts. In some districts, however, it depended entirely on the Inquisitors. In the kingdoms of Aragon and Valencia, for example, these magistrates of faith had become the only ones competent to deal with such issues, by special delegation on the part of the sovereign. The crime was regarded as proved if witnesses said they had heard the rattling and shaking of a bed which a man had occupied with a male of suspect age; if the boy had been heard to shout or scream; if a man of bad reputation had shared a bed with an adolescent without plausible motive; if the child's shirt had been found stained; or if a boy over ten years old had been seen being kissed by a man of bad reputation, especially if this man had felt his buttocks, even through his breeches.

It was permissible for the judges to proceed through the Inquisition and use torture. No aristocratic privilege could be invoked; the accused parties were regarded as unclean. Torture was to be applied if the accused claimed that he had not intended to ejaculate, or if, after having done so, he had repented of it later in the act. Torture could also be used if he maintained that the emission of sperm had not taken place in the back passage. For these were the admissions which the theologians considered necessary as proof of the crime. Taking their inspiration from St. Thomas and Cajetan, they distinguished between sodomy and luxuriousness, the former being defined by coitus in what they called "the unnatural passage." Thus Vincent Fillincius wrote:

I said *coitus* in order to distinguish between luxuriousness obtained mutually between male and male, or between woman and woman. For if the desire for sexual enjoyment merely caused a demand for carnal intercourse, without there being coitus, this would be simply luxuriousness and not sodomy, as Cajetan said, in article II, at the second "doubt." Now, coitus is the consummation of carnal copulation, natural if it is in the required passage; unnatural if it is in the forbidden passage.

There was discussion, it is true, as to whether the punishment should be carried out only if the act had been carried through to completion. And if these discussions had not had

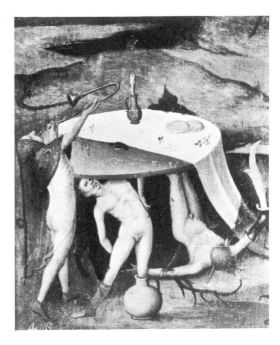

Temptation of St. Anthony. Hieronymus Bosch. Detail. Palais des Beaux Artes, Brussels.

such tragic consequences they would cause laughter today. Thus, Dominique Raynald argued that if penetration without emission of semen could not constitute complete sodomy, it was nevertheless "indecent assault" committed on a boy, the "indecent assault" being no more than the corruption of the boy achieved by penetration alone, in the same way that the rape of a virgin consists only in the perforation of the hymen, even if there is no emission in the passage. Vericelli considered that penetration alone, without emission of semen, was true sodomy. As for Antonio de Souza, he believed that if a man had introduced his member into an anus, even if he had emitted his sperm out-

St. Sebastian. Jean Bourdichon. Illustration from *Les Heures d'Anne de Bretagne.* Fifteenth century. Bibliothèque Nationale, Paris.

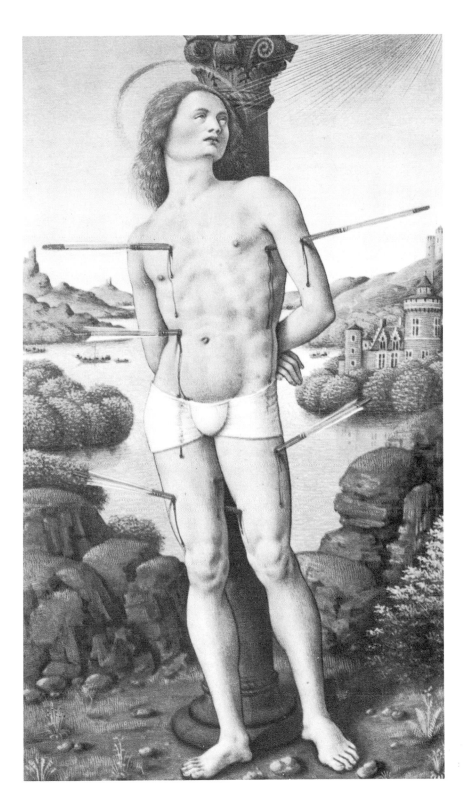

side, he should be punished by the usual sentence passed on sodomites. However, he did not want this punishment to be applied in the case of an isolated act, and demanded that there should be several of them, "for what is lacking in the completion of the sodomite act," he said, "is supplied by the repetition of the act committed against the law." So much for the Doctors.

The crime was the same in the case of both active and passive partners. If the latter was less than eighteen years of age he did, however, escape capital punishment. He was either flagellated in prison, where he had to be incarcerated for a long period, or else he was sent for a few moments through the flames of the fire used for burning at the stake. If he was less than fourteen years of age and was found to embody no dishonesty he remained unpunished. But if he was judged capable of dishonesty, he had to be beaten with an iron rod in the dungeon (even children of ten), or beaten within the prison courtyard. Even those who had not reached the age of puberty suffered this indignity. They all lost their aristocratic privileges, saw their possessions confiscated, and were forbidden to make a will. No mercy could be shown them.

Women do not seem to have escaped the ruling, although feminine sodomy was considered less frequent. Clarus and Gomez assert that women were burned alive for this crime, and Farinaccius says that in Rome he saw several women executed in the Campo di Fiori for this reason. At that time it was regarded as even more serious to have sodomitic relations with a woman than with a man. "Women, in fact, possess a passage destined for copulation," the Reverend Father Sinistrari of Ameno said later. "As a result he who rejects this passage concerns himself with the other, reveals himself as possessing a more than savage brutality, and his crime is more to be condemned as a result." Therefore no distinction was made if sodomy, that is to say "coitus in the back passage," was committed between men or between women or between persons of different sex. Various authors relate that a man was burned with his wife, for the sole reason that he had had sodomitic relations with her.

On this point, too, long discussions divided the Doctors who, like the captain of police in *The Thousand and One Nights*, wondered between two periods of officiation how women could operate without a penis. The unfortunate men did not possess much humor and wondered among themselves how the semen of the incubus could be ejaculated into the passage of the succubus. Some authors discovered that coitus between women was achieved thanks to an instrument of glass, wood, or leather, made in the same shape as the male member, which the incubus, after attaching it between the thighs, introduced into the succubus. Nuns who transgressed in this manner were therefore burned alive. But the Doctors had to recognize that these instruments were not always used. It is true, they say, that a person may have vainly introduced a finger into the front or back passage of a woman or a man, but it does not follow that the two participants can be said to have had intercourse, even if the introduction of the finger is followed by emission of semen. Neither, according to them, could an inanimate object determine coitus or copulation. The discovery of the clitoris solved the problem for them. The clitoris, they stated, swells with the flow of the seminal fluid and from that point onward becomes, in women, the organ of amorous delectation, to the extent that certain writers called it the "Sweetness of Love" and the "Tick of Venus," *dixit* Thomas Bartholinus in his *Anatomical Tables*. For, our theologians stated, all women have not discov-

Charles Eisen. Illustration for *The Fables of La Fontaine*.

ered the clitoris they possess; in many of them there can be found only a small eminence protruding above the neighboring parts when, through the effect of amorous titillation, the member in question is swollen from the inside. And they added that if in certain women the clitoris is not larger than the middle finger of the hand, in others it acquires the size of a goose's neck, as was found in the case of a Venetian courtesan. In 1671, in Pavia, a nun had to ask for the attentions of a doctor, after trying in vain to reduce the stiffness of her clitoris with soothing ointments. It was admitted from that time that women in whom the clitoris developed and who, incapable of resisting through continence the sensual titillation which lead them to the act of sodomy, must also be examined by midwives if the judge ordered it. As a result, if they were found to have a clitoris, if it was proved that they had made love with other women, they were tortured, as happened many times in the convents.

Clerics, however, received more indulgent treatment, the link between homosexuality and holy orders being thus disguised in one more way. Originally the Constitution of the Lateran Council ruled that any cleric surprised in the act of unnatural incontinence should be removed from office and thrown into a monastery to do penance. Later, in 1566 and 1568, the Constitutions of Pius V ruled that one so accused should be handed over to the secular Curia, although the Sovereign Pontiff reserved for himself the right of pardon on his behalf. It was also admitted that the cleric could not be convicted if his crime remained hidden, and the latter had to be common knowledge in fact and in law. Friars who were members of regular orders obtained even more remarkable privileges. Thus a Franciscan sodomite found himself called to the chapter, made to strip (his hands tied, and wearing nothing but his breeches),

and was severely beaten; after having recited the *Miserere mei, Deus*, his flesh was singed by small flames placed here and there around him. He was then condemned to life imprisonment. After seven years the general Master could free him if he found enough recommendations for mercy. However, even if he was freed, the culprit found himself deprived forever of the right to vote and barred from carrying out religious tasks. If he relapsed into crime he was sent to the galleys for life. Sometimes three years was sufficient for the expiation of his sins. However, torture could only be applied to friars in symbolic fashion. They were often submitted to ordeal by fire, and only underwent it after their feet had been smeared with grease, and then for a very short time, so that they were not rendered incapable of walking. This torture could be prolonged throughout two *Miserere*. While these were recited a plank of wood was held over the fire in order to moderate the heat.

One can imagine to what extent these canonical regulations—horrible enough in themselves—found, in the obscurantism of the period, the most absurd reasons for convicting anyone. In countries like France and Germany a subterranean current stemming from paganism continued to manifest itself beneath official Christianity. Homosexual customs had existed there before the establishment of Christianity, as well as in Italy or Greece. Tacitus offers proof of this in the case of the Germans, Strabo in that of the Gauls, and, later still, traces of homosexual inspiration can be found in poets such as Notker Balbulus or Marbode du Mans, even in certain *chansons de geste*. As late as the Middle Ages the Duc de Berry, known for *Les Très Riches Heures*, made no secret of his liaison with the young Taque Thébaut and the Comte de Blois with a certain Sohier. But generally speaking, homosexual-

illio mare occeanu sep fluit requesfluit requesfluit requestal fluuuo uocar ab habitatoxibz tre fi otto. Vn air autor intrxeu.

Cemendolsioteo ebenuet loz sauenta. facaunt ar istoo aggeres ne fluuimario uemeno loca culta denaster. Poit realia silitudine dicco qira eunte facet illi aggeres sie sunt illi quoo facaunt paduani uix fluuiu biente qui descedit de alpibz cannebie. Cu e alpes alamanie sint p totam byeme nuubz coopte. cu uetrex tuiu tpo qn solesao nutes resoluit iago tunc dictuo fluuiuo biente redundat i

bz multum eximie. Vz ex phesulaio q funt boies ualde dun. ingrati. maliuo li realiag. Na sicut legitur in ystoria bu romuli phm phesulani ep. que beat Petr apto misit de roma ad predicadu phesulas libu dei. ipi phesulani erant boies maligniss realiag. Vn ipse flo rentani qui descedit de illis monabz ab antiquo adbuc tenet mores realiag figia sesulana. Vn air fi Brunett intrxeu. Et tenancor delmore realiag delmagno. Et romaio q funt boies amabiles monge mti realiag oium gentibz adornati. Et

Priests damned. Italian miniature of the fourteenth century. Illustration for Dante's *Inferno.* Musée Condé Château de Chantilly, Chantilly.

ity was concealed or, worse still, became unaware of itself, giving rise to collective neuroses and uncontrollable rumors. It is natural that after being condemned by Christian officialdom it found refuge, more or less openly, in the heretical groups which flourished at the time and, rightly or wrongly, was put down to the Devil. On the other hand Waldenses, Catharians, Adamites, Béghards, Flagellants, and many others were accused of sexual abominations, without it being possible to prove that these groups were really tainted with it.

The most amusing (and the most significant) thing was that the heresy, or the representation of the Devil, always appeared linked to one form or another of anality. It was not only contemporary engravings which perpetually illustrated the Devil as showing his behind.[1] Legend saw anality everywhere. It was said therefore that nobody could enter the Vaudois sect without kissing a toad on the rump or the mouth, in which case the creature deposited something between the initiate's lips. It was also alleged that during the course of the ceremonies held by the Luciferians that a black female cat came down from a statue backward, its tail down, and then presented its behind to the novice who would kiss it. Upon which the president would ask, "What does

[1] R. Villeneuve, *Le Diable, érotologie de Satan* (Bibliothèque Internationale d'Érotologie, No. 10; Paris: J.-J. Pauvert, 1963) pp. 19, 179.

All that remains of Gilles de Rais are the ruins of Machecoul (dating from the fourteenth century), but the links between this homosexual Bluebeard and Joan of Arc—who was burned at the stake like him, for having worn men's clothing—have not failed to preoccupy many psychologists.

this teach?" And the reply was "The deepest peace." The lights would then be put out and a confused promiscuity apparently took place between the adepts. Under Philip the Good a rich citizen of Arras, Pierre de Carrieulx, confessed that during a Sabbath he had kissed a devil, who had appeared to him in the form of a monkey, beneath the tail. Pope Boniface VIII did not succeed in escaping these accusations. At the Assembly of the Louvre called by Philip the Fair, he was accused of having suspect relations with a demon who kept him informed of events. At the same period the Bishop of Coventry was reproached for paying homage to a handsome devil whom he consulted after having kissed him on the buttocks. After Hieronymus Bosch showed the Prince of Darkness defecating the world, Luther was able to describe the devil as a giant anus and thus present himself as a ripe turd ready to drop, the Holy Ghost having granted him his supreme revelation in the latrines in the monastery tower of Wittenberg. In his *Faust*, Part II, Goethe could still describe how Mephistopheles became enamored of the angels' backsides and through this distraction lost his companion's soul, which Marguerite was able to save in the end.

This anal obsession assumed a political and European dimension when Philip the Fair brought a lawsuit against the Order of the Knights Templar. The Templars, as is well known, had been founded early in the twelfth century in order to constitute the advance guard of the Christian armies in the East. However, in view of the donations from which they benefited, they became transformed, in the West, into great landed proprietors and also into bankers for the pope and various kings. The envy which they aroused resulted in a trial, no doubt the most famous in Christendom, and one which led to their condemnation as individuals and to the dissolution of their order. Among the principal accusations leveled against them, homosexuality was one of the most serious.

It is no doubt worth-while to recall that St. Bernard, whose devotion to the Marian cult and feeling for brotherly love had reached a kind of frenzy, was in fact the man responsible for drawing up the rules of their Order. During the interrogation of the four Great Dignitaries of the Order, Geoffroy de Charnay, preceptor of Normandy, stated that he had embraced on the navel the man who received him and had heard Brother Gérard de Saujet, preceptor of Auvergne, say that it was better to have carnal intercourse with one's peers than with women. And Hugues de Pairaux, visiting brother for the Order for the whole of

France, admitted that he had kissed on the lips the man who received him, had caused candidates to kiss him at the base of the spine, on the navel, and on the mouth, and finally stated that if any ardor drove them to incontinence, they had permission to express it with other brothers. Jean du Tour stated on his side that he was kissed three times, first at the base of the spine, then on the navel, and finally on the lips, that he was forbidden to sleep with women, and that if he

felt driven by any urge he could always have intercourse with his brother knights. Pierre de Bologne also admitted that he had been kissed on the lips, on the navel, and on the private parts. The enquiry on behalf of the Pope was very much concerned with knowing whether the brothers kissed each other on the mouth, the stomach, the anus, or the spine, *in ano sen spina dorsi.* One of the brothers admitted that when the man who initiated him had stripped himself in front of him, he refused to kiss him *in ano,* as he had been asked to do, but did so on the naked flesh of the shoulder. Although others denied the fact, notably the Grand Master Jacques de Molay, some of them asserted that a member of the Knights Templar, after having been a prisoner of the Saracens, had introduced the following prac-

Engravings. Abraham Eleazaris. Leipzig. 1760. These figures from alchemy which associate two men within one body are reminiscent of the homosexual *Coniunction* which is described in a document relating to alchemy.

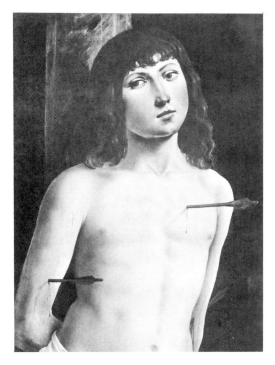

St. Sebastian. Lorenzo Costa. Galleria degli Uffizi, Florence.

tices into their own countries: the rejection and trampling of the Cross, spitting, and kisses on the buttocks. This confession raises the problem of relationships between Templars and Moslems, and more particularly between Templars and Ishmaelites.

In his book, *Le Secret de la Chevalerie*, Michelet noted that Moslem chivalry was suppressed by Islam, just as the Templars were suppressed by Christianity. On both sides Johannine gnosticism is said to have led to the encounter. Whatever the truth may be, and even if it is not admitted that the Knights Templar might have been initiated by the Haschichin, it can easily be imagined that soldiers who were lost in a world of which they had no understanding had finally been seduced by a conception of life that was wider than that of medieval Christianity. People have always been

tempted to justify the Knights Templar by denying the crimes of which they were accused. But the question has rarely been asked whether these "crimes" were really crimes, if the Templars, through their contact with the Arabs, had not envisaged a theology and a morality which were inaccessible to the barbarous world of the Middle Ages, and whether it was not natural for soldier-monks to have carnal relations when they renounced women. If we think of the Foreign Legion or other combatant military organizations it must be admitted that such aspirations would appear today to be so obviously natural and sensible that we still find it difficult to understand if not the trial of the Templars then at least the moral acrobatics through which attempts were made to absolve them. The innocence of the Templars can no doubt be established without there being any need to deny the actions of which they were accused; these actions are evidence perhaps of a premature or inadequate orientation of the medieval conscience which the Renaissance achieved at less expense, but one which the average man of the period must have been quite incapable of undertaking.

There was no need, moreover, for the men of the West to go to the Holy Land in order to make contact with a civilization whose criteria differed from their own. Arab civilization had sent some of its most eminent representatives to Sicily and Southern Italy, and their influence on the Emperor Frederick Hohenstaufen of Sicily and his court is well known. In Spain there were no courts of the Kings of Taif which were not noted for their homosexual customs. *Gulâm wasîm, fatâ wasîm* or *fatâ gamil* described the handsome boy as compared with the beardless youth, *gulâm amrad.* When the favorites began to grow beards, they were called *mu'addir*, because of the down or hairs which covered their cheeks. Famous love affairs linked together well-known people: al-Mu'tamid loved Ibn Ammar and his page Saïf; al-Mutawakkil loved a youth; Rafi ad-Dawla loved a favorite whose name has not come down to us; al-Mu'tamin of Saragossa loved one of his Christian pages. Following the example of Agu Nuwas, Bassar, and d'Ibn ar-Rumi, the Arab poets sang of their loves. In this way, al-Mu'tamid celebrates "the cupbearer who, with slender waist and provocative looks, rose to pour out the wine." Abu-l-Oâssin Ibn al'Attar compares the looks of his friend to arrows, his eyebrows to a bow, and the pupil of his eyes to an archer. Abu-l-Hasen Ibn al Hâgg weeps for his favorite who has just died and asks him why his cheeks are full of sorrow, why, after having made the flowers grow in spring, love now produced only brambles, why the full moon was also stricken by the universal upset, and if he belonged to the Omeyyades, whose black emblem was one of death. Women cupbearers tried to imitate the adolescent boys by dressing in men's clothes and cutting their hair. "She was an antelope, without being entirely one," said Ibn Saud, "for after having cut her hair she came with a long slim neck surmounting the body of a boy."

It is difficult to say to what extent Arab customs influenced Christianity, the latter having made contact with them not only during the Crusades but also beyond the Pyrenees and the straits of Syracuse. But it would be surprising if these influences, which are known to have been decisive in the realms of philosophy, medicine, and mathematics, were not equally so in that of social life as well.

When Joan of Arc was condemned to be burned at the stake she was expressly reproached for having, through her mascu-line dress, "practiced the customs of the pagans and the Saracens." Although these masculine clothes and her short hair did not prevent her from receiving posthumous canonization, it is curious all the same to find that the only man she asked for in 1429 when she was wounded outside the walls of Orleans was the marshal of France, Gilles de Rais. It is interesting to reflect that some intimate affection might have linked together the Maid—in whom the taste for male attire and the absence of any deep masculine attachment could have indicated some unconscious Lesbian tendency—and the man who was accused of having massacred a hundred and forty-four children, mainly of the male sex, after having abused them in appalling circumstances. The parallelism of their destinies, the heroic and warlike vocation that they had in common, their common revulsion for so-called normal sexuality, the accusations of heresy and sorcery which they both had to answer until they were both burned at the stake, led psychologists to propound the inevitable hypothesis that there was something complementary in their make-up, a profound similarity in their tendencies. This complementary quality can be observed even in the reactions of the ordinary people to the martyrdom of the two former comrades in arms: the crowds were indifferent or even hostile toward the saint who had saved them; they revealed sympathy and emotion for the criminal who, after having enjoyed his lovers, still found pleasure (once he had strangled or decapi-tated them), in sitting on their bodies so that he could feel their final shudders. *Sancta simplicitas*, if it is not the mystery of the communion of saints and the revertibil-ity of sins, so dear to the hearts of believers.

If, because of his outsize personality and the fame of his conviction, the name of Gilles de Rais is inseparable from the history of homosexuality and pederasty, it is only for marginal reasons. For his criminal frenzy was no more representative of these tendencies than the criminal behavior of Landru or any other murderer of women was representative of heterosexuality. But the abyss into which Joan of Arc's companion fell might have appeared to be, during a period full of prejudices, a kind of exemplary confirmation of the very criminality of homosexual tendencies. The people of the period did not see that such chasms must yawn more easily within Christian souls than in others, since the pure and icy world of religion could offer no way out for their natural barbarity. Much time was to pass before a more human, if not more everyday vision liberated itself from the terrors of the Inquisition, the frenzies of the witches' Sabbath, and the clandestine behavior imposed by the complete disapproval of society.

This vision is already developed in a curious way, although in timid fashion, in Dante's *Inferno*. And indeed the sodomites presented by the great Florentine writer in Canto XV are all damned and condemned to walk eternally beneath a rain of fire, without ever having the right to stop. But they are not considered the most guilty of the guilty, or even as receiving the most serious punishment. "A troop of spirits . . . were coming alongside the bank; and each looked at us, as in the evening men are wont to look at one another under a new moon; and toward us sharpened their vision, as an aged tailor does at the eye of his needle. Thus eyed by that family . . ." (16–22); Dante takes care not to increase their unhappiness by condemning them. "Not contempt, but sorrow, your condition fixed within me," he said later, "so deeply that it will not leave me soon" (XVI, 52). For to him sodomites are less guilty than blasphemers—while the latter show violence against the very person of God, the violence of the former is only being exercised against one of God's possessions, nature. He does not present them as criminals or frantic men, but as famous people tainted with the same sin: "They were all clerks and men of such education," he says, "and with great reputations." Some of them can be recognized: Brunetto Latini (who had predicted to Dante that he would be famous), was the Florentine ambassador, took refuge in France because he had supported the Guelphs, and returned to his country to carry out important functions after the battle of Benevento; Priscian from Caesarea in Cappadocia, the famous Latin grammarian; Francesco d'Accorso, the jurist of Bologna who taught at Oxford; Guido Guerra, the leader of the Florentine Guelphs who "in his lifetime did much with counsel and with sword" (XVI, 37), and others, too.

These names suffice to show that in the fourteenth century in Italy it had not been possible to destroy homosexuality after a thousand years of moral and physical punishment. It was widespread in the most varied, cultivated, and socially important milieux. It reigned even on the throne of Peter. Although this was not proven in the case of Boniface VIII, it cannot be forgotten that Philip the Fair wanted to condemn him as a heretic and set in motion an army of witnesses who stated under oath and with an infinite number of details that the defunct Pope believed neither in the immortality of the soul nor in the doctrines of incarnation and redemption, that he worshiped demons and nurtured "unholy and unnatural passions." These witnesses were men of the Church and of "good" reputation. And if the King of France was less successful in this case than he had been with the Knights Templar and found himself obliged to renounce his attack, it was because the usual rules of procedure had been neglected. However, it was proved that during the fifteenth century Sixtus IV, who was, moreover, known for the way in which he sold ecclesiastical offices to the highest bidders, also rewarded young men who had honored him with their favors by giving them rich bishoprics. The Christian world of the Middle Ages ended in total disaster and the very head of the Church revealed its contradictions and the admission of its failure.

The Martyrdom of St. Médard. Lucas Cranach.

Illustration for a modern French edition of the poetry of Paul Verlaine.

114

VIII

Fissures in the Renaissance

If Dante was able, as far back as the fourteenth century, to reflect the homosexuality which already reigned in Florence at this period, it can be imagined that with the trend of ideas which gradually led Italy back toward Antiquity, the "vice of Florence," as it had been called at first, rapidly became "the vice of Italy." Its importance during the Renaissance was crucial, as it had been in Greece in the past.

At the outset of these major changes stand two famous names: Leonardo da Vinci and Michelangelo. It is true that the private life of the former remains shrouded in mystery and as a result we are reduced to reconstituting it through his art, isolated outbursts scattered throughout his *Notebooks*, and occasional legal documents. For it is a disturbing fact that the Archives of Florence, of which the official records were published for the first time in 1896, describe a lawsuit brought against Leonardo and two other young men because of illicit relationships with a certain Jacopo Saltarelli, aged seventeen. The denunciation had been deposited by an unknown hand in one of the letter boxes known as *tamburi*, which at this period existed within the Duomo for the purpose of approaching the authorities. Leonardo and the three others accused were acquitted on April 9, 1476.[1] This incident, which was followed by the reproach that he had painted a boy "of bad reputation," would be mere scandalous gossip if it did not help us toward the understanding of the general orientation of Leonardo's life and the essence of his art. The fact that the latter revealed a certain degree of preciousness and even more so a deliberate quest for heramphroditism, assumes a dramatic significance in the light of the incident we have just mentioned. For Leonardo da Vinci had been influenced by Marsilio Ficino and the Neo-Platonist school in Florence which had attempted to link the philosophy of the Beautiful—inherited from Greece—to the demands of the Christian faith. This is the reason for those faces of David, John the Baptist, Jesus

---

[1] R. and M. Wittkower, *Born under Saturn* (London: Weidenfeld and Nicolson, 1963).

115

Adolescence. Leonardo da Vinci. Drawing. Louvre, Paris.

Himself, and even of "La Gioconda," which reveal a strange combination of harsh masculinity and feminine tenderness, the serious gaze born of contemplation and the formal perfection in keeping with the pagan aesthetic approach.

It is possible to believe that the development shown in Leonardo's work was based on experiences which are echoed in the bitterness of many of his confessions. For, although the artist wrote that "if the soul encounters someone who resembles the body it has invented, it falls in love with it," and that "a beautiful face should be comparable to a music of harmonious thoughts," he also knew the irreparable degradation experienced by anyone who falls in love with someone who does not deserve it: "If the object is base," he wrote, "the lover debases himself." And he cried: "Oh false glow of light, how many others before me,

in times past, have you wretchedly deceived! If I wanted to see the light, should I not learn to tell the sunlight from the unreal glow of the smoldering candle?" He also states precisely: "If you are thinking further about satisfying your desires for luxuriousness, consider those who have followed only the base desires of the body like brutish animals: what memory do they leave behind?" And one of his contemporaries quotes him as saying: "The act of copulation and the members employed in it are so ugly that if it were not for the beauty of the faces and the attributes of those taking part, and the preservation of the human species would no longer be preserved." It would be absurd therefore to regard Leonardo da Vinci as a libertine and it is more likely that his entire life was a painful struggle to achieve reconciliation between his homosexual tendencies and his lofty moral demands. If in the early part of his existence Leonardo revealed a *joie de vivre* recorded by his contemporaries, along with gaiety, eloquence, and amiability which corresponded with the extreme beauty of his face and person, it looks as though he must gradually have lost his illusions as he grew older. "Hate is more clear-sighted than love," he wrote in the end, "it ruins and destroys love."

A certain tranquillity, however, must have been made possible for him through the custom which allowed painters to welcome young pupils of their choice into their own homes. Leonardo selected them more for their beauty than for their talent. As a result, hardly any of their names are significant in the history of art, not even those of Cesare de Sesto, Boltraffo, Andrea Salaino, or Francesco Melzi. It is true that the last named showed Leonardo an affection which lasted until death and meant that he became his heir. As for Andrea Salaino, the account book has transmitted to us, with the exactness shown by a paterfamilias, the details of the expenses into which this boy led Leonardo. Thus on April 4, 1497, he noted eight yards of cloth of silver, green velvet for the trimming, ribbons, fastenings, and all for a cloak he was giving to the scamp. "This is really the last time, dear Salai, that I am giving you more money," which in spite of this formal statement did not prevent him from living with Andrea for eighteen years longer. Salaino seems moreover to have been merely a nickname for Saladino, or little devil, for this young good-for-nothing never stopped robbing Leonardo and Leonardo never stopped forgiving him.

Freud, as we know, in the *Childhood Memory* that he wrote about Leonardo, attributed the artist's homosexuality to a mother fixation of which he considered the proof to be in the famous recollection of the vulture that is said to have kissed the artist on the lips and that is unconsciously described in the drawing of the Virgin and Child. Although he does not reject a priori the possibility of sexual relationships between Leonardo and his pupils, Freud believes it more likely that the former remained in a state of "platonic, solitary, and tragic homosexuality" which even from the moral point of view, he wrote, was of greatness never achieved by any "normal debauched man." Otherwise, the father of psychoanalysis denies in lofty fashion that he ever wished to include Leonardo da Vinci "among the neurotics" and restricts himself to placing the artist "close" to the neurotic type described as obsessional. However, he considers that Leonardo's Platonic homosexuality may have been an obstacle to the completion of his artistic work. It is well known, in fact, that as he grew older Leonardo found himself progressively in-

Bacchus. Leonardo da Vinci. Louvre, Paris. The homosexuality of Leonardo—of which records can be found in the archives of Florence and which Freud rediscovered in his analysis of Leonardo's works—was sublimated through the passionate search for the hermaphrodite, as revealed in his portraits of St. John the Baptist, Bacchus, St. John, and Jesus.

capable of finishing his paintings and worked with increasing slowness. This incapacity and slowness seem to have been due to a liking for investigation that preferred knowledge to love and action, even to creation. His Platonic homosexuality, which at first inspired his art, finally therefore hampered it and favored on the contrary a tendency to scientific research which made him the first man after the Greeks to be the great violator of the secrets of nature, the father of those who revolted against tradition but also the founder of modern thought.

Unlike Leonardo da Vinci, an introvert if ever there was one, Michelangelo revealed a tumultuous and frenzied but equally Platonic homosexuality, which only became calmer during his last years, due apparently to the friendship of the serious-minded Vittoria Colonna. While the art of the great Florentine revealed a hidden and obstinate quest for hermaphroditism, that of Michelangelo abandoned itself to a passionate exaltation of the most exasperated virility. Before his time Luca Signorelli had introduced the fashion for muscular, tanned, male nudes, youths who could be seen in painting even as late as the "Resurrection of the Dead" at Orvieto, preserving the memory of an eternal Arcadia which, according to Chastel, perpetuated the ancient world. However, in spite of the example he drew from this painting, in which graceful naked adolescent boys with

The Last Judgment. Michelangelo. Detail from the Sistine Chapel, Rome.

Studies for the nude male figures in *The Last Judgment* at Orvieto. Luca Signorelli. Musée Condé Chateau de Chantilly, Chantilly.

curly hair can often be seen embracing each other, Michelangelo soon gave up the apparent tranquility that dwelt within them in order to abandon himself to the fury of his desire and his failure to accomplish it. The *ignudi* on the Sistine ceiling have been compared to aristocratic Blackshirts of the seventeenth century, because of their astonishing leather-like coloring, their muscles, and their inspired, even cruel beauty. And there is no doubt that by painting men in this exasperated fashion, Michelangelo tried to reveal a kind of uncompromising truth, symbolized by absolute nudity. But it was at this period also and as he approached forty that

his search for truth could assume the power of his unsatisfied desire and project it on the ceilings that he painted in a real frenzy, alone, and lying on his back.

At the same time 1522 saw the declaration of his passion for Tommaso Cavalieri, for whom he was to write sonnets of undying fame: "My sweet Lord whom I desire for ever in the eager embrace of my unworthy arms." But before this he had already fallen in love with Gherardo Perini, for whom he had written, "Here, my love ravished my heart and life. Here, his fine eyes promised me succor, yet took it away from me. Here, in infinite sorrow, I wept and saw the departure of this stony-hearted man who had revealed me to myself and no longer wanted me." In 1533 it was the turn

of Febo del Poggio, whose mediocre nature would only respond to the artist's frenzy through demands for money. In 1544 Michelangelo met Cecchino Bracci, whose premature death inspired him to write forty-eight epigrams: "I who was only given to you for an hour, I am given over to death forever. The more deeply beauty bewitches us, the more tears it leaves behind:—it would have been better if I had never been born" (LXXIII, 29). His love for Tommaso Cavalieri, who was handsome, distinguished, and devoted to art, lasted until death. "It is an infinite sorrow to me," Michelangelo wrote to him on January 1, 1533, "that I cannot give you also my past, so that I could serve you longer, for the future will be short: I am too old." And later, "What I desire, what I learn from the beauty of your face, cannot be understood by ordinary men. He who wishes to understand it must first die." (*Poems*, L.) Cavalieri made his friend decide to finish the wooden model for the cupola of St. Peter's. It was he who preserved his plans for the building of the Capitol and worked to carry them out. It was also he who, after Michelangelo had died in his arms on February 18, 1564 (thirty-two years after their meeting), made sure that his wishes were carried out. "What stimulus there is for me in the strength of a face," the creator of "David" and the "Bound Slave" had cried, "nothing in the world gives me such joy." (*Poems*, CXLI.)

It would have been surprising if homosexuality had remained on these heights which only genius rendered habitable. It

Study of a Man. Pollaiuolo. Musée de Bayonne, Bayonne.

was inevitable that it passed into anecdotes, if not into commonplace existence, as moral or penal prohibitions became less strict. But Italy only gave the lead to a movement that was felt throughout the whole of Europe. It would certainly be going too far to attribute to Montaigne any conscious homosexual leanings, or, even more so, any homosexual practices. But it would be naïve nonetheless to overlook in his conception of friendship one aspect of this movement and the expression—controlled or sublimated, if not repressed—of a personality-structure of which homosexuality is the evident expression. Although Montaigne's friendship for Étienne de la Boëtie was virtuous, and his references to Antiquity more literary than real (and did not prevent their authors from expressing gallantry toward women), there was nonetheless a passionate character about this friendship which places it in the same line with the dubious friendships of Antiquity and the Christian Middle Ages, and no psychologist can be deceived by it. Montaigne writes:

If I compare all the rest of my life to the four years during which it was granted to me to enjoy the delightful company and society of this person, it is nothing, it is no more than dark and tedious night.... We were lacking half of everything; it seemed as though I was taking half his share away from him.... I had become so accustomed to being his second self in everything that I seem now to be only half a man. . . . If I am pressed to say why I loved him, I feel that I could only reply because it was he, because it was I. (*Essays*, Vol. 1, 28.)

It is true that although he considers friendship a passion, Montaigne never intends to compare it to love. He finds it much too superior to the latter. "The former," he says, keeps to its path with a proud and lofty flight and watches with disdain the latter "passing far below." This does not mean that love in the Greek manner was unknown to him: "If such a type of acquaintance could be established, in a free and voluntary way, in which not only the mind could partake of this total delight but where the body also could play a part in the union, in which the whole man could be engaged: it is certain that friendship would be fuller and more complete." In the face of such a confession it matters little that contradictions have been found in an author who was still disconcerted by the liberties of behavior in Greece and who found himself

Hercules and Anteus. Baccio Bandinelli. Louvre, Paris.

The Deluge. Michelangelo. Detail from the Sistine Chapel. Rome.

St. Sebastian. Anibale Carracci. Galleria Doriz, Rome.

torn between his admiration for that country and the taboos he had inherited from his Christian education. He recognized nonetheless that some animals indulged in love between males (*Essays*, II, 12), and Tallemant des Réaux reports that when his spiritual daughter and executor, Mademoiselle de Gournay, was asked if homosexuality was a crime, she replied, "Heaven forbid that I should condemn what Socrates practiced" (*Historiettes*, Vol. I, p. 380). Contradictions of this sort form part of the greatness of writers standing at the crossroads of two eras, caught in the trough of the waves but whose "proud and lofty flight" could not remain that of ordinary men solicited by homosexual tendencies.

On a much more earthbound level there appeared a form of homosexuality which genius no longer maintained on the heights and to which Shakespeare alone paid honor, as is shown by the Sonnets, which

Apollo. Raphael. 1509. Louvre, Paris.

Terrible, the Opritchnicks, whom Eisenstein showed in visionary style with haloes of a strangely homophilic nature; Prince Serebrenni, after his victory over the Tartars, is seduced by Prince Basmanov. The latter, who was valiant in battle, also displays his beauty, his earrings, his suntan, his concubines, and his male favorites. He admits dancing before the Czar in female dress and to being called by the peasants "Ivan's Fedora."

In France, it is true, things took a more lighthearted and frivolous turn. After Henri III and his favorites came the Great Condé, victor of Rocroi, Nordlingen, and Lens, the Maréchal de Villars, conqueror of Friedlingen, and Denain, savior of France in 1712. In a series of remarkable studies, Marc Daniel (*Arcadie*, nos. 36, 37, 38, 39, 40, 41, 42–44, 45) has devoted himself to rediscovering the traces of this kind of love throughout the entire Grand Siècle. In addition to Prince Eugene of Savoy, who, as the Prin-

were dedicated to an unknown young man. But in the different cases of James I (the son of Mary, Queen of Scots, of whom it was said: *Habuimus regem Elisabetham, habemus reginam Jacobum*—We have had King Elizabeth, now we have Queen James), William III and Queen Anne, a commonplace type of homosexuality developed in England which is remembered only through its anecdotal side. In Sweden it was said that Queen Christina had been perverted by her doctor, who was an intimate friend of the Great Condé. Germany did not escape the contagion and even in Russia, if we can believe Count Alexis Tolstoy, homosexuality reached the steps of the throne. His novel, *Prince Serebrenni,* reconstructs Russian society of the seventeenth century. The hero of the work finds himself at grips with the famous guards of Ivan the

The Thermi. Girolamo Macchietti. Florence.

Adoration of a Faun. Luca Signorelli. Fragment.
Alte Museum, Berlin.

Man. Raphael. Drawing. British Museum, London.

cess Palatine recalls in her *Correspondence,* was called Madame Putana, it is said that these tastes were appreciated by the Prince de Conti, the Maréchal de Guiche, the Maréchal de Gramont, the Comte de Guiscard, and the Duc de la Ferté, without counting Louis XIII and the Duc d'Orléans, whose incredible bravura did not prevent him from applying "imperceptible amounts of rouge." It was inevitable that this freedom attracted the wrath of the conformists. The Compagnie du Saint-Sacrement took charge of this under Louis XIII and the entourage of Madame de Maintenon under Louis XIV. On Christmas Day, 1684, Bourdaloue demanded the King's zeal against "these monsters whom the Scriptures forbade him to name." And if the Sun King was somewhat disposed to lend a consenting ear to such propositions, he found an unexpected adversary in the person of Louvois who, according to what the Princess Palatine says in her *Memoirs,* believed that sodomy "was more worthwhile for serving His

Jealousy. Lucas Cranach. Detail.　▶

124

Majesty than the love of women, for when it was necessary to go to war and take part in campaigns, [the soldiers] could not break away from their mistresses...while if they had other inclinations they were delighted to leave the ladies and go on campaigns with their lovers." He added moreover that if the King wished to show proof of his severity, he should have begun with removing this type of love from the very bosom of the Jesuit College.

Primi Visconti, in his *Mémoires sur la Cour de Louis XIV*, gave evidence of the change in attitudes when he described the opinions of the Abbé del Carretto as follows: "One must feel sorry for men with inclinations of this sort because they are

Justice and Peace. Flemish School. Sixteenth century. Fragment. Musée Thomas-Dobrée et Musée Archéologique, Nantes.

born with them just as poets are born with a sense of rhyme"; yet accusations of homosexuality still led to prosecutions.

One of the most disturbing of these cases, apart from those involving Jacques Chausson, Jacques Paulmier, or Benjamin Deschauffours, was certainly that of Jérôme Duquesnoy, who in his time had acquired a European reputation as a sculptor and an engraver of medals. Born in Brussels in 1602, a member of a family of famous artists, he had become known through his remarkable productions, outstanding among which are the great statues of the apostles at the Collegiate Church of St. Michael and St. Gudule in Brussels, many works in the churches of La Chapelle, Le Sablon, or Saint-Josse in the same city, busts acquired by the Empress of Russia, and works at Malines, Ghent, and Antwerp. He had become friendly with Nicolas Poussin, and

Van Dyck had painted his portrait. He had made long stays in Rome, Florence, and Spain, where Philip IV had ordered several works from him. In 1645 he had become assistant to the court architect of the Archdukes Albert and Isabel. We then find that this artist of European reputation, whose statues are still admired today as those of the greatest sculptor of his period, was accused of having abused two boys in the chapel of Ghent, where he had arrived on July 6, 1654. He was interrogated on August 31 and September 1. In spite of an appeal to the King of Spain and a plea by the Bishop of Trieste, the Council of State decreed that his effects should be seized; sentence of death was pronounced and carried out on September 28 of the same month. He was lashed to a stake, strangled, and his body reduced to ashes in the city Grain Market.[2]

A tragedy of this sort could no doubt only have occurred in that part of the Netherlands which, through submission to the Roman Church, had failed to gain its independence. In the Northern Provinces which, on the contrary, had snatched their freedom from Spain, their hero, William the Silent, was no stranger to customs for which the obscurantism of the Southern Provinces still sent men to the stake. Germany also struggled with old taboos. Although the young Duke of Wolfenbüttel, according to the Princess Palatine, was nearly killed first by Charles-Ludwig of Bavaria and then by the Prince von Eisenach for having made propositions to them, Frederick the Great was the hero of a romance which affected his entire life. When he was fifteen he had fallen in love with Frederick von Borcke, to whom he had written, "My heart is filled with you and can only be soothed if you are fully convinced of my affection, I adore you." Later he became intimate with a page by the name of Keith, after having experienced pleasure with women after the Countess Orzelska, mistress of Augustus II, had initiated him. After von Borcke and Keith had been exiled by his clumsy father, who did not fail to refer to his son as a dandy and a fop, Frederick fell passionately in love with one of his officers, Johann von Katte. He found him to possess musical tastes similar to his own, the same freedom of thought, and refinements quite foreign to the court of the Sergeant-King. The Crown Prince therefore took it into his head to run away. His friend advised him against this

[2] *Bibliographie nationale de l'Académie royale de Belgique* (Brussels: 1878), Vol. VI.

Sketch after a painting by Giotto.

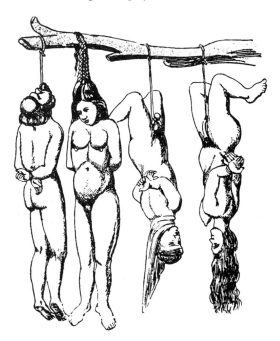

Figures in the church of Santo Biagio. Melozzo. Forli.

to shout, "Forgive me, Katte! Forgive me, forgive me, in the name of God, Katte, my dear Katte!" Upon which the prisoner, after his friend had kissed him through the bars of his prison, bowed to him and shouted in his turn, "I would die a thousand times over, a thousand times, with joy, for you, my Lord!" And he added, "I have nothing to forgive you, no, no..." When his head fell, Frederick fainted. He never recovered from this ordeal. And God alone can say what might have been the fate of "old Fritz," Prussia, and Europe, if this massacre had not occurred at the outset of that tragic life. The King whose youth had been trampled on became in the future insensitive to pity; cynical, debauched, and bantering, he could no longer seek his ultimate compensations in anything except heartbroken "greatness."

Through a paradox frequent in history, it was a somewhat ridiculous personage, although a great jurist, who was more or less responsible for the ending, in France at least, of the most repressive aspects of French legislation against homosexuals. Cambacérès, "Tante Urlurette," is said to have been the author of the penal code we possess today. However, in reality, things were different and in any case not quite so straightforward. For the basic reform (which abolished the death penalty and even all punishment for relationships between consenting adults committing no offence against decency in public) was only possible because of the general intellectual progress which had begun during the Renaissance and which culminated with the Revolution. Voltaire had finally been able to regard as aesthetic the idea of two youths in each other's arms, although the thought of "Dutch sailors" or "Muscovite stall-keepers" in a similar situation still shocked him. But the thing that in the Middle Ages

escapade but once the decision had been taken did not want to abandon him. They spent a wild night of love together among the bushes in the gardens of Potsdam. The attempt failed, the Prince was placed under arrest and Katte was accused of treason. The King himself quashed the sentence which had condemned the young man to life imprisonment, and condemned him to death instead. Frederick had to attend the execution of his friend, which took place on November 6, 1730. On his knees he begged for forgiveness, which was refused. Officers forced him to watch the torture with his head raised. He was heard had been called the silent sin, because it was regarded as so shocking for honest ears that it was detestable to mention, had later acquired a certain dignity, since it had now become the philosophical sin.

Groups such as the Black Cravats in Frankfurt or the White Cravats in Paris, which remained more or less clandestine, attracted those who had these tastes. A Lesbian organization, The Vestals of Venus, had chapters all over France. The candidates had to take off their clothes and undergo an examination, and possess at least sixteen of the thirty charms that had been sung by the old French poets. The Lesbians were divided into pairs, made the necessary verifications, and transmitted their conclusions to the president, who announced the results. Once they were admitted, the candidates had to renounce under oath all sexual relationships with men and promise that they would never reveal the secrets of the organization. There even existed certain publications for extolling the forbidden practices, and it was in this way that in 1779 a periodical entitled *L'espion anglais* had published an "Apologie de la Secte Anandryne," written by a certain Pidansat de Mairobert. As a result the Constituent Assembly of 1791 introduced legislation inspired by the spirit of enlightenment and showing perhaps excessive confidence in the goodness of man, but it made no mention of the "unnatural vice"; for the first time, in Europe, homosexual and heterosexual crimes were placed on the same footing. A decree of April 17, 1801, entrusted a Commission of five members to revise this legislation passed in 1791, in view of the definitive establishment of a penal code. Cambacérès, whose personal contribution was limited to the civil code, was not a member of it. The jurists who belonged to it were for the most part *grands bourgeois* who belonged to the liberal tradition, revolutionaries who had settled down and whose way of life was essentially orthodox. Their names were Target, Treilhard, Oudard, Blondel, and Bieillard. Their work proceeded slowly and was not completed until 1808. It was on this occasion that Cambacérès, in his capacity as President of the Council of State, had to be apprised of it on the twelfth and fifteenth of November of that year. After discussion with the legislative body, the penal code was finally published in its present form on February 22, 1810, no objection having been made to the articles dealing (or rather not dealing) with homosexuality. However, it could be regarded as more severe than the legislation of 1791.[3]

The arrangements dealing with debauchery or with the corruption of young people were all the more necessary because

---

[3] This is how, according to Monsieur Marc Daniel (*Arcadie*, January 1962, 27–29), the various sexual crimes and offenses were punished in France after 1791.

1. Rape.—1791: 6 years in irons.—1810: imprisonment.—1832: forced labor for a given period.

1a) Rape committed against the person of a child.—1791: 12 years in irons (if the victim is a "girl less than 14 years of age").—1810: forced labor for a given period (if the victim is "a child of less than 15 years of age").—1832: the maximum term of forced labor (if the victim is "a child of less than 15 years of age").

2. Indecent assault with violence.—1791: the Code makes no mention of it.—1810: imprisonment (crime treated like rape).

2a) Indecent assault with violence committed against the person of a child.—1791: 12 years in irons (if the victim is a "girl of less than 14 years of age").—1810: forced labor for a given period (if the victim is "a child less than 15 years of age": crime treated like rape).

2b) and 2c) Aggravating circumstances in the case of rape and indecent assault with violence.—1791: if the guilty party has been assisted in his crime "by the violence and the efforts of one or several accomplices," 12 years in irons.—1810: if the guilty party is in a position of authority in relation to the victim, if he is a servant in the house, if he is a functionary or minister of religion: forced labor for life.—If the crime has been comthe more indulgent attitude that had come into being only benefited those who were most intelligent. At this period, as at other times, dignity and dishonor went hand in hand. The Commissioner Picquenard, in a report to the president of the executive Directory, on 5 Prairial of Year VI, had drawn attention to the trade which went on in the evening beneath the circus sheds in the Palais-Royal where mothers brought their children, sometimes under the age of ten, in order to hand them over to debauchery. But male prostitution did not date from the Revolutionary period; during the Ancien Régime, Paris already possessed picking-up places that had acquired an international reputation. Under the reign of Henri III the "knights of straw," so called after the pieces of straw which they placed between their teeth as a sign of recognition,

used to meet in the very doorways of the Louvre. Later, the Allée des Veuves—now the Avenue Montaigne—had become the terrain reserved for homosexuals. Toward the end of the monarchy, homosexual prostitution had even been regulated by the police, who had authorized it in places which they kept under control. Mirabeau points out in this connection that a real hierarchy had been instituted among young men who sold their charms. After an examination, those whose bodies were beautiful, pink, and chubby were divided into a first category, those who were capable of being both active and passive; this category was reserved for aristocrats, and extremely high prices were charged to bishops and financiers. The second category was made up of young men deprived of testicles who, according to the language of the art, "were

---

mitted with the help of one or several accomplices, *idem*.

3. Indecent assault against the person of a child, without violence.—1791: the Code makes no mention of it.—1810: the Code makes no mention of it.—1832: imprisonment (if the child is less than 11 years of age).—1863: imprisonment (if the child is less than 13 years of age).—1945: imprisonment (if the child is less than 15 years of age).

3a) Aggravating circumstances in the case of indecent assault against the person of a child, without violence.—Nothing before 1832.

b) If the guilty party is in a position of authority in relation to the victim (if the guilty party has influence over the victim, if he has authority over him or her, if he is a servant in the house, if he is a functionary or minister of religion): forced labor after 1832. In 1832, age limit of the victim: 11 years; 1863: age limit of the victim, 13 years; 1945: age limit, 15 years.

c) Crime committed by a person possessing influence over the victim, if the latter is a minor but over the age set out in the above paragraph and is not emancipated by marriage: case not allowed for prior to 1863. After 1863: imprisonment.

d) Crime committed against a minor of the same sex as the guilty party: case not provided for earlier than 1942. After 1942: imprisonment from 6 months to 3 years plus fine if the victim is between 15 and 21 years of age (imprisonment if the victim is less than 15 years of age).

4. Indecent assault in public.—1791: a maximum of 6 months' imprisonment plus fine.—1810: imprisonment from 3 months to 1 year plus fine.—1863: imprisonment from 3 months to 2 years plus fine.

4a) Aggravating circumstances in the case of indecent assault in public.—None before 1960.—Edict of 1960: imprisonment from 6 months to 3 years plus fine if the assault committed in public consists of "an unnatural act" committed with an individual of the same sex.

5. Procuring and the incitement of young persons to debauchery.—1791: the Code only takes into consideration the crime consisting of handing a girl over to prostitution by means of violence.—1810: imprisonment from 6 months to 2 years plus fine for having "incited, favored or facilitated regularly the debauchery or corruption of young persons under the age of 21." Penalty increased if the guilty party is a relation or tutor of the victim.—1903, 1917, 1922, 1946, 1960: increasingly heavier penalties against procuring.

6. Soliciting in public.—1939: imprisonment for 5 days or longer (apart from the infliction of heavier penalties if called for).

7. Propaganda against the birth rate. 1920: imprisonment for a period of 1 to 6 months plus fine.

8. Outrage to public morality by means of the press, pictures, etc.—1791: a maximum of 6 months' imprisonment plus fine.—1810: imprisonment for a period from 6 months to 1 year plus fine. (Many other forms of wording after 1881.)

The Consummation. Hans Baldung.

rubbed with camphor. Those who came through these tests and gave no sign of erection were used as passive partners at a third of the pay only.

The French Revolution and the Empire had the merit of abolishing this semi-official prostitution and instituting legislation which for the first time granted a certain amount of freedom to homosexuals capable of using it with discretion among adults, and this legislation also protected young people against corruption of all types. Any intervention by Cambacérès in such a delicate piece of work would no doubt have lacked authority. For this "notoriously

Man and the Earth. Pollaiuolo. Drawing. Galleria degli Uffizi, Florence.

not up to standard" but were still capable of giving and receiving; these remained expensive because women used them as well as men. The third class was composed of those who could no longer be anything but purely passive, and were so worn out that they were no longer capable of an erection, although they possessed the organs necessary for pleasure. The impotence of such a young man was checked by a severe examination. He was placed naked on a mattress of which the lower half was open, two girls plied him with their most skillful caresses, while a third struck him gently with nettles at the seat of amorous desire. After this test had been tried for a quarter of an hour a long red pepper which produced considerable irritation was introduced into his anus; the stings left by the nettles were covered with fine Caudebec mustard and the glans was

Two Men. Luca Signorelli. Study. Louvre, Paris.

Mademoiselle Guizot, looked so much like a boy that as a result of this liaison his most Serene Highness, who had developed a corporation in the meantime, merely offered an additional target to his detractors. The ridicule Tante Urlurette never succeeded in entirely escaping did not however alienate the esteem in which he was held by the Emperor, who had good understanding of men and was not concerned with the prejudices of the common people. The fact that Bonaparte kept his confidence in Cambacérès while fully aware of his way of life shows to what extent contemporary attitudes had changed. Napoleon was a woman's man as far as anyone can be, but he was man enough to sense all possible aspects of masculinity and to allow their existence. He had known the passionate love of Junot, duc d'Abrantès, with whom he had lived, and it will never be known how he responded to him. His friendship with Jomini had been a kind of fascination. He knew therefore the mystery that one man can represent for another, and to what feelings the attraction of this mystery can lead. In the *Journal Secret* Lo Duca made him say in 1798:

> I shall not have lived on this earth in vain if it is granted to me to find a friend, a being who is more than a brother and more than a wife, unchanging and just, a measure of my soul as I shall be of his.... I knew when I was ten years old that another man carried within himself, perhaps unknown to him, a part of my soul.[4]

After such a revelation it is impossible not to understand homosexuality, even if one refuses to accept it as one's destiny. Napoleon had grasped its essence.

thoughtless person," whose competence was not in question, had provoked too many jokes, caricatures, and songs in Paris and throughout the whole of Europe for him to act with any efficacy in such a matter. The walks taken by the Arch-Chancelor in the Palais-Royal (we have already described the kind of encounters that took place there), when this Great Eagle of the Legion of Honor would appear decked out with his decorations, cordons, diamond badges, ceremonial sword, embroideries, and laces, had become legendary among Parisian society gossip. Napoleon, in order to limit the amount of damage he did, had indeed forced him to take a mistress, but the lady,

---

[4] *Journal Secret de Napoléon Bonaparte* (J.-J. Pauvert, Paris: 1962).

The Surprise. J. H. Füssli. 1820. Hochbauamt der Stadt, Zürich.

PART THREE
The Contemporary Eruption

Opposition is and always will be the best stimulus for great amorous vocations, for with these the part played by instinct is very important. Now, there is no better tonic for the instinct than an attempt to suppress it. This is the reason for the basic aphrodisiac meaning of prohibitions and limitations in love and for the soothing effect of liberty.

Gregorio Marañon
Don Juan et le donjuanisme
1958

The Couple Taken by Surprise. Thomas Row-
landson. 1803. Albertina Graphische Samlung,
Vienna.

IX

The Testimony of Art and Letters

There is no need to pursue our inquiry into the realms of ethnology or history beyond the period we have already reached. Today homosexuality is clearly apparent to anyone who has eyes to see. The main burden of our earlier inquiry was to demonstrate that, in one form or another, this is a phenomenon belonging to all times and all places, with a universality that argues for its existence as a fact of nature.

So it would be absurd to ask of ethnology or history more than they are capable of giving. Such disciplined studies are well able to uncover facts and describe universal values to a greater or lesser degree, but they cannot, of themselves, establish values or types of significance. Disease, for example, is a phenomenon found in all times and all places, but it does not follow that it must not be combatted. Plague, cholera, and war equally are manifestations of nature; this does not mean they should be free to propagate themselves. Felony and murder occur in all levels of life; we do not measure their importance from that fact. Need homosexuality be equated with these scourges of nature? What position does it occupy in the hierarchy of vital phenomena? Need it be condemned as a crime, tolerated as an unavoidable evil, treated as an illness, consented to as an act of foolishness, or even encouraged as a benefit? This is what ethnology and history cannot prove.

It is a reasonable assumption that a phenomenon which exists in all epochs and at all latitudes cannot be treated with levity or contempt. It deserves the dignity of all natural phenomena, and repressive attitudes have little chance of suppressing it or modifying it. So we must pursue the investigation through new ways, adding to the enlightenment derived from ethnology or history inquiries which are less quantitative, more profound, more delicate. Above all it must be emphasized that, for anyone who does not believe in a revealed morality, ethical values begin only at the point where the individual, accepting or rejecting his fate,

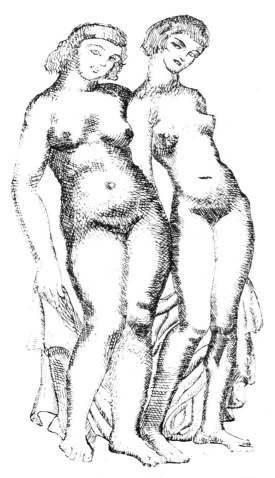

Guide to Frolicking. Maillol. Etching. Bibliothèque Nationale, Réserve, Paris.

ticularity. The second, in science, arose from studies in the pathology, medicine, psychology, statistics, and phenomenology of homosexuality by some of the greatest minds of our time. The third and most recent is indeed the effort made by homosexuals themselves to organize responsible associations for establishing themselves in the world as a minority aware of its fate.

It is useless to emphasize to what degree similar events constitute phenomena of a complete originality; statements by Leonardo da Vinci, Michelangelo, and Shakespeare can in no way be put on the same footing with those by Proust, Gide, Cocteau, or Genet. The studies of theologians or casuists cannot be equated with those of Magnus Hirschfeld, Freud, Jung, Kinsey, or Giese. And if one can find in them some link with the opinions of Plato or Aristotle, with classical or Arabic poetry, they differ, by reason of this one cardinal fact: between these two phases, the Judeo-Christian repression has taken place. Two

attempts to define himself within the world and in reference to himself.

The institution of the Code Napoléon and the transformation resulting from it encouraged in France, if not a development of homosexual behavior, at least a readier expression of its existence, a more relaxed study of its nature, and a franker acknowledgement of its phenomenology. From the nineteenth century to our own day, three important events occurred which furthered this tendency. The first, in literature, derived from the increased openness with which some great writers spoke of their par-

Mariette Lydis. Illustration for *Les Chansons de Bilitis* by Pierre Louÿs (Fasquelle).

thousand years of condemnation have left their mark on the mind. Even if Christianity has been only an interlude, it is improbable that whatever follows the interval can be similar to what went before. A mere comparison between the homosexuals of our time and those of Greece and Rome is enough to measure the extent of the difference. For if the modern type is neurotic, devious, always ashamed of being what he is, ill at ease in society, and often impotent with women, the ancient was nothing like this. Sartre has written, "It is impossible to 'liquidate' one's Catholicism. If one succeeds in tearing one's self away from it, one escapes half dead and marked for life." Is it perhaps that the homosexual of our time, having torn himself away from his faith in order to control his destiny, is no more than half alive?

Undoubtedly, what is principally revealed by homosexual literature, or at any rate by the literature of homosexuals, is a sort of vast wound—a gaping, suppurating wound, far removed from the assurance, gaiety, and enthusiasm of the ancient or Arab pederast. Verlaine and Rimbaud were wounded, Lautréamont was wounded; so was Oscar Wilde in spite of his defiance, Gide in spite of his appearance of Goethean serenity. Proust was wounded, as well as Cocteau, Genet, and Jouhandeau, together with a long roll of other great names. The wound is there, under our very eyes, despite all the efforts of certain people to treat it, or the wish of a few of the sick to cure it. These are no longer merely the cries stifled by the crackle of the pyre, the confessions lost in the course of some furtive frolic, the slanderous gossip of some drunken chronicler, as was the case in the Middle Ages and also in the Renaissance. These are works running into some thousands of pages, lives whose most minute details are often made known to us.

Anonymous. Illustration for a Lesbian novel. (Feile Weib.)

It is pointless now to return to the gossip attending these works and these lives, in the swamp of tatty "queerness" which lies at the feet of these great names. They are the great wounded beings who disclose the very reality of homosexuality better than ethnology or history can do. What does it matter if, from that time on, the Restoration and the Second Empire increased their police vigilence toward homosexual debaucheries? that at the period the favorite club of homosexuals was in the rue Doyenne, in the old district of St. Thomas du Louvre? that sodomites went dancing at Number Eight Place de la Madeleine? or that the authorities published the names of a

Caresses. Otto Schoff. Retouched drawing.

hundred and fifty of the best-known homosexuals in Paris? More significant, perhaps, because it renewed events for which the Crusades and the Knights Templar had furnished precedents, was the contagion induced by the conquest of Algeria, under Louis-Philippe. Had not the Marquis de Boissy complained of the "unspeakable pederastic flood" which, from contact with the Arabs, had entered into the French regiments and from them spread through civilian society? According to the "Dossier of Homosexual Malpractices," first compiled at that time, the Petite Rue des Marais had become the Paris recruiting ground, particularly busy after the theater. The Allée des Veuves had retained its notoriety to such an extent since the Ancien Régime that no policeman dared go there. Ropes tied from tree to tree marked off the known areas and armed thugs harassed the unwary. Victor

Hugo received a drubbing there. In 1864 the pages of *La Petite Revue*, published by Loredan Larkey, and a letter from M. Castagnary in *Le Progrès de Lyon,* discuss the adoption of "this vice" in "a number of military formations." The study of this line of military homosexuality could be of great interest. It led, in France, to such names as Lyautey, the builder of Morocco; in England, to Cecil Rhodes, the founder of Cape Colony, and to Lawrence of Arabia; in Germany, to Eulenburg, commander of the Berlin garrison, and to von Moltke, servant of Wilhelm II. Even the life of Oscar Wilde remains, from this point of view, lacking in true enlightenment, divided as it was between the hypocritical arrogance of the aesthete and the decline that followed the trial.

At the end of the nineteenth century and in the opening years of the twentieth, homosexuality remained under a cloud of dissimulation which is partly explained by the state of legislation in countries such as England, and the state of public opinion in the majority of Western countries. Even more so, Christianity had left its mark in the very depths of the soul, imposing hypocrisy or broadcasting the idea of culpability which events in society brought forth. Many homosexuals called themselves "bimetallists," in the phrase created by Wilde. They acquired mistresses as well as male lovers and veiled their deeper desires under the cloak of marriage. Proust, who, in *Sodom and Gomorrah* and *The Past Recaptured* depicted homosexuality with the objectivity and precision of an entomologist, could not help femininizing the leading characters whose pederastic adventures fill *Within a Budding Grove.* And his work, like that of Jean Lorrain, discloses nothing more about this sort of love than the depths of absurdity into which a decadent and neurotic society can founder. This hothouse atmosphere is not, of course, unique to homosexuality, but characterizes an epoch and an aristocracy whose arrogance and pretensions can find an adequate compensation only in the homage of coachmen, valets, and milkmen. It is, in the last analysis, this mutual fascination between the prince and the ruffian which forms the basis of Proust's interest in the psychology of homosexuality, a fascination which grew in him, if one can believe Maurice Sachs, from his frequent visits to a bathhouse of dubious reputation in the rue Boissy-d'Anglas.[1]

Nevertheless, this literary setting for homosexuality, concealed and partial though it might be, formed a new departure to which trials like those of Wilde and Verlaine suddenly give a tragic, human notoriety. But it is clear that the typical homosexual work of the period is still no more than a tentative avowal, an allusion which only the initiated can perceive. *The Portrait*

[1] Maurice Sachs, *Witches' Sabbath* (New York: Stein and Day, 1964).

Malices. Otto Kopp. From Dr. H. Lewandowski, *Les "Enfers"; Domaine Allemand, Bibliothèque Internationale d'Érotologie, No. 9* (Paris, 1963).

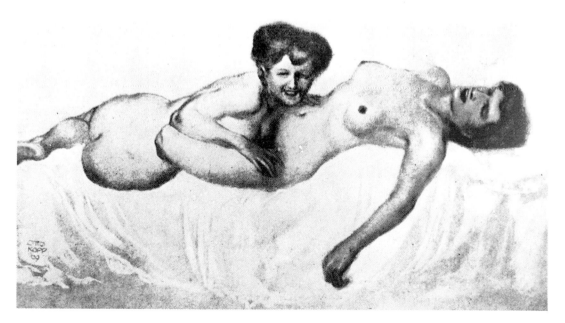

The Schoolmaster and his Pupils.

of *Dorian Gray* remains a philosophical tale whose homosexuality was imperceptible to anyone who had not been warned of it. Similarly, in spite of the Charleroi scandal, Rimbaud's *Illuminations* and *A Season in Hell* were written in such an esoteric style that they called forth ecstatic and superficial interpretations from Paterne Berrichon and Claudel. Verlaine, who, between 1862 and 1870 had been in thrall to early and pas-

sionate affairs in which he had hoped to discover a superior form of love, nevertheless married Mathilde Mauté de Fleurville, after he had tried out the girls in the local brothels at cut rates. He had allowed himself to be tattooed on the chest by his lover, Rimbaud, and marked by him with knife cuts. Yet none of this prevented him, after the Brussels affair, from writing *Sagesse* in prison and letting himself be swept along by asceticism and repentance. After this, he found it possible to live six apparently happy years with a boy named Lucien Létinois, whose death finally threw him into a state of near-madness in which he followed the life of a tramp for many months around barns and Gypsy caravans. In much the same way, Lautréamont, whose suicide was sufficient mark of the spiritual tension which was still the lot of homosexuals under Napoleon III, revealed his own tendencies only in a wild ecstatic mythology, recalling the work of Hieronymus Bosch. A prisoner of the Christian taboo, he worshiped "Evil" and, in *Les Chants de Maldoror*, identified his hero with the Emperor of Darkness, a divine being inhabiting the higher spheres and revealing himself more powerful even than Satan. His cruel eroticism was in the hands of those "angels" whom it had pleased him to place on the

Happy Friends. Photograph. 1896. G. Sirot Collection, Paris.

140

Intimacy. Anonymous lithograph. 1910.

Oh! if, instead of being hell, the universe were nothing but one vast anus. I'd take my fill of it! I'd stuff my weapon into its bloody sphincter and smash its frame to pieces with the violence of my action! In its misery it would not blind my eyes with its blown dunes of moving sand. I should be able to discover the dark subterranean place where truth lies, sleeping; and the flood of my viscous sperm would find some way to an ocean wherein to lose itself.

In these passages can be recognized the tones of the Middle Ages. In them a Christian resonance still remains. These are the identical accents which can be found in Jean Genet and even in Jouhandeau. One of them a Catholic, the other an atheist; but both try to categorize homosexuality as evil, with a criminal prognosis, without considering the judgment that Christian or lay morality has never ceased to exercise on it.

In the book which Sartre dedicated to the creator of *Deathwatch, Our Lady of*

earth. But his own avowals were more direct:

Oh, how delightful it would be to snatch from his cot the child whose upper lip is smooth . . . and then, suddenly, at the moment when he least expects it, to plunge one's long nails into his soft breast!

Or, in Chant V:

I myself have developed a vicious desire for the pale youths of the classrooms and the emaciated children of the factory.

And, although a silent stranger plunges a dagger into Maldoror's back, anal reminiscences flood through other episodes, marking the emotional level on which the drama is being played, as well as establishing the hoped-for issue:

The Precious Ones. Steglitz. Postcard in "oranotypie." 1904. Isabelle Tardieu Collection.

the *Flowers,* and the short film *Le Chant d'Amour*, he emphasized how much Genet has in some manner established for himself a position both guilty and criminal which his dual situation of thief and "queer" has given to him in this world. He accepts this situation just as Untouchables accept their situation and as the Negroes of Virginia used to accept theirs. He does not wish either to change his life, like Rimbaud, nor to change society, like Marx. He accepts his criminal condition and his "claim to evil" constitutes, for Sartre, his dignity. Although this attitude may constitute a sort of sanctity, although it may involve a "sacrifice to Evil" comparable to the sacrifice made by a saint to God, although it may impose respect by virtue of the fact that inversion carried to its extreme point leans toward its contrary, nevertheless it does not make any less sterile the hope all homosexuals have for seeing their particular characteristic admitted into society. In this sense, Genet's atheism does not differ materially from the Catholicism of Jouhandeau. While recognizing the Church's condemnation of homosexuality, Genet claims to renounce neither, and keeps himself in the condition of a sinner who, by his own admission, remains in the community of believers. Thus he delivers himself up to a huge wager on God's pity, believing that He will exercise it on the farther side of mortal sin and Hell. But if this wager is to be justified for every man who is not tied to a dogmatic belief, a place cannot be found in the canons of dogmatic theology. For if, within these canons, every sinner has reason to hope for God's pardon, he has no reason to repent his faults nor to exercise a firm will to avoid renewing them. If pardon is accorded to anyone who falls through weakness and strives to redeem himself, it cannot also be accorded to him who accepts his condition and remains within it. The notion

Passion. Anonymous. From Lewandowski, *op. cit.*

that God is to be found equally at the limits of criminality as at the end of virtue is less a Christian than an Eastern idea which the *Upanishads,* the *Bhagavad-Gita* and, more recently, Vivekananda have brought to our notice. In the same way, with Genet or Jouhandeau, one arrives at a border line where intelligence itself is not sufficiently daring to question the taboos before which it wavers, but where instinct remains violent enough to subsist even in the way of evil or criminality.

The link which, with Genet, Jouhandeau, or Lautréamont, is propounded between homosexuality, theft, and crime, merits a thorough investigation. However, it must be observed that this link appears most clearly in a Christian climate, and undoubtedly derives from the fact that homosexuality cannot possibly spread in a Christian society. Louis Massignon has investigated this lack of possibility.[2] However this may be, Genet's eroticism is linked, like it or not, to a form of sado-masochism in which personality vanishes and which tends toward

---

[2] "Prière sur Sodome," in *Les trois prières d'Abraham* (Privately printed by the author, 1929).

fetishism. For, as Sartre has observed, the erotic object for the poet of *Our Lady of the Flowers* is not a boy's face, nor his hair, nor his legs, nor his backside. It is a detail of his appearance, a belt out of place, a gesture rather than a fact of flesh, a symbol rather than a reality. And what is even more significant, all his heroes end by dying, leaving him isolated, as though all the companions whom he claims to have loved have been nothing but specters or shadows. Now this is not a peculiarity of Genet alone. Most homosexuals slip from one partner to another with a disconcerting facility, seeking in each of them an interior symbol rather than a personal reality. Where classical Antiquity and Islam have passed down to us the names of those who loved one another, present-day homosexuality leaves few traces of the *grand amour*. It seems to prefer a sort of sexual communism—the promiscuity of the public park or the public toilet to the enduring engagement of finite persons.

This tendency toward sexual communism and the effacement of the personality is evident even among men like Gide or Cocteau, who have found the courage to make manifest their homosexuality by attempting to justify it and predicating a function for it. But each of them ended as great solitary figures, giving no evidence in their lives of a single love affair which swept them off their feet or which was enduring. However, the extent to which Christianity weighed upon each of them is well known and this distinguishes them from Rimbaud, Wilde, Proust, Lautréamont, Genet, and Jouhandeau, who had to force themselves to think out their peculiarity. There is no point in going over the story of Gide and his *Corydon*. Suffice it to say that this little book establishes a date in the history of general morality. Across the centuries, it links up with the images outlined in *The Symposium, Phaedrus,* and *Lysis,* while taking into account at the same time the objections set up both by Christianity and by the demands of science in our own time. Thus it is of no great moment that Gide's life remains full of ambiguity, imperfections, and hurtfulness, and that his relations with his wife have always been to some extent open to question. Jean Delay was probably correct when he pointed out the extent to which the author of *The Fruits of the Earth* was

Submission. Verheym. Lithograph. 1925. Fritz Gurlitt Collection, Berlin.

Anonymous postcard. 1919. Sir Edwin Asquith Collection, London.

always torn between a wife whom he loved without desiring and boys whom he desired without loving. However, the situation could scarcely be otherwise in the case of a prominent individual in his circumstances, and yet the extreme serenity in which Gide came to grow old and welcome death demonstrates the decisive influence he exercised on an entire generation of young men. It conferred upon his homosexuality a finality which brought him an ultimate satisfaction. So, then, even if the entire Gidean *corpus* should ever fade into oblivion, *Corydon* will remain in men's minds as the first attempt since the time of classical Greece to think out homosexuality, to raise it up from the abject depth into which Christianity had plunged it, and to re-establish it in the hierarchy of our values.

Cocteau continued in the same direction, although his literary and cinematic works contain few direct references to homosexuality and endeavor rather to uncover the byways through which this peculiarity can be brought before the public at large.

Anonymous photograph. 1896.

But if, when publishing *Escales, Musée Secret,* and even more so, *The White Paper,* Cocteau has not attempted to disguise his eroticism, his especial merit is that he has in his turn given his attention to the place that homosexuality occupies in the natural scheme of things:

. . . in spite of some attempt at an intelligent and liberal approach, the world at large is silent in the medieval darkness and goes out of its way, in its pride, to contradict the laws of economy and prodigality of which the animal and vegetable kingdoms give us examples.

He cites the example of the unbelievable

Waiting. Gustave Klimt. Drawing for the *Coutesans' Dialogue* (Lucien). From Lewandowki, *op. cit.*

The Modesty of Sodom. Félicien Rops. Bibliothèque Nationale, Estampes, Paris.

freedom of behavior which the plant world exhibits and which would scandalize a curé if he could see them in his garden in the way that time-lapse photography reveals them. And Cocteau believes that homosexuality is nothing more than the following:

. . . an interaction of forces which come face to face, a form of expression similar in many ways to the forms of art, something which integrates itself into a vast machine by means of which nature strives to maintain its equilibrium.

While one need pay little attention to the viewpoint of those who see in homosexuality nature's attempt at birth control, it is worth emphasizing once more the efforts many have made to establish it in the daily life of the world—to give it, in short, a direction. As an example of this sense of direction, one can look at the case of the woman poet Renée Vivien, of whom Colette has left a souvenir. Renée Vivien belonged to the baroque, artificial epoch which has been so precisely described by Proust, or by Peyrefitte in *The Exile of Capri,* a period when social conditions were unique to a degree that makes it difficult to discover evidence of a general application. The people of this epoch were idle, neurotic, sick creatures for whom luxury, travel, eroticism, homosexuality, and, finally, a conversion to Catholicism were no more than a pastime, a compensation for the emptiness and uselessness of their lives. One never observes them confronted by the material difficulties of life or by the demands of a profession, and this fact endows their emotional experiments with a much reduced vitality. Nevertheless,

Attributed to André Dunoyer de Segonzac. Lithograph. Illustration for Verlaine.

Renée Vivien, who died of tuberculosis at the age of thirty, had the courage to proclaim her Lesbian loves as no one had done since Sappho. She experienced a passion for a young American girl of her own time, one Natalie Clifford Barney, a passion which was shared but later brought some wild scenes and many disappointments. Nevertheless, Renée wrote for her American love:

> I fear the pearly shimmer
> of your tender breasts, trembling
> I touch your Godgiven body
> I fear the delights of your mouth.

And:

> As you pass by., with your delicate smile,
> blonde head laden with perfumes and gems
> I dream of your splendid free and naked
> body.

The two friends thought they would gather around themselves a group of women poets, much as Sappho had done at Mytilene. They took themselves off to the island of Lesbos, where they rented two villas joined by an orchard. But their wish to give birth to the old pagan rites was defeated by the mores of their own world. The social conditions which, in ancient Greece, had permitted the development of Sapphism, now were dead and could not be revived. The luxurious life of the two dilettantes of Mytilene could have no more scope than the life of the exiles of Capri. Her companion took up residence in the apartment which Renée Vivien had set up in Paris, a place described by Colette in *The Pure and the Impure.* In this fantastic house everything was artificial and exotic, even to the shrubs in the garden, the fruits of which were precious stones and the leaves crystal. Colette relates how, overcome by the odor of incense, flowers, and overripe fruit, she finally became sick of so many heavy funereal scents and tried to open a window. The window was sealed.

This sealed window could well be taken as the symbol of the Lesbian love affairs Renée Vivien experienced. Similarly, her attempt at suicide by laudanum, her conversion to Catholicism, and her premature death throw a sinister light on the lines which speak her epitaph in the cemetery at Passy:

Here lies my enraptured heart
At peace, sleeping
Since, for the love of death,
It has pardoned the crime which is life.

It is worth taking note of this avowal, particularly because it characterizes a large number of homosexuals in the moral and social climate at the end of the last century and the beginning of this one—the tendency to prefer death to life, to consider life a crime. Genet also continuously identifies death with love, going so far as to say that to love a living being is to be in love with death, that it is equivalent to killing him, that living is no more than outliving a dead child, in preparation for the funeral pomp. René Crevel described, in much the same way, his own suicide in his novel *La Mort Difficile*. The infantilism of a sincere love affair drives him to despair from which the no less sincere love of a woman cannot save him. In the majority of homosexual works, male or female, a certain funereal note is always present. Most often they end in disaster, either in parting, accident, suicide, or resignation before social conventions. This manifest impossibility of resolving homosexual love with contemporary society is equally the theme of a long, uneven, and unusual film called *Couronne d'Or,* made by Gilles Velon. It is full of magnificent imagery frequently spoiled by an overemphatic sound track. The film presents the

Zinga and Agatho. Marc Vincent. Watercolor. Illustration for Hugues Rebell, *Le Nuit Chaud du Cap français,* Edition G. Raoult (Paris, 1966).

mad love of two boys who go to the extent of celebrating their wedding in a church. Death strikes down one lover while the other sees his beloved's face decompose and his body fade away as he lies dying in his arms. This film, which has not been commercially released, is, as far as one knows, the only full-length feature that has been devoted exclusively to homosexual affairs. *Fireworks* by Kenneth Anger, and *Chant d'Amour* by Genet, are only shorts with, nevertheless, a prevailing poetic quality. But *Couronne d'Or* is still, in essence, a Christian work, although the intention of the director was very much foreign to Christianity, since it makes death triumph over life, solitude over love, the sense of guilt over the positive act of will. Another example in the same vein is to be found in the works of

Adolescent Girls. From Lewandowski, *op. cit.*
Fritz Gurlitt Collection, Berlin.

Roger Peyrefitte, in *Special Friendships* and *The Keys of Saint Peter* where, in spite of a Voltairean tone and an irony voluntarily adopted by the author, traditional morality wins out in the end. The same thing occurs in *La Ville dont le Prince est un Enfant,* by Montherlant, and in the old but still admirable film, *Mädchen in Uniform.* Those Anglo-Saxon books devoted to a study of homosexuality are no more inspired by joy. Take *The Well of Loneliness* by Radclyffe Hall, the autobiography of Diana Fredericks, Carol Hales's *Wind Woman,* or

Lillian Hellman's play *The Children's Hour.* In these works are to be found only cries of anguish and grief, conflict with society, a retreat to the psychiatrist's couch, or suicide. True, one can also find there some desperate claims for the acknowledgment of a love which must always believe itself condemned. *The Well of Loneliness* ends with this prayer for all Lesbians: "Lord, we have not denied You. So do something to protect us. Give us recognition, God, before the whole world. Give us also, the right to life."

Feelings of guilt, of disgust with life and society, the attractions of death, even perhaps the delight of criminality do not succeed in drawing a veil over the random and puerile nature, the promiscuity of the loves involved in this literature of sickness. So some moralists and psychiatrists have taken the cue to pass judgment. This is the reality of homosexuality, they say, this is its essence and meaning. It is through error that homosexuals attribute their distress to society, to its laws and its morality. This distress would have been the same even if their peculiarity was admitted everywhere. It comes to them not from outside but from inside. It results from the very malady to which it leads, from the refusal to adapt to reality, which is at its root.

The difficulty of this situation, which it is possibly too early for us to judge, lies in two facts not properly taken into account at present. On the one side, the ancient literatures of Greece and Arabia show no evidence of a similar distress: this must be taken as characteristic of the Judeo-Christian era. On the other hand, due to the extent to which laws and public opinion are not altered to convince homosexuals that they have nothing to fear from society, it is impossible to know if this distress derives from the conditions of society and morality in which homosexuals exist, or from the very nature of their being. Only complete tolerance in law and public opinion can bring to the light of day the real nature of this state, for it is really most surprising that psychologists regard two thousand years of persecution, condemnation, torture, and fire as totally ineffective. If the collective unconscious is more than a mere hypothesis, it is inevitable that this Judeo-Christian scourge must have left its mark on the minds of homosexuals to the extent that they feel themselves or wish to feel themselves in a state of criminality or, alternatively, have influenced psychiatrists to a degree that actively informs their judgment.

Two names form a contrast with those we have just discussed, and they appear to

Illustrations for a *roman de moeurs* (1904). Cf. Patrick Waldberg, *Eros Modern Style,* J.-J. Pauvert, Bibliothèque Internationale d'Érotologie, No. 14 (Paris, 1964).

bear witness to something which, without being identical with what Greece, Japan, or Islam knew, is nevertheless beyond and above the Judeo-Christian terrors. The names are those of Stefan George and Walt Whitman. It may be thought paradoxical to link the two together, since George could be considered one of the prophets of National Socialism, while Whitman is herald of a generous and universal democracy. But, while we must agree that the author of *The Seventh Ring, The Star of the Covenant,* and *The Kingdom Come* would certainly have disclaimed the politicians who called on him as witness, this linking together of the two is justified by the force, brilliance, and serenity of works which are marked by their homosexual tendencies and by the integration of these tendencies into a broad view of the world and of life. For Stefan George, the event has a name: Maximin. Of course, nothing has come down to us about the identity, the family, or the real life of this boy. The chief miracle is that he existed at all and that the poet made a god of him. But from the descriptions which George has left of him, in his verse and in the *Memorial* which he dedicated to him in 1906, one perceives a brilliance which links the physical splendors of paganism to the Christian glories of the soul:

> Child to one, friend to the other,
> While I, I see you as God.
> A shiver has told me,
> My ardor goes out to you.
>
> You came on the last day
> When, exhausted by waiting
> and wearied by prayer,
> I was sinking into the night.
>
> Your light shaft was The Sign,
> A ray into my darkness,
> and the harvests in flower
> Rose up beneath your feet.

Stefan George said of Maximin that "he had the unconscious pride of all those who have never denied their being, who have never been servants, he showed the inimitable dignity of those who had prayed much." He added that "even when he was not speaking nor moving, his mere presence in the room was enough to awaken in the minds of all present an awareness of a physical warmth and perfume." Maximin brought him the vision of divinity in the world. For, to George, he was not merely youth and beauty; he was the very incarnation of wisdom and heroism. "We had

need," he said, "of someone who could be moved by the simple things of life and who could show us these things as the eyes of the gods would perceive them." And he made of Maximin a sort of Christ of our time, a Savior in whom flesh became divine and divinity took on flesh. In *The Seventh Ring,* he cries:

> You also have known the call of heaven
> And received a kiss from the lips of a god.
>
> Come, my Savior, make me grow tall!
> You alone can look into my distress.
> Deliver me out of my winter,
> Give me rebirth in springtime.

Such accents are very far from Verlaine, Lautréamont, or Genet. Walt Whitman's voice is equally disconcerting. Indeed, in contradiction to the case of George, no single name comes to us from this life in which the faces of boys are dazzlingly clear. Whitman lived from 1819 to 1892 in the most puritan of nations, but after the scandal provoked by *Leaves of Grass,* Whitman's spirit opens out, going beyond masculine love to a love still more vast, which ends by identifying itself with the whole of humanity. It is a procedure recalling that of Plato. He begins like this:

> When he whom I love travels with me, or
>   sits a long while holding me by the hand,
> When the subtle air, the impalpable, the
>   sense that words and reason hold not,
>   surround us and pervade us,
> Then I am charged with untold and untellable wisdom—I am silent—I require
>   nothing further.

But after having listened to "the hugging and loving Bed-fellow [who] sleeps at my side through the night, and withdraws at the peep of the day, with stealthy tread"; after having asked him: "Shall we stick by each other as long as we live?", he extends his love and exalts "the republic of comrades":

> I will make inseparable cities, with their
>   arms about each other's necks;
> By the love of comrades,
> By the manly love of comrades.

And he becomes a prophet in his turn, prophet of "Democracy, ma femme." His late poem, "So Long," recalls Hölderlin writing that "if love has made the world, amity will remake it":

> I announce justice triumphant,
> I announce uncompromising liberty and
>   equality . . .
>
> I announce adhesiveness—I say it shall be
>   limitless, unloosen'd;
> I say you shall yet find the friend you were
>   looking for.
>
> I announce myriads of youths, beautiful,
>   gigantic, sweetblooded . . .

There is a fine poem dedicated to Walt Whitman by Garcia Lorca, who was, metaphorically speaking, crucified in his still medieval Spain of modern times, and who made a distinction between the "pansies" and the "doves." It is precisely this distinction—so frequent among homosexuals influenced by the Judeo-Christian tradition—which finds no place in the works either of Stefan George or Walt Whitman. It is perhaps that these two have achieved an identical serenity as the result of a continence which many remark, but of which no one has proof. The roots of the matter seem otherwise. If, as Jung asserts, the kernel of all neurosis lies in the loss of a sense of universal belonging, it might be thought that every existential species which looks into itself and finds itself in this world will find in this rapport a feeling of peace, a consolation, a justification, and, no doubt, a finality. Were Lautréamont, Verlaine, Genet, Jouhandeau, and many others neurotic because they accepted, consciously or otherwise, a conception of the world which condemned and rejected them? Does Peyrefitte perhaps extract himself from this situation without too much damage because his superficiality led him to believe that he could achieve an accommodation with Heaven? Did Gide and Cocteau glimpse new horizons, perhaps in hope, because they attempted to free themselves from their Christian burden? Stefan George and Walt Whitman perhaps arrived at a sentiment of plenitude, light, and happiness because they made their eroticism into a foundation for a new humanity, a new world view. These are the questions which homosexual art and literature pose today, and which must be examined from the point of view of doctors and psychologists.[3]

---

[3] *The Encyclopedia of Sexual Behavior, op. cit.* See also *Dictionnaire de Sexologie, op. cit.*

Sphinxes. Edvard Munch. Lithograph. 1899.

151

Ganymede and Eros. Louise Janin.

X

The Uncertainties of Science

At the time when the French Revolution had abolished the legislation of the Ancien Régime, the first scientific treatise on homosexuality was published. In 1791, Moritzen in his "Magazine of Experimental Psychical Studies," published the story of two men inspired by a passionate love for members of their own sex. And although Moritzen was a German, there is another coincidence which deserves to be described as significant in the Jungian sense; for specific similarities display the spirit of the age more readily than any amount of commentary. Moreover, it is worth noting the fact that while most of the worthwhile literature in this field is French, by far the greatest part of the scientific work has been done by the Germans and Anglo-Saxons. Moritzen's work was a point of departure. Throughout the nineteenth century, certain commentators had touched on the question: Caspers who, in 1852, published *Über Notzucht und Paederastie* and, in 1863, *Klinische Novellen*; Ulrichs, a magistrate who was affected by homosexuality, whose writings, published in 1865, appeared under the pseudonym of Numa Numantius; Griesinger, who studied the question from the point of view of heredity; and Westphal, who tried to integrate it all under a general proposition he called "the method of perceiving the sexual opposite."

Studies made during this epoch remained embryonic and tentative, strongly marked by the need for justification when the authors themselves were homosexuals, but coldly medical and psychiatric in other cases. There is a predilection for the idea of congenital transference for homosexuality, there are observations of the disgust felt by pederasts for the opposite sex, or discussions of the variety of erotic technique. Ulrichs went so far as to say that "homosexuals have a woman's soul in a masculine body," that they constitute a race of "hybrids" and that the state should recognize the legitimacy of their unions.[1]

Krafft-Ebing was the first to elaborate a theory of homosexuality.

---

[1] *Dictionnaire de Sexologie, op. cit.*

Paris Bordello. Jules Pascin.

He was, of course, the author of a celebrated work, published in 1869, entitled *Psychopathia Sexualis*. This book set out to describe for the first time the entire range of anomalies or sexual perversions, based on clinical observations. He endeavored to discover causes, to attempt a diagnosis, and to propose a method of therapy. He also tried to look at the matter from the medico-legal point of view. Homosexuality, therefore, was placed under the banner of pathology, amid the whole gamut of sexual troubles, and alongside such states as sadism, masochism, fetishism, exhibitionism, erotic paedophilia, gerontophilia, or even zoophilia. Krafft-Ebing, as a professor at the universities of Strasbourg, Graz, and Vienna, was an alienist and his observations all referred to mentally ill patients. His studies no longer considered homosexuality a sin or a crime, but a sickness which could be cured. Dr. Alexander Hartwich, who prepared a new edition of *Psychopathia Sexualis* in 1949,

denied the place of moral verdict toward sexual perversions. "They are 'illnesses,'" he said, "and that's all there is to be said, from the moral viewpoint."[2] But nowhere do Krafft-Ebing or his disciples discuss the concepts of illness or the norm which must constitute the basis of their conception. This discussion was undertaken later by medical practioners with a philosophical understanding and awareness of psychology, history, and ethnology, a knowledge lacking to the psychiatrists of the previous century. Karl Jaspers outlined it in his *General Psychopathology*, while it informed the whole of Jung's work.

Without calling into question the philosophical presuppositions of the psychiatry of the period, Krafft-Ebing attempted a classification of many differing types of homosexuality with a theory of their nature and their origins. This attempt at classification was useful in order to dissipate the superficial notions which had sprung up about homosexuals and which equated the males with effeminism, as "queers" or "marys"; and which identified the women as basically masculine viragoes. Throughout these pages, it has been the aim to emphasize that, among the innumerable historical examples that one may identify as homosexual, and where the common denominator is the physical and spiritual attraction toward one's own sex, there are men and women of very different levels of behavior and character. Krafft-Ebing began by dividing homosexuals into two groups—those whose homosexuality is congenital and those who have acquired it. Then he emphasized the importance of the age of the loved one. For the masculine homosexual, he noted a first group which was attracted to young boys of

    [2] R. von Krafft-Ebing, *Aberrations of Sexual Life*, Alexander Hartwich, ed. and Arthur V. Burbury, trans. (Springfield, Ill.: C. C. Thomas, 1960).

less than twelve years of age, or those on the verge of puberty at, say, fourteen. This, according to Krafft-Ebing, is merely a variation of a much more general incidence of erotic paedophilia. A second group, the most numerous, is oriented toward adolescents of fifteen to nineteen years. A third is affected by adult men. Another group is attracted by old men and corresponds to heterosexual gerontophilia.

Among the cases he delineated as congenital, Krafft-Ebing distinguished four divisions. The first, sexual hermaphroditism, is characterized by its tendency toward both sexes, homosexual and heterosexual inclinations existing side by side, one succeeding the other according to prevailing circumstances, education, will, and so on. The second division consisted of homosexuals in the strict sense, uranists, among whom the attractions of the same sex are unchallenged. The third group is comprised of those whose spiritual make-up relates closely to that of the other sex, such as effeminate men and masculine women. The fourth consists of those cases where the physical conformation itself approaches that of the opposite sex, such as in androgyny and gynandry.

Krafft-Ebing believed that "true homosexuals" differ from other men only by reason of their sexual sensibility, while their character and mental individuality conform to the general characteristics of the sex of their anatomical conformation. Among them are to be found saints and sinners, heroes and cowards. Contrary to these, the "effeminates" will not only be attracted by their own sex, but will feel themselves to be feminine in the presence of men. Often, from infancy, they seek out the company of small girls, they enjoy cooking, sewing, and embroidery, and they choose feminine toiletries. When older, they do not smoke or

Drawing. Jean Cocteau. From *Arcadie*. 1954.

drink or engage in sports, but find their pleasure in fabrics, perfumery, adornment, and the arts. They delight in dressing up, they behave like women toward those they love, and their way of walking is frequently feminine, even if the conformation of the pelvis and the skeleton remains normal. If they meet one another, they chatter like gossips and feminize their names. The Baron becomes the Baroness, Monsieur Meunière becomes la Meunière. Krafft-Ebing observes that, contrary to what is believed by the average man, these "queers" are far from being the majority among homosexuals. They are less numerous than the group he calls "true homosexuals." He adds that

Rebellious Wasps. Eza.

Krafft-Ebing made a point of noting the complications that are part of homosexuality, and how perversions such as masochism or fetishism are associated with it, as they are with heterosexuality. He cites the frequency of boot fetishism, or fetishism concerning velvet, fur, and leather. One of the patients had drawn up a list of all the people he had ever met who wore boots. When the boots corresponded to his ideal, he would seek out every opportunity he could to make the acquaintance of their owner. Once in possession of these fetishes, he would take to bed every night a pair of boots which would give him voluptuous dreams and enable him to evoke the owner. Jackets and trousers of leather, breeches and gloves of skin, umbrellas, chains, bracelets, close-shaven necks and brilliantined hair, can all be counted among the most frequent fetish accessories of homosexuality.

In the case of feminine homosexuality, Krafft-Ebing drew a similar picture. He

many of the effeminate ones are attractive and manly toward women, while the importance given to the majority of transvestites is out of all proportion to the publicity they promote. Effeminate homosexuals behave like women during the sexual act. They play their part with a succubus or a passive ring held *inter femora,* through passive masturbation or *ejaculatio viri dilecti in os.* Some of them seek out a passive form of pederasty, but rarely an active one.

The androgynes are not distinguished solely by the orientation of desire for, or personality traits belonging to the opposite sex, but by an anatomical conformation which is nowadays called pseudo-hermaphroditism. There is no question of any true hermaphroditism; embryonic bisexual organs are not in evidence. There is however a tendency toward the secondary physical characteristics of the opposite sex, such as, in a man, heavy hips, a rounded figure due to an abundant development of adipose tissue, a light beard, a high-pitched voice, and so on. But here again, it sometimes happens that heterosexuals possess anatomical oddities.

Pierre Bonnard. Lithograph. Bibliothèque Nationale, Réserve, Paris.

took note of its more secretive and, usually, less sensual character. According to him, there is a category of women among whom there exists a psychosexual hermaphroditism, that is, a tendency toward both sexes. In this category some adopt homosexual practices out of habit, arising from a hypersexuality which forced them first into masturbation, or from lack of opportunity for relations with men, as is the case with prisoners and girls at boarding schools, or, with some young girls, from fear of pregnancy. In others it arises from the impotence of their husbands or, as in the case of prostitutes, from disgust with men who compel them into the performance of repugnant acts. A second group would be those possessing "true homosexuality." In the third, to whom he gave the appelation "viraginity," the characteristics, apart from sexual tastes, closely approximate those of the opposite sex. As children, these little girls strive to outdo the boys, disdaining dolls, playing with soldiers, dressing in outfits which are negligent or eccentric. Later they prefer the sciences to the arts, they drink and smoke, despise hairdos and perfumes, experience penis envy, and love men's clothes. The fourth group is comprised of those whose physical form relates closely to the male physique. There are cases of gynandry where the bone formation, the pelvis, the walk, features, and voice are very far removed from the notion of the eternal feminine. And, in all these categories, the love-object ranges from very small girls, to young and then mature women. Satisfaction is obtained by mutual masturbation, by one-way or reciprocal cunnilingus, and sometimes by means of an artificial phallus. The idea of using an enlarged clitoris as a penis is, according to Krafft-Ebing, nothing but a myth. Very often sadistic tendencies, with a taste for flagellation, are associated

Candida Poyarsky and Rita Cadillac of the Crazy Horse Saloon, Paris. Photo Bélorgey.

with feminine homosexuality. More often than with men, the awareness of the deviation remains latent, and the women dispense with genital satisfactions, replacing love more easily with friendship.

This is the clinical picture established by Krafft-Ebing. And, at any estimate, the picture remains useful, its descriptive value genuine. However, the distinction between congenital and acquired homosexuality has not gone unchallenged. One of the old master's pupils, Dr. Albert Moll, in the edition of *Psychopathia Sexualis* which he prepared

157

The Dance at the Moulin Rouge. Henri de Toulouse-Lautrec. Engraving. 1897.

One can bring up a healthy boy in a manner as effeminate as one would wish and a girl in a similarly virile manner. They would still not become homosexual in any degree. The natural disposition is the determinant factor, not education or other hazards such as, for example, the influence of debauchery.

It is as well to leave this question in abeyance and to see how the later discoveries of biology and depth-psychology endeavor to clear it up. However, we might mention briefly Krafft-Ebing's point of view, nowadays abandoned, on the essence and origin of homosexuality. Krafft-Ebing considered it to be a functional stigmata of degeneration and part of a pathological state which is most frequently due to hereditary causes. He considers the following to be symptoms of this neurotic taint: precocity, the abnormal strength of sexual impulse, the romantic conception of love and obsessional desires, the presence of other symptoms of functional or anatomic degeneration, the presence of neurosis and, nearly always, a temporary or permanent neurasthenia. He considered further indications of homosexuality to be the uncontrolled and vibrant psyche glistening with brilliance, in states of imbecility or moral folly. He believed that onanism is responsible for acquired homosexuality. This last point has since, however, been refuted by Stekel in his great work *Onanism and Homosexuality.* As for the pathological character of homosexuality, it has been denied by other investigators, notably Hirschfeld, Carpenter, and Ellis. Ellis estimates that more than fifty per cent of homosexuals belong to families which are perfectly normal, and that two thirds of them are in a good state of health. Not more than eight per cent are genuinely ill. Moll, for his part, has observed that the concepts of morbidity and hereditary "taint" are variable, and that Krafft-Ebing's viewpoint

in 1931, makes a point of the difficulty that exists in separating the hereditary factors from the acquired factors. He prefers to speak of a latent rather than acquired homosexuality, although this new expression does not specify whether the direction of the instinct is innate or acquired. Phenomena which appear late in life can be innate, while other precocious characteristics can be acquired. And Alexander Hartwich, another disciple of Krafft-Ebing, has gone so far as to claim that "homosexuality is congenital in all cases"; and that in "latent homosexuality" the essential and determining role is always played by predisposition. Krafft-Ebing wrote:

derives from the fact that he was consulted only by individuals who were sick. Moll recognizes that in many of the cases he encountered as a doctor he could discover no hereditary tendencies, in spite of very precise investigation. His opinion is now the majority one. None of these scholars had asked whether neurasthenia or neurosis, from which many homosexuals suffer, does not derive rather from the moral and social condemnation which they attract.

This is the thesis adopted by Magnus Hirschfeld (1868—1935), one of the greatest sexologists of the period. He was unwilling to see in homosexuality anything more than a "variety" of nature and rejected the idea of any pathological character. It was he who invented the well-known term, "the third sex," by which he intended to place the homosexual as an intermediate being between man and woman. In his books *Die Homosexualität* and *Der Uranische Mensch*, published in 1902, and in numerous articles in the *Jahrbuch für Sexual Zwischenstufe*, he claimed that there exists a true congenital homosexuality which cannot be confused either with bisexuality or occasional pseudo-homosexuality. He looked for the physical signs that distinguish homosexuals from ordinary men and women: developed breasts, a feminine pelvis, and a fine skin among the men; developed beard and masculine traits among the women. "I have never met," he wrote, "one homosexual in five hundred who is distinguishable, physically and mentally, from a complete man, and I will not believe such a one exists until I have personally encountered him." However, he noted that there are effeminate men and masculine women who are completely homosexual.

The sources of his research are much richer than those Krafft-Ebing had at his disposal. He was the first, starting in 1903,

Orgy at the Convent. After a lithograph by Otto Schoff.

to seek his material among subjects who were outside mental homes and doctors' waiting rooms. He inaugurated a system of enquiry to which Kinsey gave full rein. He approached 3,000 male students in Berlin, receiving 1,756 replies. He contacted 5,721 metal workers and had 40 per cent response. These investigations convinced him that

Still photograph from an anonymous film. France, about 1910. Institute for Sex Research, Bloomington.

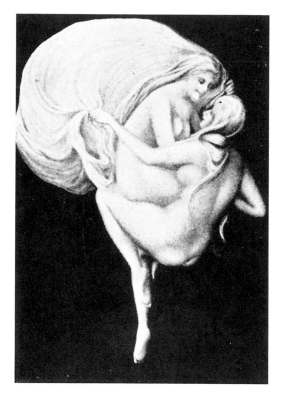

Postcard or "Arcimboldi...pos litteram."

similarity in the psychology of love between homosexuals and heterosexuals. Several of these "proofs," as we shall see, have been questioned by psychoanalysis. Nevertheless Hirschfeld in some degree anticipated these later findings by indicating a mother-fixation among homosexual boys and a very close understanding between the Lesbian girl and her father. But instead of seeing these "infantile complexes" as the cause of homosexuality, he saw them as symptoms resulting from the psychophysical make-up of these children, a congenital deformity

Homosexual Bar. Marcel Ventès. Detail from a lithograph.

homosexuality depends on "a deep and latent constitutional predisposition." And the proof he was looking for was a spontaneous eruption of homosexual sensation in place of the glorification of love directed to the opposite sex, which is the social norm. He sought out the girlish looks which, from infancy, appear in certain boys, and the boyish attitudes of some girls; he sought it in the fact that, with nearly everyone, the first conscious sexual desire is awakened by persons of the same sex; he looked for an absence of desire for the opposing sex, the homosexual content of dreams. He studied the constitutional and anatomical differences revealed chiefly by the work of Weil, the which develops parallel with homosexual development, since it derives from the same base. He believed he could find confirmation for his views in the experiments carried out by Steinach, Pézard, and Knut Sand on the modification of psychophysical sexual characteristics. The discovery of female cells in the sex glands of homosexual males and, still more, the fact that at one time it seemed likely that male, female, or intermediary types could be created at will by implanting certain sex glands, convinced him of the notion that male and female as much as intermediate types depend on the gonads. It is logical, therefore, that he looked on marriage as "the true homosexual crime" and entered the battle for the abolition of the anti-homosexual laws prevailing in Germany. He drew up against the laws a petition which was placed in the Reichstag and signed by eight hundred important names in literature, the law, medicine, and science. In spite of this effort the famous Article 175 of the German penal code remained in existence. The Institute for Sex Research which he had founded was destroyed in 1933 and it is well known how ferocious the repression of homosexuality became under the Hitler regime. The Night of the Long Knives in June 1934 and the massacre of homosexual adherents in the party, some with socialist ideals, is fresh in most memories.

Krafft-Ebing, Westphal, Moll, and Hirschfeld limited themselves to a description of the appearance of things, such as could be derived from the testimony of those involved, from the observation of their behavior, their anatomy, and their environment. They took little or no account of what went on beneath the surface and could only be revealed by biology on the one hand and deep analysis on the other. It was at this point that the theories of the congenital or innate character of homosexuality collapsed—or appeared to collapse.

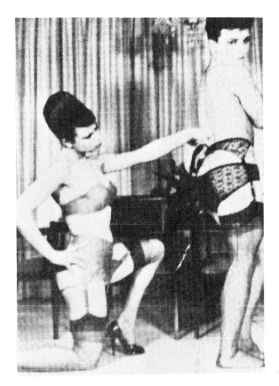

Photograph from an American transvestite publication, *Queens in Silk*.

The opinion of psychoanalysis was transformed by the early researches of Freud. His disciples, as is usually the case, have not hesitated to express views considerably less tentative than those of the master. For the average psychiatrist, the cause of homosexuality is to be found in the oldest realms of the psyche and even beyond the Oedipal phase to which it was once believed linked. It must correspond to the deepest stage of the psychic "regression," to the "oral" phase and the mother-child duality. The homosexual would be incapable of assimilating the first experience every man has of woman in the person of his mother. He would remain fixated by this experience and would never succeed in getting over the act of his weaning. For this he would hold all women responsible and his penis-hunt would conceal a dream of vengeance against all those who had refused and deprived him of the breast. He would complicate the situ-

A still photograph from the film, *La Garçonne,* by Jacqueline Audey, after the novel by Victor Margueritte. 1962.

Jany Holt and Françoise Christophe in *Mademoiselle de la Ferté*. 1949.

ation with an extreme narcissism, the dispossession at weaning provoking the need for a perpetual recompense. It goes without saying that, for the average psychoanalyst, homosexuality is without a shadow of a doubt a perversion and a sickness, a flight from false conceptions of women built up in the unconscious. There is nothing congenital about it and, in principle, analytical treatment can cure it. If you ask a psychoanalyst how this fixation comes about, he will reply most frequently that it is on account of the excessive attachment a mother has for her son, a result of her energetic and masculine character, or the premature absence of the father.

Schem. Drawing for *L'École des Biches.*

Today many psychoanalysts have abandoned this attitude and Freud himself put forward some more subtle suggestions. According to him, it is necessary to understand that, apart from the infantile fixation just discussed, "everyone, even the most normal of beings, is capable of a homosexual choice, has indeed made it at some moment in his life or at least had an unconscious tendency toward it, or else, through a vigorous contrary attitude, away from it." However, he pointed out that we do not know the forces which effect the change in one direction or the other, that we must not exaggerate the importance of psychoanalytical explanations concerning the psychic origins of homosexuality, and that there are insufficient examples to resolve the problem. He also noted that the number of cases in which one can discover conditions necessary for this homosexual type "exceed by far those in which the effect appears to derive from external influences," such that, he added, "we cannot avoid the action of concomitant but unknown constitutional factors, those which have usually been identified with the origins of homosexuality."

This opinion is fundamental, so much so that Freud himself took great care not to include, for example, Leonardo da Vinci among the number of neuropaths, pointing out that "health or sickness, normal or abnormal states" are not neatly separated; and that neurotic characteristics do not denote an inferiority of character. The number, intensity, and distribution of objective substitutes, brought on by many half-resolved repressions, would justify on the practical level the diagnosis of illness or constitutional weakness. Instincts and their metamorphoses are the last things, he has said, that psychoanalysts can get to know. Starting from this frontier it must yield to biological study. The tendency toward

The Girl with the Golden Eyes. After Balzac, with Marie Laforêt and Françoise Prévost. 1961.

repression and the capacity of sublimation must be related to the "organic bases of character," bases on which the whole psychological edifice can be elaborated. This was a return once more to the conception of a sort of constitutional determinism for homosexuality, not indeed, in the manner of Magnus Hirschfeld and his "third sex," but as a result of biological discoveries concerning sexuality.

These discoveries were made by Gregorio Marañon (1887–1960) who set them out principally in his *Evolution of Sexuality and Intersexual States.* They related essen-

Illustration for a Dutch edition of *Gamiani* or *Two Nights of Excess,* 1866.

tially to the fact that every being comes into the world endowed with two sexual possibilities, one of them developing later, under the influence of hormones, without ever completely eliminating the characteristics of the opposite sex. Geneticists have confirmed these findings. Thus, every man possesses a female component and every woman a masculine one, which remain latent, perhaps in the unconscious, the sexual dominant alone being manifest and fully conscious. It is immediately apparent that those who hold homosexuality to be a perversion can draw some support from this hypothesis. So there was to be henceforth among homosexuals only a "latent heterosexuality," suppressed, which it was possible to bring to the surface. Homosexuals become curable since all one had to do was to reverse the constituent tendencies of the individual, to make, for example, his masculine component manifest and his feminine component latent. Although Marañon had elaborated an evolutionary theory (according to which a woman is only an unfinished man, postulating that the male would always tend to become more male and the female more female), nevertheless when it comes to homosexuality, he retained notions similar to those of the average psychoanalyst:

> One is homosexual only if one has a congenital disposition so to be. And this disposition can be so powerful that it triumphs, regardless of environment, education, and moral opposition. It may also remain latent and, finally, manifest itself or not as circumstances favor or discourage it.[3]

This is to leave virtually intact the problem of the open or latent character of any homosexual tendency. It merely propounds the presence of masculine or feminine elements in every being, without coming to any conclusion which may succeed in imposing one on the other, nor yet the extent to which one may be substituted for another.

Among advanced psychoanalysts, Stekel was one of the few who drew from the theory of intersexuality some original conclusions, although sometimes they may seem to be contradictory. In *Onanism and*

[3] *Don Juan et le donjuanisme* (Paris: 1958), p. 138.

Geza Radvanyi's *Mädchen in Uniform,* with Romy Schneider and Lilli Palmer.

The Two Friends. Albert Marquet. Oil. 1912.
Private collection.

Homosexuality he insists that "all homosexuals have heterosexual tendencies in their infancy." He believes there is no exception to this rule. It must be agreed also that Hirschfeld was mistaken in imagining, for example, that the contents of dreams among homosexuals were always directed toward the same sex. "There are no monosexual beings," says Stekel. But, with logic, he adds that monosexuality could be neither normal nor natural. "Nature, having made us bisexual, demands that we behave as bisexuals."[4] Just as the homosexual is a

[4] Wilhelm Stekel, *Onanisme et homosexualité* (Paris: Payot, 1948).

"parapathic" because he suppresses his heterosexuality, so the pure heterosexual is parapathic since he suppresses his homosexuality. What is Stekel's "parapathic" being? One, he says, who has not succeeded in conquering the instincts associated with what he considers to be immoral. Thus one can no longer properly talk about a pervert or a sick homosexual. Stekel recognizes also that parapathy varies in differing countries. It is a conflict with society and civilization—or at least with the image that a majority of individuals project of themselves—because, for

165

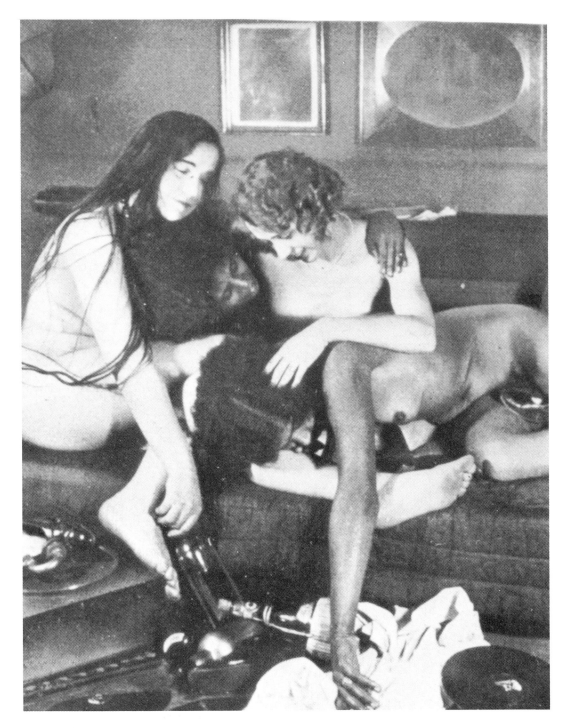

Music and Orgy. Photographic composition. Berlin. 1926. *Die Erotik in der Photographie,* Vienna, approximately 1930.

Stekel as for the majority of psychoanalysts, "society" and "civilization" are myths and taboos which cannot be discussed in terms other than "the development of humanity." It scarcely enters their heads that society is in a position to be changed. They conceive that the individual must adapt to it without realizing that what we call society is nothing more than the sum of the individual wills of those who compose it. Stekel resigns himself to the idea that one day "instinct will be placed entirely at the service of society," and that there will be a "complete domestication of the instinctive life." He accepts the ideals of the anthill. He even goes so far as to say that "the healthy man must be able to exercise a bisexual activity" and that "the normal homosexual must be indifferent to women." He does not dwell on these ideas, any more than on his notion of parapathy in the heterosexual, although he repeats that "monosexuality already constitutes a disposi-

tion to parapathy and is, indeed, the essential parapathy."[5] But Stekel shares the point of view of those psychoanalysts according to whom homosexuality is a regression. And he finds this regression to be so deep that, in his opinion, it extends even to the primitive hermaphroditic forms of animal life. But, at this point, Stekel suddenly takes off on his own. The homosexual is, most importantly, according to him, an atavistic phenomenon. He is not a superman, but a sub-man. His precociously developed instinctive life does not adapt itself to civilization. Biologically, he is closer to the primitive bisexual disposition than the "normal" man of his time. But since this conflict manifests itself in overcompensation, this primitive man "becomes a creature of the future." Stekel notes that "when nature wishes to create something grand, powerful, and elevated, it always returns to the reserves of the past." Now,

[5] *Ibid.*

Le Concerto de la Peur by José Benazéraf. 1963.

167

Heroes in Combat. Pollaiuolo. Detail. Albertina Graphische Samlung, Vienna.

the past means the power of the instinct when genius is mingled with crime. It is to this point that homosexuals (the primitives) would be driven to sublimate their antisocial instincts (which derive from past centuries) and transform themselves into creators (poets, painters, musicians, prophets, inventors, and so on) or to give rein to this instinct by becoming criminal, or even, if the sublimation or criminality are prevented, to become poor parapathics.

It will no doubt be asked why the primitiveness of the homosexual must necessarily lead to crime rather than the achievement of sublimation. And it may be observed that the so-called civilized man shows himself to be no less criminal than the primitive. But Stekel believed that the fear of the opposite sex, which the homosexual unconsciously displays, is nothing but the result of hatred shown toward himself. "Homosexual parapathy," he writes, "is a sadistic disposition toward the opposite sex, a tendency which obliges the subject to take refuge even more deeply within his own sex." With some contradiction, Stekel, who judges the pure heterosexual to be as much a parapathic as the pure homosexual, does not state whether this latter is also a sadist in spite of himself, one whose sadism exercises itself toward his own sex and obliges him to flee from the other. He does not speculate, for example, as to whether wars are not the result of a suppressed homosexuality. He is similarly inconclusive when he discusses the possibilities of curing the homosexual. If an individual is capable of sublimating his heterosexuality, he can "present the appearance of normality, and a manifest normality into the bargain. He is then very much like a normal heterosexual." But Stekel skims over the implications of this idea. Maintaining that, if one wishes to change a homosexual into a heterosexual, one is obliging him to suppress his homosexuality and become parapathic, he would rather make a bisexual of him. But he recoils in horror from this opinion which is, manifestly, the only logical end of his theories: "He would be banished completely from society." In this way, Stekel says, the cure would coincide with the suppression of the inhibitions that separate the homosexual from the opposite sex and would consist in making him *de facto* bisexual and "practically" heterosexual. This clearly demonstrates the shunt scientific thought makes toward philosophical thought, the one forming the unconscious fecundation of the other. Stekel adds, not without regret:

. . . we must decide for ourselves on a unique ideal of love. This is the monotheism of sexuality, more rigid and severe than religious montheism. The battle for a single god of love encloses the entire erotic tragedy of our civilization, the battle, that is to say, for fidelity and monogamy, a battle which in tentative form plays out the final end of the sexual commandments of civilization.

Rudolf Valentino in *The Son of the Sheikh*.
"A very good-looking boy followed me for a
quarter of an hour, and in the end he came up
to me outside the Opera....I went back with him
to his home and he kissed me with a frenzy even
on the staircase....I was wildly passionate....
We made love like tigers until dawn...." *Private
Journal,* June 5, 1924.

The phrase "tentative form" is admirable, coming as it does from this man of science who, without being able to restrain his
doubts at least a little, welcomes such
unscientific and dubious concepts as those of
an evolution of Eros toward monosexuality
and "the final end of the sexual commandments of civilization." So he is opposed to
all idea of punishment for homosexuality
and believes that homosexuals, "by undertaking voluntary sterilization will render a
great service to society," by preventing their
sadistic instincts from making themselves

Illustration for a modern French edition of the poetry of Paul Verlaine.

evident. In this way homosexuality would even be a sort of cure for its own latent sadism. He believes moreover that the polar tension between man and woman can only multiply the number of homosexuals in the future. As for the cure, which he says conforms to the "sexual commandments of civilization," he recognizes that if analysis can lead to success from time to time, it is only "in certain conditions and in attenuated forms of sexuality." Like all psychoanalysts, he notes that failure is certain if the subject does not wish to be cured, a situation that prevails in most cases. But he does not investigate why the will for a cure is, precisely, so often absent.

Havelock Ellis' position is not noticeably different, although he is less rigid in his attitude to monosexuality. Ellis, while he continues to refer to homosexuality as a deviation and perversion, believing that it must be the object of therapeutic and prophylactic measures, ends by admitting that "the criterion of a deviation cannot be discovered in the acts of the individual but in the mind which informs them." For him the majority of sexual activities labeled as perversions are only special forms of behavior that have aroused puritan reactions in certain periods and in certain countries. The fetishistic and obsessive character of any tendency, even the heterosexual, is, in his opinion, neurotic. He judges Greek pederasty to be normal because it did not prevent the homosexual from having relations with women and did not have the obsessive character which contemporary homosexuality has acquired.

In *L'Accord des Sexes*, Forel refuses to class homosexuality among the perversions and thinks that it is a term which should be reserved for those cases only where a fetishist attraction occupies the dominant position in the love of a person. This notion is rare

The Adolescent Boys. Otto Schoff. Drawing. Fritz Gurlitt Collection, Berlin.

among psychoanalysts, who appear to concentrate rather on the notion of abstract entities or processes than on living persons. The average psychoanalyst will immediately affirm that the pederast is a Narcissus incapable of loving. This viewpoint is theoretically necessary to him because, at the "regressive" stage where homosexuality subsists, there can be no openhandedness. But such a belief can be sustained only by one who has never observed a homosexual affair. If the majority of pederasts really do give evidence of an absurd infantilism and narcissism, they do not present in this respect a picture much different from the majority of married people and womanizers. Mature behavior is rare and difficult, and no evidence so far suggests that homosexuality renders its achievement unattainable by its intrinsic nature.

To put it plainly, psychoanalysts are in complete disarray when it comes to homosexuality. Freud had the modesty to recognize that it had always been a mystery to him, and Krafft-Ebing found it an enigma. Some have considered that the only therapy possible would be to reconcile homosexuals to their homosexuality, if social pressure was making it intolerable for them. Others continue to believe that it is possible, in some circumstances, to transform the homosexual into a heterosexual. The root of the debate lies among the discoveries of intersexuality and its atavistic nature. As far as intersexuality is concerned, the presence of characteristics deriving from both sexes in every individual is today established. Among male heterosexuals, masculinity is dominant and manifest, while femininity is concealed and latent. With women the reverse is the case. But with the homosexual there are at least some physical characteristics of the opposite sex which are manifest and others which remain latent. From this the psychoanalyst deduces that it is enough to reverse this combination and that in the reversal lies a cure. But he does not ask himself if the balance is stable, if the two plateaus are equally weighty, and if homosexuality does not find its cause in an instability of embryonic chemistry which would prevent the substitution of the lighter element for the more weighty. Similarly, he considers a priori that archaic ways of thinking and feeling are inferior to those of the so-called civilized man, and that from the dawn of time to our present epoch there exists a clear progression, following a straight line, in which evolution resides.

These viewpoints imply a certain naïveté, a lack of culture and worldly awareness. We have already seen that Stekel recognizes, after some difficulty, that every progression of nature implies a return to the past and

La Couronne d'Or. With this film Gilles Velon and G. Mahieu have produced a full-length feature of a purely homosexual nature, repeatedly banned, sometimes pompous, but full of admirable and frightening images.

that, in a paradoxical manner, homosexuals of the primitive type change themselves into the men of the future. A German sociologist, Blüher, who undoubtedly had read Whitman, comes to the conclusion in his book, *Die Rolle der Erotik in der männlicher Gessellschaft,*[6] is that the total socialization of humanity would be linked with homosexuality, and Bloch, for his part, has underlined how much this type of loving is often associated with intellectual superiority. But Jung, a large section of whose life was devoted to the study of the ancient world, revived its significance.[7] And although he did not devote a systematic

[6] Iena: Eugen Diederichs, 1917 and 1919.

172

Scene from *La Dolce Vita*. Film by Federico Fellini. 1960.

course of study to homosexuality, which was remote from his own temperament, he has thrown some useful rays of light on the subject. His position is not so very different from that of Freud and his disciples, as far as the description of the phenomenon goes, but he differs from them in interpretation.

Jung, as is well known, has called the unconscious part of man the *anima,* and it is also his feminine part. Homosexuality reveals itself, for him, as an identification of the *anima* which the heterosexual projects

upon woman. What does the homosexual project so that an amorous gratitude can intervene equally on his behalf? Jung did not say so, but one may conceive, if one follows him into his psychological geology, that it is the *umbra,* the double. Here we are led right into the *Epic of Gilgamesh,* and into ancient Egypt, although for Jung, the *umbra* merely symbolizes unconscious processes, certainly less deep than those of the *anima,* but which express a no less important section of the personality, a part that is repressed or germinal. From this follows the fascination exerted by the contrary (frequently also complementary), which is

[7] C. G. Jung, "Archaic Man," in *Civilization in Transition,* R. F. C. Hull, trans. (New York: Bollingen Series XX, Pantheon Books, 1964), Vol. X.

found so often in the origins of homosexu-ality; of, for example, the bourgeois for the adventurer, of the aristocrat for the lout, the dandy for the ragamuffin, the saint for the criminal, the intellectual for the self-taught, Don Quixote for Sancho Panza. The homo-sexual in this way pursues his *umbra,* a mirror of himself, as the heterosexual pur-sues his *anima,* also the mirror of his uncon-scious. So, if cure there be, that of the hom-osexual can be achieved at least theoretically by an integration with the *umbra* and by the detachment of those projections drawn upon real women by the *anima.* In the one case as in the other, the problem of love is born at this moment, when the mirages of passion are extinguished and the loved one appears, not as desire paints the picture, but as he is in reality. This *umbra,* for Jung, is "primi-tive," but without doubt is criminal only in so far as we fear to confront it and integrate with it. Thus the master of Zurich notes that "the interpretation of homosexuality as a pathological perversion is very much open to challenge." And he adds:

> From the psychological viewpoint, it is more a question of an incomplete detachment from the archetypal hermaphrodite, combined with an open resistance to unilateral sexual behavior. A similar disposition is not to be judged as negative in all circumstances, to the limit where the original human type who, up to a certain point, is lost by this unilateral sexual behavior, merits being saved.[8]

Indeed, Jung has not rejected the possibility of therapeutic action for the homosexual; he has shown, rather, how homosexual imagin-ings can transform themselves in dreams into heterosexual imaginings.[9] He has,

"Specialty" drawing.

moreover, underlined the frequently de-structive character assumed by the mater-nal complex, as much in homosexuality as in extreme libertinism, and which can extend as far as impotence, castration, and suicide; but he also noted the constructive aspects. The differentiation of Eros in the Platonic manner, an aesthetic refinement, elegance, a historical sense, a delicate taste for friend-ship, religious sentiment—these are the

---

[8] C. G. Jung, *Archetypes and the Collective Uncon-scious,* R. F. C. Hull, trans. (Bollingen Series XX, No. 9; New York: Pantheon Books, 1959).

[9] "Analyses de deux rêves homosexuel" in *Les Homo-sexuels* (Paris, 1955).

Eternity. Léonor Fini.

traits a homosexual finds in his nature.[10] Jung considers, furthermore, that the psychological treatment is difficult to impose, or at least must be undertaken with extreme prudence at the moment when sexual particularities appear to be linked with exceptional creative gifts. He respects art and poetry, as much as the primeval mold from which they stem, and there is never to be found in his writings those affectedly simple judgments which, in the case of so many psychoanalysts, are only a disguise for their creative impotence.[11]

Kinsey's reports confirm the extreme variety in sexual behavior sketched by Krafft-Ebing. They confirm the theory of intersexuality by showing, in a great number of subjects, the alternation or simultaneity of heterosexual and homosexual behavior. The significant figures are those which relate to homosexual experience: 80% of women and 50% of men of forty-five years of age have had such experience, 26% of single women and 50% of single men form the largest group which has had such experience. Among married subjects, there were only 3% among women and 10% among men who have had such experience. Relations culminating in orgasm were less numerous among women than among men: 3% against 22% between the ages of sixteen and twenty, 10% to 40% between ages thirty-six and forty, 4% to 36% between ages forty-six and fifty among the unmarried. The percentages are markedly less high among the married. However, among those who had once been married, the percentage

Postcard signed by Cocteau and Peyrefitte noting *Viva Arcadie!* Paris.

varied from 3% to 7% in women and 5% to 28% in men. Certainly, many of these experiences were only occasional. Kinsey does not give the number of years involved in these figures for men, but for women he mentions 47% within one year, 25% from two to three years. One of the most remarkable sets of statistics relates to the number of partners. It turns out that the Lesbian is more faithful than the male homosexual. While 71% of women content themselves with one or two partners and 4% report having more than ten, the corresponding figures for men are 51% and 22%. Investigating the correspondence between cultural levels and other social or physiological elements, Kinsey notes among women, a higher proportion from university circles while with men the proportion was very nearly equal throughout the different educational levels. However, a greater frequency of orgasm appears among the less well educated. The onset of puberty seems to be without influence from this point of view among women. The contrary is true of men. Nevertheless, an urban background is more favorable to male homosexuality. Religious devotion encourages female homosexuality. At the end of his tally, Kinsey draws up a

---

[10] C. G. Jung, *op. cit.*

[11] As an example of aggressive envy disguised as pseudo-scientific objectivity, see Dracoulides, *Psychanalyse de l'Artiste et de son Oeuvre* (Geneva: 1952); compare with this Jung on poetry and art in "The Spiritual Problem of Modern Man" in *Civilization in Transition, op. cit.*

Werner Hilsing. Pencil drawing. Hilsing is a contemporary German artist.

comparative table for subjects between twenty and thirty-five years of age.

So if Jung's work in the psychological field confirms those biological discoveries pertaining to intersexuality, it puts in question the idea of a necessary "evolution" toward "monosexuality" as a final end of civilization. On the contrary, his work shows to what degree all unilateralism in behavior is of dubious benefit and how much the clear acceptance of the primitive in oneself can be a salvation.

It is not a fruitless investigation to verify the extent to which so-called civilized man has achieved this monosexuality which Stekel wished to establish as the supreme sign of civilization. A statistical inquiry was suitable for this purpose and Kinsey set to work on it with vast means at his disposal. We shall not examine in detail here the methods which produced a systematic exposé in *Sexual Behavior in the Human Female.*[12] More than sixteen thousand persons were consulted, rather more men than women.

[12] A. C. Kinsey, *Sexual Behavior in the Human Male* (Philadelphia: Saunders, 1948) and *Sexual Behavior in the Human Female* (Philadelphia: Saunders, 1953).

These subjects were interrogated sometimes at intervals of years and, for each of them, a biographical dossier was drawn up. Over and above the verbal testimony, the investigators had at their disposal sex calendars, personal diaries, private correspondence, albums and photographic collections, paintings, drawings, and so forth. The statistical tables were drawn up in accordance with a sampling method which, in theory, enabled the compilers

to a greater or lesser degree. And this has been done.[13] Some psychoanalysts have pointed out that exhibitionism, unconscious motives, and a propensity to lying are to be found in subjects who lend themselves to this type of inquiry. The matter is open to question. As a last resource, some American psychoanalysts—Edmund Bergler for example—bring out the specter of the use of

Category	Percentage	
	WOMEN	MEN
Completely heterosexual		
Unmarried	61-67	53-78
Married	89-90	90-92
Formerly married	75-80	
Slightly homosexual	11-20	18-22
More than occasional homosexuality	6-14	13-38
Homosexuality—equal or more than heterosexuality		
To the largest extent, homosexual	3-8	7-26
± exclusively homosexual	2-6	5-22
Exclusively homosexual	1-3	3-16

pilers to determine mathematically the reasonable limits of error committed in extrapolating the findings to the whole population. Without doubt, Kinsey's report related to the entire range of sexual behavior in men and women. Homosexuality was only one element in it along with many others. But the results which were obtained have continued to provoke surprise.

One may smile at the passion which has pinned down with statistics behavior patterns where secrecy is usually the main characteristic. One may contest the precision

these statistics "by foreign politicians and propagandists hostile to the United States." Such a nationalistic intrusion into a scientific inquiry introduces a comic note hitherto absent from the discussion. But it must be understood just how far Kinsey's conclusions are of a nature likely to affront a nation of puritans. "You would have to isolate a third of the male population from the rest of the community if you wanted to give treatment to all those who have homosexual leanings." When it is remembered that a course of analysis can last on the average from two to three years and costs a fortune, it is evident how Utopian such a wish to "treat" homosexuals must be.

So what is the answer? Other psychotherapists, such as Clara Thompson, have

[13] *Dictionnaire de Sexologie* (*op. cit.*). Here is to be found (pp. 247–249) the opinions of both Catholic and Protestant theologians on this inquiry, opinions which (the Catholic in particular) confirm the precision of the Kinsey figures.

ended by asking whether or not too great an importance was being attached to homosexuality. And, indeed, this importance is largely the result of the fear displayed toward homosexuality by those medical men who are prisoners of the taboos of the society they represent. She went on to ask, "What would happen if an individual could develop within a civilization in which there were no sexual restrictions?" and she observed that in every respect, adult love is rare in our civilization. "It is possible to believe that, theoretically at least, adult homosexual love is possible." She contended that homosexuality procures a sexual satisfaction and helps to solve the problems of solitude and isolation. After all, she has said, "this may be the best form of human relation of which one individual is capable and to this extent is better than isolation." In the same way, according to her, the homosexual's way of life can have a constructive or destructive character, according to the use which is made of it and the personality of the individual.

Thus, then, following Forel, one returns again to the conception of the importance of personality and to the idea that it is less a question of knowing whether a person is or is not homosexual than of determining the way of life produced by homosexual tendencies. This new method of approaching the problem has been devised by two scholars who, in different ways, have found a way out of the impasse toward which this discussion was leading. The first is Dr. Hans Giese,[14] director of the Institute of Sexological Research at the University of Hamburg; the second is Dr. Szondy, the celebrated author of *L'Analyse du Destin* and *Diagnostic Expérimental des Pulsions.*

In the preface he wrote for Giese's *Homosexuality in Man,* Dr. Hesnard (a veteran practitioner of psychoanalysis who was once president of the French Society for Psychoanalysis and who published *Homosexual Psychology* in 1929), acknowledges that homosexuality remains "a human problem without a solution, as much in research circles as in the ways in which society regards it." And he praises Dr. Giese for having "freed the problem from its clinical stigmata" by bringing it out into the humanist milieu of a concrete philosophy for a being-in-the-world. Giese, while emphasizing that the homosexual phenomenon represents "the Achilles' heel of sexological science," sets out to delineate the "very real blind alley" into which the various disciplines have been led by a wish to discover the causes of homosexuality. There is one blind alley for the psychoanalyst, another for the geneticist, and yet another for the endocrinologist. In this way, it is time to build up a "sociology of the phenomenon, to discover its anthropological structure," and to recognize the importance of personal decision and development of style in this matter, as in all others. Giese thus locates his researches in the domains of phenomenology and existential philosophy which are characteristic of our epoch.

The material used in his studies was considerably less extensive than Kinsey's work, so much so that it is valueless from the statistical point of view. But the intention was different. The investigation set out to explore in depth, rather than in breadth.

---

[14] Dr. Hans Giese, *Der Homosexuelle Mann in der Welt* (Stuttgart: 1957). Dr. Giese is one of the most oustanding living sexologists. For some years, he has striven for the foundation of an International Congress of Sexology from which can grow a real International Center of Sexology. Reticence in various countries, arising from "modesty" campaigns, has prevented the undertaking up to now. The wishes of Dr. Giese on this matter are given in the *Dictionnaire de Sexologie* (*op. cit.*), aims formulated also by Prof. Dr. Bürger-Prinz.

The Hermaphrodite-Angel of Peladan. Czanara. Drawing.

Nevertheless, its scope is by no means negligible and was built up in two ways: first, by the author's interviews with homosexuals who had come to consult him medically (131 cases in six years); and second, from 401 replies obtained from a questionnaire sent to 5,000 homosexuals in Frankfurt.

More than half the subjects analyzed by Giese had practiced heterosexual cohabitation. About one-third desired treatment, either because they wanted a home and children (15%), or because they desired to recover an inner peace (13%), or for moral and religious reasons. The other two-thirds had no wish for treatment. Most of them considered that homosexuality responded to their deepest natures, some gave evidence of their aversion to women (8%), others, of an advanced age, mentioned the superiority of male beauty, or referred to an unsuccessful attempt to find a cure.

Having observed that juridical condemnation had no effect on the desire for treatment, Giese considered that, among the varieties of homosexual behavior, it was necessary to distinguish the ways in which a partner is chosen. He noted three principal types of behavior—continence, free homosexuality, and settled homosexual relations. According to Giese, continence could be complete or partial. The first case is largely that of priests or pastors whose ministry constitutes a kind of acceptance of their particularity by society, which recognizes the value of their sacrifice. Not that priests are exempt from sexual problems, and Giese cites one case of a priest who admitted that he saw Christ as a beautiful young man, and experienced voluptuous sensations concerning him. But this continence is by way of being a device for conferring a certain moral superiority and social authority. It belongs to the pedagogic Eros and to the sacred domain which was touched upon ear-lier in this book in the discussion of the sacerdotal vocation among the shamans. Giese writes:

The despair which results from biological sterility creates a world peculiar to itself, producing a love directed toward the community, priestly authority and so forth, as a mediation between the individual and society. The social or cultural utility of this intention by the homosexual to experience "a new birth" enables him to make a place for himself, a refuge which belongs to him, and to him only.

As for the partial continence frequently found in homosexuals who behave in an exclusively heterosexual manner without being able to renounce their homosexuality or, again, of those homosexuals who content themselves with masturbation, Giese judges them in a less optimistic manner. He quotes the evidence of one of his patients who made up his mind to marry only as a means of escaping a sort of anguish when confronted by the male body. And, to emphasize the drama created by marriages of this sort, "the atmosphere of conjugal life cannot modify or suppress a fundamental sexual deviation," any more than the irresponsibility of mediocre psychoanalysts who push the homosexual toward women. In this field, absolute continence alone can be satisfying, since it alone can offer, through ecstasy, an equivalent for the impulse to seek orgasm.

Sublimation of this kind remains exceptional. Giese then passed to the study of homosexuality without a regular liaison, a state which is, no doubt, the most frequent. In this type of homosexuality must be included affairs between adolescents of similar age, those existing between prisoners, sailors, prostitutes, and so forth. Such liaisons are distinguished by the fact that they do not bring about a modification of the conscience, nor a need for repetition. But

The Texture of Symbols. Czanara. Drawing.

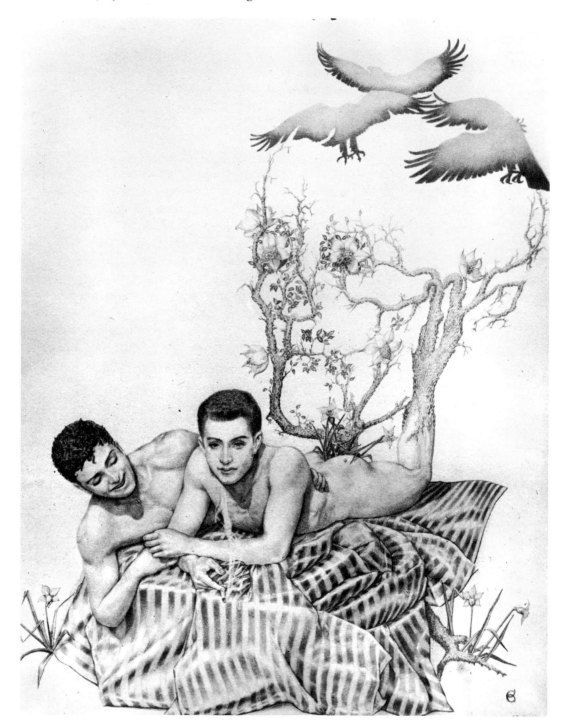

when it comes to relationships which are not forced on the subject by circumstance, the situation becomes graver. Such relationships no longer offer any personal characteristics. They shade off into promiscuity and anonymity. They are established in public conveniences and other public places. It is immaterial who is replaced by whom, so long as he possesses a fine phallus; obsession becomes dominant, and finally solitude wins. The situation is exactly paralleled by womanizers and insatiable Don Juans.

However, formal liaisons do exist, liaisons characterized by faithfulness, life together, and a sense of durability. Out of 393 cases, Giese noted 171 where the liaison was stable. The majority had been going for one, two, three, or four years (118). He mentions twelve which had been effective for eighteen to twenty-five years and even one which lasted for forty years. In some cases the couples adopted children, the majority discovered a common interest in the arts, in most of them sex relations occurred once or twice a month, and in some of them between twice and four times a week. Giese contends that those of his subjects who have adopted such a fixed way of life present fewer tendencies toward extreme behavior patterns than the rest. Their desire for medical treatment diminishes proportionately with the success of their way of life. In setting up their relationships, "they share in the world with us, they make an effort to adapt themselves to us." Their scales of values correspond to ours: Fidelity and maturity are constituent elements or, at least, ideals to be aimed at. Specific and responsible experiments arising from the desire for paternity correspond to irresponsible impulses toward reproduction in the heterosexual. In the homosexual it sets in motion a tendency toward activities of an aesthetic nature. Charitable works, kindergartens, youth clubs, the education of protégés chosen by the couple—these are the sort of interests felt by the partners in such liaisons, to which are frequently added interests in theater, cinema, literature, collecting, and clothes. In this picture of life, the prostitute himself is not to be scorned, since he can be one who relieves others of taboos, and can awaken them to the true relationship. "If only," said one of Giese's subjects, "I could erect a monument to the boy who sells himself, as one might do in the case of the grandest savior!" Inversely, the "savior" is often saved by the one whom he rescues from solitude.

Giese considered the question of the "authenticity" of homosexual behavior. Frequent examples of aestheticism would indicate that the individual has not found his own manner and must content himself with imitating others. The essence of aestheticism is, indeed, to provide "images of reality rather than reality itself." But it is here, in the "cultural stakes" that the homosexual tries to seize some compensation for his physiological sterility. His paternal attitude itself represents an aesthetic behavior pattern of a special type. It becomes a substantial substitute for the family, for the creation of a world of one's own, by a cultural act which creates a paternity by adoption, wherein the methods are identical to those of so-called normal paternity.

It may be supposed that after such observations as these, Giese found himself obliged to forsake the ideas of perversion or sickness. In their place he substitutes "deficiency." Perversion, he says, can be justified only where the deficiency is directed against the norm, where it is based on destructive impulses in a fetishist form, promiscuity, etc. Lacking a relationship with a woman, the homosexual displays a deficiency, not a perversion. This deficiency

Two Women. Maillol. Bibliothèque Nationale, Éstampe, Paris.

is a setback to the established order, while perversion is a revolt against this order. Finally, Giese considers that the essential thing is to take one's destiny into one's own hands. He who makes himself responsible, says Giese, has no need of a physician.

However, it may be thought that in the general realm of the metaphysical destiny of man, there is a great deal to be said on the question of this distinction between constructive and destructive behavior patterns, each of them seeming essential to the economy of the universe. Yet the fact remains that, in the realm of social reality, Giese's viewpoint shows itself to be a fruitful one, because in this area it is true that the homosexual lacks biological rapport between the sexes. But he does not lapse into perversion unless he refuses to take responsibility for a liaison. In this case, his efficiency is a destructive one; in the other case it is constructive. So Giese advises doctors to use all their skill in the service of the alternative continence-liaison and to direct the anomaly toward rational human possibilities. "If pederasty is a conscientious choice," wrote Sarte in *Saint Genet*, "it becomes a human possibility."

Szondy does not have Giese's breadth of vision. As a believer, he does not question the Christian taboos. As a medical man, he does not depart from pathology, but within its limits puts forward some "ways out," indicates the "valves" about which it is useful to ponder. Szondy's genetic theory will not be discussed here, although it has merited comment. What is essential to this Hungarian scholar's theory, and what cannot really be contested is that the source of impulses, innate in the individual, resides in specific genes. These impulses set themselves together in antagonistic pairs, one of which would be humanized and the other not. The pathological individual is he in whom the "I" dragged into the whirlpool of a specific impulse, would not be able to find the valve which corresponds to it. These "valves" reside in certain centers of specific interests, of a professional order, or adhering to chosen pastimes, or again in the genotropic choices of friendship or love. Each of us finds himself determined to specific impulses through hereditary predispositions, so that he is never able to escape their dangers except by "rescue attempts," equally specific. We cannot escape our impulses, but we can live with them on differing levels. What is needed is a "guided fatalism."

Szondy distinguishes humanized impulses from those which are not. And along the path of humanization, he indicates two methods—socialization and sublimation. According to him, socialization is realized when the Ego, remaining fixed at a lower lovel, does not live and will not externalize its needs in their natural forms, but "de-natures" them by causing them to enter a realm of activity and assuaging them in a profession. Sublimation comes about when the Ego does not live out its needs in their natural form but spiritualizes them.[15] Thus it is that homosexuals—at least those who are dominated by the maternal complex with its need for warmth, tenderness, the desire to receive presents, to beautify oneself with make-up and frivolities, lyrical tastes, and childlike confidence—can come to terms with society in a great love for nature and humanity. They will become, for example, hairdressers, bath attendants, hoteliers, servants, pastry-cooks, lingerie-makers, fashion designers, dancers, artists, or spies. At the higher levels, they engage in such vocations as that of music, poetry, gynecology,

---

[15] Szondy, *Diagnostic Expérimental des Pulsions* (Paris: Presses Universitaires de France, 1952), pp. 185–86. See also Henri Niel, *L'Analyse du Destin* (Brussels: Desclée De Brouwer, 1960).

and the medical studies of sexual pathology. Sublimation operates above all in the directions of culture and literary humanism. Those forms of pederasty which are marked by sadism, coldness, harshness, aggression, daring, and the spirit of destruction and criticism, can be brought into a relationship with society in a civilizing spirit, careful of protecting and defending others. People of this type can be found in professions such as butchery, manicure, surgery, sculpture, dentistry, animal-taming, veterinary medicine, wrestling, gymnastics, and massage, or they become racing-car drivers and soldiers. They find their sublimation in technicalities and in the work of the State.

Indeed, Szondy recognizes the extreme difficulty of achieving sublimation—in which Jung, for example, did not believe—if it is defined as a total transposition of genital activity. But it is not necessary to consider socialization or sublimation in such Utopian terms and it is enough to see how far similar orientations, no matter how simplistic or skeletal they may be, are inclined to extend the sexual tension by diverting to it one part of the libido and, even more, by allowing a fruitful and social relationship with the world. For all neuroses find their origin in that absence of intimate social rapport, in the loss of direction such as Keyserling conceived; and we can be certain that we are starting upon a therapeutic route from the instant that some psychic or physical particularity becomes linked to the totality of the individual and the world—that is to say, from the instant when these individuals are no longer lost, alienated, or damned.

The centuries of sexual investigation that have passed could well be summed up in the following manner: descriptive pathology will set itself to draw up a clinical picture of the types of homosexuality, varied as they are, and among which only a part can be identified by the preponderance of feminine characteristics in men or masculine characteristics in women; biology, genetics, and depth psychology have demonstrated the existence of intersexual states and the existence of the characteristics of the two sexes in each individual. These studies have not, so far, established the reasons for the passage of intersexuality to homosexuality, nor have they found out whether there is a possibility of reversing the constituent elements in every individual. Psychoanalysis has described the history of a type of homosexuality which for men derives from an excessive attachment to the mother, and for women comes from an overpowering attachment to the father—an attachment which, however, remains unconscious, thus provoking a fear or hatred for the opposite sex. Psychoanalysis has not, however, been able to explain how identical family circumstances fail to produce homosexuality in all the individuals affected, just as it has been unable to present any theoretical explanation for homosexual acts in the animal and vegetable kingdoms. Neurotic troubles are often, though not always, linked with homosexuality. It has not been demonstrated that such troubles are inherent in homosexuality and are not the result of the social condemnation our civilization loads upon it. In the face of this uncertainty, and given the enormous increase of homosexual tendency as revealed by statistical studies, there now exists a consensus for the abolition of penal measures which, in certain countries, are directed against it. And there are some doctors who continue to believe that the transformation of homosexuality into heterosexuality is both desirable and possible, at least in some cases, while others believe it to be unrealizable or at any rate dangerous. The nearness of the homosexual to certain primitive modes of life and action makes it possible to think of some for whom an extreme danger and an immense "cultural chance" are contradictory issues of the same destiny. Furthermore, the most recent researches invited the homosexual to come to terms with his deficiency in an organized manner, that is, to structure his personality in a way useful to the world. Absolute continence or a permanent homosexual liaison will allow this method of character-building, while those ways of socialization and sublimation can be discovered in the direction of adopting a profession and of cultural integration.

I would not wish to end this chapter without mentioning one last discovery of a kind which, at one and the same time, is likely to make the supporters of a natural solution think again and the lovers of science fiction speculate. This discovery was made in 1935 by the French biologist Albert Peyron and confirmed by R. W. Evans in 1957 and by L. C. Stevens in 1960. It refers to the existence of a male parthenogenesis which could be the counterpart of the female parthenogenesis discovered by Loeb in 1911. Since his experiments, it has been known that the male is not necessary for reproduction and that a simple physico-chemical agent in the female is enough to bring it about. But, what is even more odd, the male can produce germ cells comparable to those of the female and capable of giving spontaneous birth to embryos. This male parthenogenesis is accompanied by a polyembryonism, the embryonic buds each multiplying on its own account and giving birth, by division, to two embryos. Embryos discovered in malign tumors of testicles can be cultivated *in vitro,* with the result that Jean Rostand has pointed to the possibility of one man having some thousands of offspring without a mother, who would be identical in all respects to the original progenitor. These are possibilities which give rise to wild speculation. But do they not correspond to the myth of generation by division that Plato described long ago—at the deepest level of desire for a homosexual, to create an identical being without the intervention of the opposite sex? It is no more ridiculous to imagine a time when this ectogenesis[16] would become a reality than it is to believe that one day man will arrive on the moon, Mars, and Venus. The dreams of men are only the memories of the past or intuitions of the future. Such a futuristic perspective can suggest, indeed, that the instinct for reproduction seeks to show itself by ways which are not necessarily those imagined until now by the average man. And, in a similar conjecture, homosexuals could well be as Stekel saw them—primitives in whom the memory of ways of ancient men live on, and futurists in whom possibilities hardly dreamed of until now are being born. But the reader must not exaggerate what we have said. It is mere speculation, and there is no cause for alarm.

---

[16] *Dictionnaire de Sexologie (op. cit.)*, pp. 133–34.

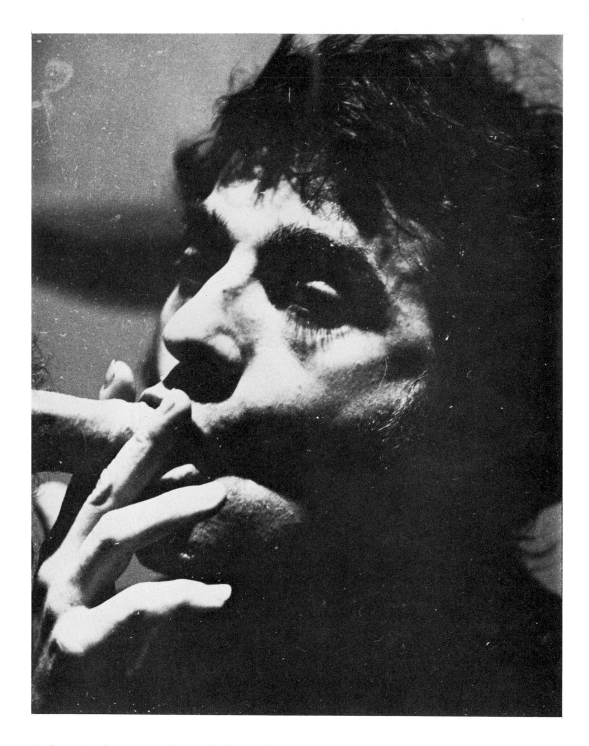

Ondine, the hero of Andy Warhol's novel a.
Photographed by Billy Name during the taping
of the novel.

XI

The Claims of Homosexuality
and the Penal Problem

As an inevitable result of the French Revolution, homosexuals began to regard their problem as part of the problem of the Rights of Man, to consider themselves as a persecuted minority, and to claim a place in society that would not force them into acts of dissimulation. The literary explosion and the scientific research of the past hundred years have prepared the ground for similar action today, and it is being pursued with a vengeance.

This is undoubtedly a historic event; because it is the first time in the Western world (and probably anywhere in the world) when homosexuals have tried to organize themselves for what they are, and to do so publicly according to the principles on which modern society is based. This movement extends beyond the vast underground network that has always existed among homosexuals, permitting them to find their counterparts in the most varied places—those bars, restaurants, and other public places which constitute accepted centers for introduction and meeting. It is very much an international organization, similar to what exists in the trade-union movement.

The movement has been under the aegis of an International Committee for Sexual Equality, whose first congress was held in Amsterdam in 1951. The first participants came from the Scandinavian countries, and from Germany and Holland. Soon they were joined by members from Italy, Switzerland, France, Spain, Portugal, Belgium, the United States, and Syria. At the third congress, which was attended by some five hundred delegates, the statutes of the new organization were drawn up. They established that the Committee would undertake to encourage the scientific study of homophilia and, above all, to try to bring the social position of homosexuals, in law and in practice, into line with the principles of the Declaration of Human Rights adopted by the United Nations. According to the Committee, these principles give all individuals the right to the liberty of opinion and expression, the right to meet and associate together undisturbed, to be protected from arbitrary interference in their private lives and against any attack on their honor or reputation, regardless of race, color, sex, language, religion, or "any other situation" which might differentiate them.

It is not easy to assess the number of homosexuals who support the work of the Amsterdam Committee. In West Germany, the subscribing organization has more than a thousand members, the Dutch association more than twenty-three thousand. The French review *Arcadie*, which has announced its support of the Amsterdam principles, prints more than ten thousand copies, a fact which puts it among the most widely distributed of French magazines. *Arcadie* is published by a "Club of the Latin Countries," under the direction of André Baudry. The Club has a bar, restaurant, library, legal-aid services, and gives its members a great deal of useful information about employment, accommodation, holidays, etc. It organizes evenings at the theater or cinema, lectures, courses of study, and even tea dances. One can see fifty or so young men dancing the Twist, letting themselves go to the sound of rock-and-roll music. The sight is an unusual one, yet it has a decorum that verges on the unreal, possessing a tender and melancholy dignity. The directors of the Club have very strict rules about members' dress, and one of the more frequent reproaches directed at them by their homosexual members is "you can't get away with anything." Their major concern appears to be to protect the great majority of their members from the dangers of blackmail, prostitution, and promiscuity in public places. Their moralizing tendencies incline them toward paternalism, with something of a boy scout, parsonical style that irritates many of the members. They reveal the characteristics of a parish priest, filled with the pertinacity, devotion, and condescending authority that are characteristics of the Protestant or Catholic hierarchy. Every month *Arcadie* publishes scientific articles of some distinction, and historical studies of undoubted value, together with poems and short stories of a more mediocre quality. It has not succeeded in attracting contributions from homosexual writers of higher repute. Only Jean Cocteau and Roger Peyrefitte have agreed to publish messages and articles in it. Marcel Jouhandeau has contemptuously refused to allow his name to appear. Jean Genet has remained unrepresented. *Arcadie* is, however, neither the first nor the last of the homosexual magazines. It follows *Der Kreis*, a Swiss paper established in Zurich and published in three languages. It is also very close in style to other periodicals, particularly *One* and *Mattachine Review* in the United States. All these publications are characterized by pretensions to scientific, moral, and sociological study and are very different from the wide-circulation illustrated periodicals, such as *The Male, Physique Pictorial*, and *Star Models*, which disguise their erotic intentions beneath sporting or artistic fronts. So organizations like the Amsterdam Committee or the magazines among which *Arcadie* can be numbered, stand in the same relation to the homosexual movement as the first trade unions did to the working classes or the first anti-racist organizations do toward Jews or Negroes. Their actions are often considered to be inopportune, useless, even dangerous by those whom they intend to benefit. It is, however, impossible to appreciate their significance without knowing the penal and moral situations in which homosexuals find themselves in different countries.

It is necessary to draw a distinction between those countries like France, where homosexual acts in themselves are not punishable, and those where the reverse applies. Again, the legal situation varies radically within each of these categories. In Europe, Belgium, Denmark, Spain, Italy, Holland, and Sweden fall into the first category; Greece can also be added because, although homosexual acts are punishable, conditions are such as radically limit the application of the law. The following are the current legal positions in the principal European countries and the United States.

Austria: All "indecent unnatural acts" committed by persons of the same sex are punishable. Maximum penalty: five years' imprisonment (except in cases of threats, violence, or where drugs have been employed to render one of the parties incapable of resistance—ten years' imprisonment; twenty years if the victim is gravely wounded, life imprisonment if the victim dies). Detention of from one week to six months for indecent acts which are not "unnatural" (mutual masturbation).

Belgium: Homosexual acts are not offenses in themselves. Acts committed against boys of less than sixteen years old are considered to be "an assault against decency" (maximum of fifteen years' imprisonment). With a consenting young man of sixteen to twenty-one years of age homosexual acts are not punishable unless the "assailant" is a relative of the victim and on the condition that he is unmarried (maximum of ten years' imprisonment). With other unconsenting partners it is a matter of an "assault against decency" (five years' maximum). Public outrages against decency are punished by a maximum of one year's imprisonment and 500 Belgian francs fine (three years and 1,000 francs fine if a boy of less than sixteen years is involved).

Denmark: Homosexual acts are not punishable in themselves. With children of less than fifteen years of age a maximum of six years' imprisonment. The same penalty for acts accompanied by violence, deception, or drugs. With a partner of less than eighteen years, four years' imprisonment maximum, but in the case of young people of the same age the court has license to acquit. With a partner of from eighteen to twenty-one years, three years' maximum if the act is committed by an abuse of authority or by persuasion. Acts committed against the will of the partner or in public: four years' imprisonment.

France: Homosexual acts are not punishable in themselves. With a partner of less than twenty-one years: imprisonment for three years and 100,000 francs fine. With a partner of less than fifteen years: ten years' imprisonment, and forced labor in cases of violence or where the "assailant" is a relative of the victim or is in a position of authority over him. Public offences against decency: two years imprisonment and 5,000 francs fine, maximum.

Great Britain: "Buggery" or anal connection: life imprisonment. Attempted buggery: ten years' imprisonment. Grossly indecent acts between men: ten years' imprisonment unless the victim is less than fifteen years of age. Indecent acts between women: two years' imprisonment. Indecent acts between men: two years. Persistent solicitation with intent to commit buggery: ten years. Solicitation or importuning men for immoral practices: from six months to two years.

Greece: Homosexual acts between men are punishable with five years' imprisonment: (a) if the "assailant" is in a position of authority over the victim or (b) if the "assailant" is adult and the victim aged less than seventeen years.

Holland: Homosexual acts are not punishable in themselves. An indecent act on a child of less than sixteen: a maximum of six years' imprisonment. Acts achieved by violence or deception: a maximum of eight years. Special laws obtain for indecent acts committed by relatives, teachers, tutors, etc. Outrages against public decency: a maximum of two years' imprisonment.

Italy: Homosexual acts are not punishable in themselves. Indecent acts: ten years' maximum penalty. Attempted acts of gross indecency: a maximum of ten years. Acts committed through an abuse of authority: a maximum of five years (penalty reduced by a third if there has been no physical connection). Acts committed on a boy of sixteen years or less or in his presence: a maximum of three years, but only following a complaint by the victim, his parents, or his tutor.

Norway: Homosexual acts are prosecuted and punishable by a maximum of a year's imprisonment, but cases are not tried unless the public interest warrants it. Carnal knowledge of children, boys or girls, is punishable by fifteen years' imprisonment if aged less than fourteen, with five years if aged between fourteen and sixteen. With adolescents of sixteen to eighteen, such acts are not punishable unless the "assailant" is in a position of authority over the victim. "Indecent acts" which are distinguished from "carnal knowledge or union" can be punished by three years' imprisonment if the victim is less than sixteen. Outrages against the public decency: a maximum of three months' imprisonment.

Spain: Homosexual acts are not punishable in themselves. Six years' imprisonment for "acts against decency." Six months and a fine of 5,000 pesetas for acts "causing a public scandal." Those who fall "noto-

riously" into homosexual practices can come under the jurisdiction of the law by being "dangerous and homosexual."

Sweden: Homosexual acts are not punishable in themselves. With a boy of less than fifteen: four years' maximum. With adolescents of less than eighteen and where the "assailant" is older; with adolescents of less than twenty-one where the "assailant" is more than eighteen or abuses his authority over the victim; with irresponsible persons; with prisoners in jails, invalids in hospital, orphans in children's homes where the "assailant" is a member of the staffs at one of these places: a maximum of two years' imprisonment. Acts committed by an abuse of a position of authority can be punished with a maximum penalty of six years' imprisonment. Outrages against public decency: a maximum of two years.

West Germany: All homosexual acts are punishable by five years' imprisonment maximum. Female homosexuality is not forbidden by law. Further maximum penalties are ten years' imprisonment if: (a) the victim is less than fifteen years of age; (b) the victim is less than twenty-one and the other party is over twenty-one; and (c) the accused is in a position of authority over the victim.

United States: The laws vary from state to state. Some of them adhere to the customary law which limits sodomy to anal penetration, whether it is performed between men and women, or men and men. In certain states, such as Mississippi, oral practices are not forbidden. Half of the states forbid "any carnal knowledge by means of an orifice other than the sex organs." In other states, such as New Hampshire and Vermont, homosexual acts fall within the meaning of laws concerning "offences against morality" and "offences against public morality." Penalties vary according to the state.

Of all these countries, Sweden has the most liberal legislation. Homosexual acts between young men of the same age cannot be prosecuted, a position which echoes the findings of psychoanalysis in respect of the normality of homosexuality during adolescence. At the other extreme, Germany, Austria, Great Britain, and Norway prosecute homosexual acts with more or less severe penalties. It is much the same in the U.S.S.R. and the U.S.A. While on the other side of the Atlantic legislation varies from state to state and includes homosexuality in the general group of practices deemed to be "unnatural" or "indecent," in Russia, where homosexuality was licensed by the Revolution at the same time as facilities for divorce and abortion were increased, the liberal legislation was abolished in 1934, when Stalin asserted his dictatorship.

In those countries where homosexuality between consenting adults is still punished by imprisonment, those organizations which we have already mentioned alert public opinion to the iniquitous character of the existing legislation, in an effort to accelerate its abolition. In Great Britain, such action has obtained results which, without being decisive, have been widespread and beneficial. It resulted in the creation of a Royal Commission which published a report, remarkable in many ways. The creation of the Commission was made easier by the public feeling aroused by the case of a member of the House of Lords, Lord Montagu of Beaulieu. His trial gave rise to an outcry similar to that about Oscar Wilde in 1895. For the first time in British history, a peer of the realm was judged and condemned by a criminal court. Public feeling was even stronger because Lord Montagu, a friend of the Royal Family, a guest at garden parties and of the Royal Enclosure at Ascot, was undoubtedly the victim of a blackmail conspiracy organized by two members of the R.A.F., described by the judges themselves as "debauched and perverted in the lowest degree." Whereas the young lord was condemned to a year's imprisonment, his accusers were able to leave the court as free men and to enjoy the fruits of their betrayal. Public opinion was even more concerned on hearing that the affair had been going on for two years. Evidence gave proof of the relentlessness of the pursuit, which finally threw doubt on the value of the relevant legislation. However, the tyrannical process of law and the confusion brought to light by this trial were by no means unusual. Between 1953 and 1956, not less than 480 adults had been sentenced for nonviolent homosexual acts, committed in private with partners both consenting and adult. Thanks to his name, and his position in the royal circle, Lord Montagu had involuntarily attracted general attention to a problem affecting persons of all conditions.

The Royal Commission set up in 1954 was under the chairmanship of Sir John Wolfenden, vice-chancellor of the University of Reading. The Commission consisted of twelve members, including a judge of the High Court, an ecclesiastic, two medical practitioners, three women, two M.P.s, and a member of the House of Lords. The task of the Commission was to study the law and the practice relating to the offence of homosexuality and to propose an eventual reform of the law. The Commission held sixty-two meetings, of which thirty-two were devoted to the hearing of evidence. Among those giving evidence were representatives of more than forty official organizations, including the Association of Police Officers, the Davidson Clinic in Edinburgh, the National Council of Women, the Society of

Labour Lawyers, the Institute of Psychoanalysis, the British Medical Association, the Boy Scouts Association, several municipal councils, the Catholic Consultative Committee on Prostitution and Homosexuality, the Ministers for Air and War, and the First Lord of the Admiralty. The report of the Wolfenden Commission finally concluded that homosexual acts committed in private between consenting adults should no longer be considered criminal. This relatively undramatic conclusion merits less attention than the arguments which led up to it. The report constitutes the most complete official document on homosexuality anywhere in the world. Both by virtue of the circumstances surrounding its publication and the personalities of those who signed it, it reflects the moderate views which every cultivated and informed person must hold on this subject.

In the first place, the Commission had to define the extent to which legislative penalties should apply. It considered that the law's object should be to preserve good order and the public decency, and to ensure the protection of individuals against exploitation and corruption by others, but not to interfere in the private lives of citizens nor to force them to live in any particular way. Adultery, fornication, and prostitution are not crimes in Britain, although many will consider them to be sins. Unless sins are identified with crimes according to the rules of any particular religion, "there must remain an area of private morality and immorality which is not the concern of the law." The Commission observed that, by adopting this sort of attitude, one can do no more than insist on the personal and private nature of morality and immorality; and it emphasized the responsibility of every individual. It also distinguished between homosexual crimes and homosexuality itself. "A sexual attraction between persons of the same sex," said the Commission's report, "is indeed a condition, and, from that position cannot come within the purview of the law." It is clear, for example, that solitary masturbation of a homosexual nature has never been considered a crime, even in the worst periods of the medieval terror.

The Commission certainly recognized a wide variety of homosexual behavior. It noted the existence of a "potential" homosexual in every person, even to the extent of the "observer whose exaggerated indignation against homosexuality is often a sign of a suppressed homosexuality." It recognized that there are gradations by which heterosexuality shades off into homosexuality, that homosexuality is a normal stage in development and that, as much as with heterosexual love, all the stages of vice and virtue exist within it. Homosexuality is not linked to a particular social stratum and it can be found among fools as among wise men. But by refusing to consider homosexuality as an illness, the Wolfenden Committee made its most significant point. According to its report, there is no merit in removing judges and bringing in doctors to examine the criminality of homosexuality. In the majority of cases, homosexuality is compatible with perfect mental health. Neither biochemical nor endocrinal research, nor those investigations into the somato-morphological realm have been able to point to a pathological character. So far no causal explanation has been put forward which can be entertained as valid. All the factors brought out can apply equally to heterosexuals, whether it is a matter of hereditary predisposition, seduction in youth, eccentric family life, a faulty sex education, or a lack of heterosexual contact during adolescence.

If homosexuality were a malady, it would have to be postulated that even acts committed in public or against minors could not justifiably be prosecuted in law. This is not the viewpoint of the Commission, which considered that the protection of the young and the weak, as much as the preservation of public decency, must be its concern. That is why it has sought to legalize only acts committed in private and between consenting adults.

To those who believe that homosexuality, whether private or public, is a menace to social well-being, the Wolfenden Commission replied that there is no proof whatsoever for this belief; and that the phenomenon has existed to an equal degree in periods of high influence as in the decline of civilizations. Moreover, if it has harmful effects on family life, the damage done is no greater and no less than that caused by adultery, debauchery, or prostitution. As for the possible risk that homosexuals will now attack minors, the Commission observed that those of them who prefer relations with adults rarely have any dealings with minors, and that it is scarcely probable that they will abandon practices which are now permitted in order to adopt new ones which could continue to be criminal. Otherwise, the Commission thought that the effect of the law on human behavior is overstressed and that, in its present state, the law has shown that it has lost its restraining influence.

Setting out to define what must be understood as "private" relations between "adults," the Commission thought that consent in homosexual acts must be the same as in heterosexual cases. Threats or deception would reduce it to nothing, as would the use of drugs, and the mental incapacity of the partner. On the other hand, the giving of a present could not be considered a means of illegal extortion. As for the private nature of these relations, they also should be the same as in heterosexual relations. A place would cease to be private when a third party might be able to view the act and the courts would have to decide whether a location is private or not. Although the legal age of consent in England between boys and girls is sixteen, the Commission thought they must fix an age limit of twenty-one for relations between boys. They thought that it would be absurd to condemn automatically homosexual acts committed between boys of less than twenty-one. Prosecutions should only be initiated when acts of this kind were accompanied with "clearly criminal or vicious acts, such as brutality in a school or other teaching establishment, or the abuse of his position by a superior in the armed forces, by blackmail or prostitution." They were, moreover, of the opinion that homosexual offences should only rarely be considered by the courts and that no prosecution against a young man of less than twenty-one should be mounted without the agreement of the Solicitor General, unless there had been rape or an outrage against public decency.

When the Wolfenden Report appeared on September 4, 1957, the British press was clearly surprised by its lofty tone. *The Times,* the *Manchester Guardian,* the *Star,* the *News Chronicle,* the *Daily Mirror,* the *Sunday Times,* the *Observer,* and the *News of the World* approved its conclusions more or less enthusiastically. The report was discussed on television. The only papers which were openly hostile were the *Evening Standard* and the *Evening News,* both of Conservative opinion. In the meantime the Homosexual Law Reform Society had been set up, under the presidency of Mr. Kenneth Walker, and included some of the most prominent names in Britain: the Archbishop of York, the Bishops of Birmingham, Bradford, Exeter, Reading, and Ripon; numerous members of the House of Lords; writers such as Graham Greene, Rosamund Leh-

Le bel âge. Archimboldi. Collection particulière, Montecassino.

mann, J. B. Priestley, Angus Wilson, and Philip Toynbee. Cardinal Griffin, the Catholic Archbishop of Westminster, published a report which, while emphasizing the fact that homosexual practices are a grave sin, concluded that the domains of the law and morality are distinct, and that it is neither possible nor desirable to see approval given to acts of immorality committed in private, if no one is hurt. In spite of this support (the Church of Scotland, and the Salvation Army, and the Archbishop of Canterbury declared themselves in favor of the maintenance of the *status quo*), the legislative reform proposed by the Commission was rejected by the House of Commons on June 29, 1960, by 213 votes to 99. Electoral considerations, objections sustained by a long prejudice, were pre-eminent.*

The defeat, no doubt temporary, suffered by British homosexuals, furnished arguments to all those who have blamed the above-mentioned organizations for bringing to light problems which are more easily left in darkness. By bringing the problem into the full light of public opinion, homosexuals took the risk of provoking a reaction capable of sweeping away the *de facto* toleration which they all enjoyed to a limited degree. Other people observed that it is ridiculous to form organizations in the name of a sexual particularity, since it constitutes merely one element in life; one might as well, they say, form organizations for heterosexuals. Others expressed the opinion that organizations of this kind tend only to isolate, within a limited and artificial world, beings who, more than any others, need to be snatched from their solitude and put in contact with so-called normal people, and, above all, people of the opposite sex. Nevertheless, the urge to bring the debate out into the open exists and it is too late to stop it, if this could ever have been done. The problem is not, moreover, merely one of legislation. It exists equally in customs and habit. In his book, *The Lesbian in America,* Donald Webster Cory gave evidence about the performance which homosexuals were forced to put on in public because they are outcasts, and the impossibility of getting civil-service jobs, of serving in the Navy or the Army, of using ordinary media of mass communication. In three years, he said, fifteen thousand persons were arrested in New York under the charge of immorality and the majority of them were homosexuals

* On July 27, 1967 the Sexual Offences Act 1967, Chapter 60, made homosexuality legal between consenting adults in private. Legal majority in Great Britain is twenty-one-years old.—*Editor's note.*

whose sole crime had been to propose to some stranger a meeting in a bar or a park. For this reason he calls not merely for the abolition of the American legislation against homosexuality, but for "liberty of thought and expression on homosexual matters." And he concludes that the homosexual has "two historic missions to perform"; whether his political opinions tend toward democracy or totalitarianism. He says, "he is forced by historical circumstances to join in the fight for increased liberty of expression." And whether his religious and moral convictions tend toward continence or license, "he is compelled by history to engage in a fight for the liberation of sexual mores in our modern civilization."

Clearly, in those countries where homosexuality between consenting adults is tolerated, the organizers of homosexual organizations hesitate to compromise a situation already achieved by making demands which are no longer urgent. For this reason it is normal for homosexuality to be less of a talking point in Latin countries than in Anglo-Saxon or Germanic ones. Regarding

legal plans, there can be no other aim than to ensure that male and female homosexuality are placed on the same footing, or to see that the penalties relating to young people of less than twenty-one years are relaxed, as in Sweden. But for the rest of the former Christian world, there remains a difficulty that inhibits legal action. This difficulty lies in the social contempt in which homosexuals live, and in the social and professional discrimination of which they are victims. A climate of opinion like this can be transformed only by slow and thoughtful action which, no doubt, may result only in transforming the homosexuals themselves. By setting out to make them conscious of their individual and social responsibilities, by shedding light on the juridical and therapeutic problems that concern them, by removing them from that sexual promiscuity which constitutes their greatest temptation, the Amsterdam Committee and similar organizations perform a useful task, as much for those whose defense they are undertaking as for society, which must either integrate them or destroy them.

Hell. A fragment. Orvieto Cathedral, Orvieto.

197

The Lonely Kiss. Roland Bourigeaud. 1965.

XII
Conclusions

Many will find "integration" or "destruction" to be false alternatives. And they will add that a third way is open—the possibility of cure. However, as has been shown, neither endocrinological nor psychological methods have given decisive and really satisfying results. There is no serious psychotherapist who fails to recognize that a determined wish to be cured must be the first precondition of a cure. This determination rarely exists and, where it does exist, it is seldom brought to a successful conclusion. There are many homosexuals of both sexes who have followed innumerable courses of treatment and have discovered them to be merely a means of knowing themselves better and coming to terms with themselves more successfully. The few accredited successes—and by this must be understood a stable, definitive, and healthy orientation toward the opposite sex—are insignificant compared with the vastness of the problem thrown up by statistical research. American and Swedish research has shown that, counting only men, there exist between one and four per cent of exclusive homosexuals; so it is absurd to think that enough psychoanalysts can be set to work on these ten to forty million individuals, even supposing that these had enough time and money to be able to undertake treatment whose average duration is one or two years.

The impasse is identical with the difficulty in which the moral theology of the Middle Ages found itself engaged. Efforts to suppress homosexuality by medicine are just as much wishful thinking as trying to do so by means of judicial fire or the fear of hell. The reason is simple. In their hearts, homosexuals are not convinced that they are either sinners or invalids. And if they often exhibit signs of culpability, social inhibitions, or even an anguish that can border on despair, they will attribute these symptoms to the ostracism to which they are subjected. Psychoanalysts can reply in vain that neurosis displays itself precisely in just such a refusal to adapt oneself to the demands of society and by the contrary desire to adapt the world to oneself. But such a position is facile. If there were never any men willing to assert their own opinions above those of the multitude, we would still be living in caves. Civilization and progress are created from these ruptures and conflicts. The root of the problem lies deeper, at a point where the very ideas of illness and pathology can themselves be questioned.

The average psychoanalyst does not discuss these ideas. He accepts them just as society passes them on to him, limiting himself, by reason of temperament or self-interest, to extending them to the detriment of the moral situation. But it is not enough to say that it is difficult to establish a dividing line between health and sickness. One must also add that, above all in the psychological field, we do not know *a priori* who is healthy and who not. Physical malady can be defined more easily; pain and incapacity show themselves in a clearer, less contestable manner. By what criterion then can one declare as sick a homosexual who is content with his situation, whose amorous experiences are satisfactory, and whose social success is beyond reproach? Cases of this kind are more frequent than might be thought, even if the average psychoanalyst believes that they are founded on an illusion and that their sickness lies in the unconscious—that is to say, their cure must begin with the inevitable destruction of the precarious well-being which they have achieved. But by what right can one justify such a destruction? By what right can it be decreed that this well-being is illusory and not genuine? By virtue merely of an ideal conception of normal health held by the majority of individuals in a particular society at a particular moment? In his *General Psychopathology*, Karl Jaspers has shown brilliantly how "to be normal is also to be somewhat lacking in spirit," and how

also the ideas of health and sickness can become inverted since it must be admitted that poverty of the spirit is, in itself, morbid. In the last analysis, psychology does not provide us with a concept of reality sufficiently apparent to establish objective criteria. There is no ultimate measure of judgment which we can bring to bear on the most wayward fool. The only legitimate answer is that his mental processes escape our understanding and, in some cases, his behavior shows itself to be socially dangerous. In our time, St. Francis of Assisi would be immured in a mental hospital. This would not, of itself, enable us to declare him insane or in a state of mental health.

Homosexuality is not found at these lost horizons. It is frequently accompanied, as we have seen, by suffering and inhibition. And, as Giese has suggested, it certainly constitutes a deficiency to the degree that it lacks a biological rapport between the sexes or, at least, the rapport with that half of the world represented by the other sex. But it must be borne in mind that the essential thing is not to know if one is or is not deficient, but to know what one can make of one's deficiencies. Jaspers and Stekel have shown, from the study of eminent people, how illness seldom has the effect of interrupting or destroying. Further, illness not only does not prevent certain productive activities,. it positively assists them. Jung has gone as far as to say that we will not cure neurosis, neurosis is itself a curing agent. Because the human being does not have to get rid of these complexes which are more or less independent forms of his aspirations and his richest potentialities, it is all the more important that he live with them, try to place them in a position of fecund accord with that other complex which is constituted by the Ego, and, thanks to these experiences, develop his potentialities and open out the total personality in the direction to which it is destined.

At this point, one of the most useful questions to be faced is the one the psychoanalysts have raised: Does homosexuality denote a lack of maturity and is it no more than a stage toward a monosexuality which might be part of general evolution? Again, there is nothing to furnish objective criteria for "maturity." And if it can be admitted that maturity should consist of a certain capacity for loving beings as they are, a certain aptitude for constructing a durable and really free association with a flexibility of reaction to the most contradictory circumstances, and a certain *sang-froid* in adversity, it is not clear how the problem of maturity can present itself any differently for homosexuals than for heterosexuals. It is true that the majority of homosexuals are infantile, but so are the majority of hetero sexuals. It is true that a good number of pederasts are narcissistic—no more and no less than the majority of women, and one never hears that psychoanalysts wish to cure them of this amiable fault. It is scarcely probable that the possession of a spouse and an abundant family confers, in itself, greater maturity than celibacy or a homosexual liaison. Ostentatious "queers" are absurd people; but then so are rabid skirt-chasers. The average heterosexual mocks "queens" and "nances." The average homosexual mocks Don Juans and pimps. Up to now, it has not been shown that maturity is more inclined to one sexual orientation than to the other. The majority of married people assume their conjugal responsibilities like sleepwalkers, and it must be admitted that it needs a greater courage to adopt a mode of sexual behavior which has been condemned by society than to sustain the burden of this somnambulism. And does maturity appear to be linked rather with the attitude adopted by each individual toward his sexual tendencies, than to the tendencies themselves? As has been shown, both the finest and the most loathsome aspects of love exist equally among homosexuals and heterosexuals. And only a comparative study of each aspect, on the condition that each is placed in identical social and moral circumstances, could indicate whether maturity is found more in one state of being than the other. However this may be, it would seem that a certain degree of maturity, as well as a certain degree of cure, can be attained from the moment when an individual succeeds in integrating his most secret personality traits into his personality as a whole, and so begins to discover their significance.

The essence of all psychotherapy lies where Bleuler and Freud discovered it: A psychic element of any kind is a disturbing factor only insofar as it remains unconscious and is dissociated from the complete whole of which it should form a part. As soon as the link with this complete whole is re-established, its disturbing character vanishes. Beyond this dialectical relationship are confusing visions of hypostatized structures which lead directly to the worst pretensions of medieval dogmatism. The idea of monosexuality propounded by Stekel and others corresponds to concepts of this kind. Again, this is a question of an ideal concept which has no basis in historical observation and reflects the Judeo-Christian Superego which dominates the thinking of many psychoanalysts. It goes without saying that in this field we are still in a state of ignorance. Many observers can claim, with many clear justifications, that woman is becoming masculine and man feminine.

It is as well to turn away from such idle speculation. A more fruitful line of investigation lies in considering the customs of other civilizations or other epochs of

Western culture. We have shown that certain primitive peoples, as well as the Greeks, Chinese, Japanese, and Arabs have hardly considered homosexuality a crime or an illness. Is it possible to imagine Plato, Aristotle, Alexander, or Caesar consulting a psychiatrist? And what of Greek philosophy, Hellenic civilization, and the four centuries of the Pax Romana? One shudders to think of it: pre-Oedipean ruminations, oral-masochists, guilt complexes, and the rest. One thing is too often overlooked. The theories of the average psychoanalyst are themselves inherited from the Judeo-Christian tradition, and it is essential to measure its character in accordance to limitations of space and time. In the historical and literary documents we have studied, there is nothing to assign a neurotic character to homosexuality beyond that attributed to it by this tradition.

On the contrary, pederastic literature and life are distinguished from the majority of artistic endeavors by good conscience, *joie de vivre*, and the creative fire. In order to explain homosexuality, it is necessary to postulate a theory inclusive of all civilizations and even the vegetable and animal kingdoms from which man derives. There is no such theory. So the point of view of the average psychoanalyst remains provincial. If we cannot imagine Plato or Caesar consulting a psychiatrist, no more can we think of baboons, porcupines, or bats under the care of some veterinary-psychoanalyst because they dare to mount partners of their own sex. The matter is less trivial than it appears. A type of behavior which is present in all forms of life and is not even unique to the human species, cannot easily be regarded as a sickness.

Can it be said the Western mind may one day view homosexuality as it once was seen outside the Judeo-Christian tradition? It seems unlikely. Twenty-five centuries of moral condemnation are a reality from which it is impossible to escape and, however barbarous this may have been, it must have some significance. This condemnation is personalized in every individual, homosexual or not. Reason might find no foundation for it, there is always some part of oneself where fear, intolerance, and conformity find obscure accomplices. Homosexuality, where pre-Christian or para-Christian, gave evidence of an innocence inconceivable today. It must even be admitted that, with the universal spread of Western ways of living, this innocence is liable to disappear from those places where it still exists. Western guilt feelings can influence reactions which so far have remained spontaneous. And we do not speak only of that sort of innocence which is linked to primitive conditions of life or to a low state of mental evolution. One must bear in mind the homosexual state in ancient Greece or Japan. Neither Plato nor the lords of Bushido would have been able to understand the depths of hatred, disgust, and cruelty homosexuality can arouse in those who have fears of succumbing to it. The gulf of Judeo-Christian morality had not yawned at that stage, and they were able to live in an atmosphere of serene tolerance, in the belief that pederastic love was superior to any other. But since then the abyss has opened, and each individual must cross it before reaching new horizons. In the chapter on contemporary homosexual literature, we have shown to what extent it has been hurt and remains trammeled by thoughts of culpability and nightmares of criminality. So henceforth the homosexual problem must be approached as a double reality: by keeping a check on the barbarous condemnations to which homosexuality is subjected in our civilization and which any excesses can awaken; and by recalling that this condemnation has never been universal and, in fact, constitutes a historical anomaly.

If the essential achievement of Christianity was to establish a dramatic disassociation between the body and the spirit, between celestial and material love, this disassociation finds its meaning in the enlargement of conscience which it permits and makes essential. The reason for this is that the reconstruction of unity and reconciliation of opposites cannot be achieved without the full and open awareness of what separates and opposes them. In this sense, homosexual organizations that demand a public examination of their problem find themselves, clearly, in a righteous cause, however great the dangers in their course of action. They are certainly worthier than those pederasts and Lesbians who prefer darkness, dissimulation, and secrecy. The world is moving toward the light, or at least the light is growing stronger and reveals itself as the only way out of the abyss. A homosexual is, therefore, no longer under the obligation of living out his peculiarities in ignorance of their deeper meaning and of what they represent for others; he must make of them an open awareness of the existential difficulties and possibilities in the world.

At this point, we have seen, one must show humility. The present state of science has not solved the mystery of homosexuality, but on the whole this mystery cannot be much different from the mystery of love itself. The little evidence we possess throws some light on the intersexual nature of man. This is the most undeniable conclusion of contemporary science. How some people pass from this initial and ever-present intersexuality to heterosexuality and others to homosexuality is still unknown. Are con-

Examination of the Herald. Aubrey Beardsley. 1896.

genital predispositions responsible, or educational circumstances? We do not know. The clearest evidence is that the homosexual is little different from the androgynous archetype, as Jung has noted. If we agree with him that man, in his original state, is worth saving from a one-sided orientation toward the opposite sex, then the homosexual's vocation lies in the way he compensates for the unilateral nature of the average man. The "contrary" sexual orientation can become a "contrary" way of seeing and acting in the most general sense. The homosexual, whose feelings tend to be opposed to those of the average man, is adept at uncovering the unknown face of things, the face in the shade, the far side of

La Poupée. A film by Jacques Baratier. 1962.
Transvestism in the cinema.

the world. From there stems his predisposition toward criticism, counsel, and education in their widest sense and at all levels, even toward liberty and the fight against all conformity. Plato's pedagogic Eros is no doubt too limited to explain the problems of homosexuality, particularly since it restricts itself to relationships between the older and the younger partner. However, since it extends to all situations in life where a rapport of initiation must be established, it still constitutes one of the most royal ways toward homosexual safety. This kind of love can plunge into unimaginable depths, by reason of its proximity to those most primitive sources of emotion which are also the sources of the sacred. The link established in many archaic societies between priesthood and homosexuality acquires its full significance in this connection.

Can it then be inferred that, by reason of his disposition toward the sacred, the homosexual would be more inclined toward continence than the heterosexual? There is no evidence for this. If we agree with Giese that this way of thinking shows itself to be socially comfortable in the Western Christian world, nothing proves that it is often practicable. Indeed, the complete sublimation of homosexuality is possible, but occurs without causing harm only in those cases where it comes about in an almost spontaneous fashion through the fascination of a superior love. The physical and mental decline that overwhelms so many members of the clergy is evidence enough that it cannot be advised generally. The man of today is no doubt less inclined than Plato to escape from the responsibility of an individual love in favor of a universal one. Rather than sublimate the flesh, he seeks to reincarnate himself. After so many centuries of metaphysical musing, he suspects that the choice of an individual, in body and soul, and fidelity to this choice, are inclined to make him locate the divine in himself rather than lose himself in an abstract love of the universal. In this way, for homosexuals as for other men, an established liaison, as proposed by Giese, remains the way of life most desirable in its accomplishment. Nikolas Berdyaev denied the possibility of a homosexual "married" couple. Positive and negative electrons, he said, cannot unite with their equals; they can only meet their contraries. This is a theoretical point of view. Homosexual couples do exist, and we have talked about them. They are rare, but they are not a myth. Some endure for a long time, as do heterosexual couples. Berdyaev did not perceive that active and passive tendencies exist in the heart of every individual, and that among the inverts these tendencies can bring about a relationship which is the reverse of that existing between a heterosexual couple. In such cases, it is not two active individuals who come together, nor two passive ones. Each of these partners will finally establish himself in an active or passive position, complementary to the other, a position which can be permanent or allow of change.

A homosexual liasion always runs the risk of being more stormy, more fragile, and more unhappy than heterosexual liaisons, partly through the difficulties caused by environment as by difficulties provoked by the instability of internal balance. But this can even be a source of delight or exaltation. Only those who do not succeed in overcoming the difficulties of their state must be induced to follow a course of treatment whose merit will be, at least, to show them the possibilities and limitations of that state. Among the weak, those who are destined to homosexuality or who conform to social circumstances will be able to discriminate with precision only if society gives them proof of tolerance in law and morality. As long as such tolerance does not exist, anything that can be said concerning the pathological nature of homosexuality remains without scientific value and without ontological significance. More serious is the opinion according to which the "overaesthetic" attitude of homosexuals, or at least of pederasts,[1] prevents them from attaining the deeper things of life and limits them to formalized behavior, "copies of life."

It is true that an exaggerated cult of the Beautiful leads to a preference for perfect form rather than richness of being, the container rather than the contents. But this is only a question of a defect of quality, when the aesthetic sense consists precisely in giving form to the formless. However, this tendency has other outlets beyond the arts, arts such as the cinema, theater, painting, or

Transvestism in real life.

---

[1] This tendency to aestheticism is seldom to be found among Lesbians. Sappho's human failure would seem to indicate rather that the aesthetic road was, for them, an impasse, and that their identification with the *animus* would bring them rather toward a sado-aggressive attitude whose archetype is the Amazon. However, if Plato's reflections (like the contemporary ideas of Jung, Giese, and Szondy) have cleared the way for more sublimation and a wider socialization of male homosexuality, it must be said that nothing similar has been achieved for female homosexuality. Dr. Caprio's recent work (*op. cit.*) on this subject is conformist and poverty-stricken in imagination.

sculpture, all of which can be called—even in a naïve manner—"copies of life"; but these are the activities in which it is important to work with reality and give it style. One has only to turn to the roles played by pederasts in *haute couture*, decoration, hairdressing, town-planning, and in the design of cars or planes to notice the extent to which this tendency can be interpolated into the most ordinary activities of life, imparting a brilliance it could not possess by itself. But this Apollonian Eros is formal only in appearance: It frequently brings to the surface some rich vein which has been buried in the past, or else it brings into existence creative notions invisible to the generality of men. We should not forget that the pederastic Apollo of Delphos was a sinister Apollo whose qualities were very similar to the Python he killed. His nearness to the abyss and his criminal element allowed him to accede to the rank of God of Light, Beauty, and the Arts.

Once more, we must go back to Giese. The tendency toward the overaesthetic must be integrated into the sense of responsibility which the homosexual must offer to the world. If he is justified in demanding his rights, it is important that he should also think of his duties. Whether his particularity is a deficiency or not, he must serve others. The essential thing is that he should not use his homosexuality merely to escape from the world, but as a means of chosen self-definition and self-affirmation in the world. This is the only way in which he can ensure the respect of others and assess his own limitations for himself: His very failure could only make him turn to other things and achieve a greater maturity.

In the face of such realities, theories about the finality of nature are absurd. There are more things in nature than in our ideas about it. Reproduction is not the sole purpose of the sexual instinct; that is clear to everyone today. We are beginning to suspect that there exists in nature an equilibrium of living phenomena in which biological sterility has its place, a sterility which is also the necessary condition for great cultural creation. We may even wonder whether, deep within homosexuality, there is some hint of that parthenogenesis which existed at the beginnings of life and which the most recent scientific discoveries are now showing as a possibility of the future, a possibility which would also furnish the very greatest liberty of the individual. However, such speculations are without immediate significance.

The immediate problem is the situation of the homosexual in the contemporary world. On one side, the liberty that society must accord him; on the other, the responsibility that he must assume toward the world. The average man must learn to consider that his own sexual tendencies belong only to the average experience; and that other people exist whose character, con-

Friends. Marc Chagall. 1961. Casino de Knokke.

structive or destructive, depends in a large degree on his behavior toward them, on his tolerance and his respect for all who live. He must admit that the dazzling image of men like himself, and the tenderness and love it can awaken, are universals and have no connection with the sordid impressions that some people have of homosexuality. It can never be repeated to him too often that, among homosexuals, the most virile of men cling to the effeminate ones; and that you can find among them conquerors, sages, strong characters, and men of genius just as often as you find the vanquished, the decadent, the weak, or the stupid. He must realize that this orientation which he finds repugnant exists potentially within himself, and that unforeseen circumstances can cause him to succumb to it. He must remember that his very repugnance constitutes an anomaly and that exclusive heterosexuality, just like exclusive homosexuality, is just as capable of driving him to neurosis. The repugnance he shows must convince him rather that he is living in ignorance of his own latent homosexuality and his own secret femininity (or, in the case of a woman, of her secret masculinity), and that he has not succeeded in integrating them, so that his personality continues to be incomplete and fragmentary. Above all he must bring himself to the realization that a homosexual orientation can be useful to society to the degree that the attraction of like for like can lead to an awareness less frequently found in the projection of contraries. The Lesbian is less indulgent toward women than is a man; the pederast has less feeling for a man than a woman has. Each of them has descended into the abyss of the similar, into the hell of the Doppelganger and the Shadow, myths we have already discussed. The so-called normal man does not see himself, does not know himself. He is seen and

Here Dali rediscovered something of the Platonist inspiration of Greece.

known only by the woman who, alone, looks at him, but sees him often without being able to understand him. And the contrary is true.

The homosexual, in opposition to the above, sees not only his counterpart face to face; he sees right inside the other and can understand him by virtue of their similarity. That is why he is capable of bringing to human awareness a dimension which escapes casual awareness and which, indeed, does not replace the conventional but enriches it. He must nevertheless always assess to what degree he remains vulnerable, threatened not only by reason of the repulsion he arouses or the condemnation that bears down on him, but also by the position which the most archaic impulses have marked out for him. He must know that, more than anyone else, he inhabits a territory threatened endlessly by the ocean, and the tidal waves are the unordered force of his own unconscious strength. With more ardor and haste than others, he must raise defenses that will preserve this interior world from the storm and, if he cannot succeed alone, he must not be afraid of demanding from others the necessary therapeutic help. He must remember that in the depths of his personality he also possesses a latent heterosexuality which must be brought out into the open by one means or another if he does not wish to become completely unbalanced, lacking even the accomplishment of such completeness as is allowed to him. He must even ask himself if the image he pursues so relentlessly in others is no more than a projection and crystalization of a part of himself that he has never had the strength or courage to integrate or realize. He must attempt this integration or realization in order to know if the forces that move him are only mirages derived from his weakness or cowardice. But if, after having considered these problems in their entirety, he chooses homosexuality as his destiny, he must take thought and assume it with courage, make it as dignified as he can and, as far as is conceivably possible, extract from it all the potentialities that will be useful to others. He must desire maturity—one in which he does not search for partners in bars, parks, or public conveniences—but in the gift one being can make of his person to another. Such a maturity is foreign to facile promiscuity, since it actively desires to avoid scandal and to perform all possible services for everyone.

An attraction for one's fellow, the exaltation that can be achieved through a complementary quality in similitude, produces an enchantment resembling that produced by the contemplation of orchards in springtime. It consists in finding, in one being, the contrasts of gentle flexibility and energetic toughness, the bright confidence that gives one partner the capacity to accomplish what he would find impossible on his own. The search, never disappointed and continually renewed, for beauty perfect in all its forms, constitutes the enigma of homosexuality. This enigma is beautiful, as are all enigmas. But whatever one might think of its exceptional character, it can integrate

Still from *Orphée*. Jean Cocteau. 1949.

itself with the exemplary and archetypal behavior patterns whose myths have been thrown up throughout history. Only the most unredeemed personality would find absurd such examples as those furnished by Gilgamesh and Enkidu, Zeus and Ganymede, Apollo and Hyacinth, Achilles and Patroclus, and even David and Jonathan, or Jesus and St. John. He would be poor of spirit who remained insenstitive to the reflections of Plato, to the stifled confessions of Leonardo da Vinci, or to the cries of that wounded titan, Michelangelo. We must search out those admirable types of human behavior which the Judeo-Christian tradition has veiled and sullied. Undoubtedly the time has come when one must no longer despise the muddy foundations essential for the most sublime of creations. Psychology has shown to what extent the high and the low are interlinked. We must not be upset by the dung that gives life to the flower. To learn that everything is beautiful, if good use is made of it—this is the lesson we must accept from Greece and Asia. The mortal sins of the Christian West remain intolerance and fanaticism. The Christians, disturbed heirs to the "chosen people," refused a place in their pantheon to that which the more courteous Romans had already admitted into theirs. Now is the time to assess what movement there has been from monotheism to monosexuality and, in spite of the greatness of certain exceptions, to measure the degree to which it contains the seeds of savagery and fanaticism.

Tolerance is more difficult at the most intimate point of being: sexuality. It is the difference between sexual behavior patterns that exacerbates the awareness of foreignness, fear, repulsion, or hatred. It is, therefore, toward those whose sexual behavior is contrary to our own that we should really practice most tolerance.

Nothing relaxes erotic tensions more than the authorization of erotic practices. Don Juan died from the facilities his epoch accorded to so-called normal love. He lived off the interdictions of eighteenth-century Spain and in fear of hellfire. Many homosexual passions were nourished in the condemnation that afflicted those who practiced them, and in the quality of secrecy that surrounded them. If we take the drama out of the problem by permitting what is already freely done to be done with everyone's respect, to be performed in the light of day, we may be sure that the snobbery which so often surrounds forbidden mores will vanish with the light and tolerance granted them. Such tolerance can have consequences vaster and deeper than can be imagined, for the transformation of attitudes toward sexuality produces repercussions on the whole of human activity.

That peace about which there is so much vain talk is impossible only by reason of the internal mobilization to which we are all subjected. It is scarcely "moral rearmament" that is needed by the West and the entire world, but a genuine moral disarmament, in which sexuality should be the first object of attention. Eros is everywhere, his visage is multifarious, and we must learn to venerate him even in those guises most strange to us. We can surely tolerate him in his most unusual manifestations from the moment he consents to assume the shape of what is most important to us: a person worthy of being loved and capable of loving.

The Sin or *Sodom and Gomorrah*. J. P. Clezen. 1965. Salon de Mai, Paris.

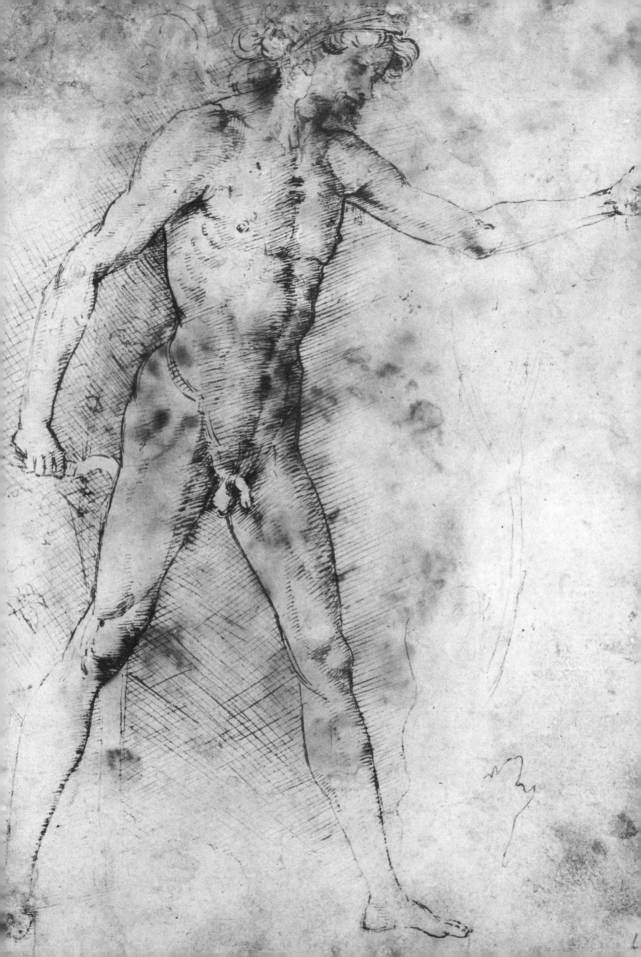